www.wadsworth.com

wadsworth.com is the World Wide Web site for Wadsworth and is your direct source to dozens of online resources.

At *wadsworth.com* you can find out about supplements, demonstration software, and student resources. You can also send email to many of our authors and preview new publications and exciting new technologies.

wadsworth.com
Changing the way the world learns®

THE WADSWORTH CONTEMPORARY ISSUES IN CRIME AND JUSTICE SERIES
Todd Clear, Series Editor

▼

Renegade Kids, Suburban Outlaws:

From Youth Culture to Delinquency

Second Edition

WAYNE S. WOODEN

California State Polytechnic University, Pomona

RANDY BLAZAK

Portland State University

Wadsworth
Thomson Learning

Australia • Canada • Mexico • Singapore • Spain
• United Kingdom • United States

Executive Editor: Sabra Horne
Development Editor: Teri Edwards
Assistant Editor: Ann Tsai
Editorial Assistant: Cortney Bruggink
Marketing Manager: Jennifer Somerville
Project Editor: Susan Walters
Print Buyer: Karen Hunt
Permissions Editor: Joohee Lee

Production Service: Shepherd Incorporated
Copy Editor: Bruce Owens
Cover Designer: Lisa Langhoff
Cover Image: © Deborah Celecia
Compositor: Shepherd Incorporated
Cover and Text Printer: Malloy Lithographing Inc.

Printed in the United States of America.
2 3 4 5 6 7 04 03 02 01

For permission to use material from this text, contact us by:
Web: http://www.thomsonrights.com
Fax: 1-800-730-2215
Phone: 1-800-730-2214

For more information, contact
Wadsworth Publishing Company.
Wadsworth Publishing Company
10 Davis Drive
Belmont, California 94002
USA

International Thomson Publishing Europe
Berkshire House 168-173
High Holborn
London, WClV 7AA
England

Thomas Nelson Australia
102 Dodds Street
South Melbourne 3205
Victoria, Australia
Canada

Nelson/Thomson Learning
1120 Birchmount Road
Scarborough, Ontario
Canada M1K SG4

International Thomson Editores
Campos Elisecis 385, Piso 7
Col. Polanco
11560 México D.F. México

International Thomson Publishing GmbH
Königswinterer Strasse 418
53227 Bonn
Germany

International Thomson Publishing Asia
221 Henderson Road
#05-10 Henderson Building
Singapore 0315

International Thomson Publishing - Japan
Hirakawacho Kyowa Building, 3F
2-2-1 Hirakawacho
Chiyoda-ku, Tokyo 102
Japan

Library of Congress Cataloging-in-Publication Data
Wooden, Wayne S.
   Renegade kids, suburban outlaws: from youth culture to delinquency / Wayne S. Wooden, Randy Blazak.
   p. cm — (The Wadsworth contemporary issues in crime and justice series)
Second edition
ISBN 0-534-52754-X
1. Socially handicapped youth.
2. Problem youth. 3. Deviant behavior.
4. Suburban life. I. Blazak, Randy, 1964–II. Title. III. Contemporary issues in crime and justice series.
HV1421 . W66 2000
362.7'4'0973—dc21
            00-034972

Youth, though it may lack knowledge,
is certainly not devoid of intelligence;
it sees through shams
with sharp and terrible eyes.

H. L. Mencken

Contents

▼

Foreword

One generation encounters another with bewilderment: How can you stand to pierce your nose? What made you want a tattoo on your neck? Isn't it annoying to have your pants falling below your waist like that? And how can you tell those songs apart—they all sound the same?

Some of this is style, of course. From long hair and love beads in the '60s to hip hop and lip rings in the '00s, each generation makes a claim to "a look," and it is nothing short of normal for the generations to look so different on purpose. This is a kind of lineage dance, in which each new generation deliberately separates itself from its predecessor by style, fashion, and priorities. And by its preoccupation with being different, each new generation signals that little has changed in the broader scheme of generational tension. It is not merely normal that young people seek to distinguish themselves from their parental generation, it is good and necessary. It is the business of Western society. Wayne Wooden and Randy Blazak call this process of inter-generational change, "youth culture."

Still, youth culture is not completely benign. Breaking norms is never a neutral act, no matter how trivial. It is understandable that we might worry about this aspect of growing up, in its more extreme manifestation. Many young people have taken a family car without permission, but joy riding a stranger's car is an order of magnitude more serious. A majority of teenagers experiment with mood altering substances, but forming a moneymaking drug delivery enterprise is not "growing up" behavior. It is common for young men to test their manhood with fights, but guns make the routines of youthful aggression lethal. So while we anticipate that each new generation of young people test norms and push against social convention, we are right to be uneasy about the limits of growing up.

In this, the second edition of *Renegade Kids, Suburban Outlaws: From Youth Culture to Delinquency,* Wooden and Blazak explore the boundary between deviance and criminality in the lives of young people who are deeply involved in the youth culture. I am pleased to welcome this new edition to the *Wadsworth Contemporary Issues on Crime and Justice Series.* The series is devoted to furthering our understanding of important issues in crime and justice by providing an in-depth treatment of topics that are neglected or insufficiently discussed in today's textbooks. *Renegade Kids* is an excellent example of the kind of work the series was designed to promote.

Wooden and Blazak write about young people with authority and passion. Part of what makes this book so useful is the way they have given the subjects of this study a "voice." They tell the stories of the troubled youths by the youths' own words, which gives the reader a richer and more sympathetic understanding of the troubled lives being chronicled between the covers of this book. The rich variety of youth cultural forms is also impressive. From the largely inconsequential deviance of the mall rats, dopers, and punks, we see the way music, literature and fashion fuse in images and social patterns for middle class youth. This generally innocuous expression of youth culture gives way to the more extreme forms: hate, guns, and formal gangs committed to violence in ways that travel the conceptual thread from rap music to gang banging; Wooden and Blazak show how youth culture is not a set of categories so much as it is a dynamic and creative response to the confusions of growing up in modern society.

These are what we call "at-risk" youths: young people whose life chances are dominated by strong possibilities of trouble, upcoming despair, and even serious failure. Many end up in trouble with the law; some in prison. But all the youths whose stories are told within these pages are products of modern society, with its pressures on institutions of socialization and informal social control: parents, schools, peers, and social life. It is important to remember that for many of the young people whose lives are described in these pages, things eventually worked out. Some are now college graduates and in good jobs, raising families. Others have shifted their attention from deviance to productive lives using their own routes. The question this book raises is twofold: What are we to make of the way the youth culture draws your young people toward deviance? And how are we to prevent the all-too-easy transition from the everyday deviance of our youth culture to the more extreme versions of juvenile delinquency?

I commend this book to you. It is a fascinating study of a critical issue in criminology. Reading it will change the way you understand "growing up" in modern, mainstream society.

Todd R. Clear
Series Editor

Acknowledgments

As is the case with most research projects, this study of suburban youth cultures and juvenile delinquencies has a history. I began work on the first edition of this book in 1986, when I was asked to teach a new senior seminar course, "Youth and Social Deviance." I wanted to focus on behaviors that involved youths in the middle-class suburban communities near where I teach (some thirty miles east of Los Angeles). The class of twenty students and I developed and field-tested the questionnaire of one hundred items that became known as the "Youth Survey." (See Appendix A for a full discussion of the methodology of this research project. Copies of the questionnaires and the summary tables appear in Appendix B.)

For the second edition of the book, I asked Randy Blazak to join me because his research on teenagers, gutter-punks, and hate crimes as well as his take on youth at the start of the new millennium added to my knowledge of the modern youth scene.

The study in general and this book in particular would not have been possible without the cooperation of many people. First I must thank the numerous university students, in addition to that initial class, who have assisted me with various facets of the study. In every chapter of the first edition—much of which is incorporated into this second edition—there was considerable input from students, including assistance with administering the questionnaires and analyzing the data. On occasion, university students took directed studies with me to assist with the interviews.

I wish to acknowledge the support of my campus, Cal Poly, Pomona, which granted me leave to complete the initial manuscript. Thanks are also in order to the entire production staff at Wadsworth who assisted with the preparation of the manuscript. And finally I want to express my appreciation to both of my editors at Wadsworth: Brian Gore, who was the Criminal Justice Acquisitions Editor and enthusiastically supported this book through its development during the first edition, and Sabra Horne, who championed the book—along with assisting me in obtaining a coauthor—for this current edition.

I also wish to thank the reviewers of this book: Gail Berlage, Iona College; Denise Herz, University of Nebraska–Omaha; Bud Levin, Blue Ridge Community College; and Gay Young, Johnson County Community College.

Wayne S. Wooden

My research into deviant youth subcultures began in 1986, when I began to notice Nazi skinheads harassing the local punk scene in Atlanta, Georgia. I began a fifteen-year odyssey to understand why young people get involved in hate groups. The 1995 edition of *Renegade Kids, Suburban Outlaws* by Wayne S. Wooden was a crucial part of my research.

As one of the first wave of Generation X (born in 1964), I grew up in the suburban punk rock subculture of the early 1980s. My work on delinquents and deviants attempts to shine a light on the creative power of youth in the face of a confusing and often disorganized society.

It has been a great pleasure to work with Wayne S. Wooden on the new edition of this book. I would also like to thank my students at Emory University and Portland State University who have kept me connected to the changes in youth culture. I would also like to thank the gutter-punks of Portland for their honesty in a harsh reality. Finally, I owe a great debt to Sabra Horne for allowing me to write about a topic that is so important to me.

Randy Blazak

1

▼

Introduction
to the Problem

The ominous signs are everywhere: kids bringing guns onto junior high and high school campuses and shooting each other; teenagers forming sex posses and racking up "body counts" of the number of girls they have "scored with" or "sacked"; mall rats rampaging through suburban shopping arcades, "streaming," as they call it, through the aisles of department stores and grabbing stacks of clothing before making a quick getaway; tagger crews "mapping the heavens," spray painting their three-letter monikers on overhead freeway signs. The cry for help of punk rockers and their offshoots, ignored by families and society that do not take time to listen. And these are just the good kids!

And what about the others? Racist teenage skinheads plot revenge on unsuspecting fellow students at suburban high schools for no other reason than that they dislike them because of their skin color, nationality, or presumed sexual orientation. White, youthful, stoner gang members wander aimlessly with their suburban "homies," or homeboys, looking for the next high, surviving on dope and booze. Juvenile Satanists, participating in a fad, find themselves caught up in a cult.

An examination of these youths and others forms the bulk of this book. For the most part, the teenagers we focus on resided within a 25-mile radius of each other in sleepy, upscale bedroom communities of the San Gabriel Valley and the Inland Empire in Southern California. Our disturbing story—and study—unfolds in suburban areas with such pleasant-sounding names as San Dimas, Diamond Bar, Walnut, Chino Hills, Upland, Claremont, and West Covina.

Our focus is not the youth of the inner city, racked by street crime, urban violence and gang intimidation, but the youth (primarily males) of more affluent, suburban, middle-class neighborhoods, situated more than a 30-minute commute from Los Angeles.

This book's intent is to distinguish between two types of troubled teens from these and other privileged areas. On the one hand, we explore the reasons or conditions under which some teenagers get caught up in the ever-changing youth styles and youth cultures of the moment. These youths are referred to as *renegade kids*—identity seekers who are relatively socially harmless. On the other hand, there are teenagers who have embraced decidedly more deviant and delinquent identities and behavior. We refer to these juveniles as *suburban outlaws*—the nonconformist and rebellious youths prone to lawbreaking.

Not all youths, of course, test the limits of authority or break the law. Most teenagers, in fact, are law-abiding citizens. They do well in school, mind their parents, and come from loving, secure, and attentive families. These youngsters, fortunately, grow up to become responsible and contributing citizens. Not enough good things can be said about these teens.

AT-RISK KIDS

The focus, however, is on the others—those not-so-good kids. These are the teens who feel isolated and misunderstood, get angry and enraged, take risks, and get into trouble. For some, these behaviors are only a stage, a "kids will be kids" kind of thing. But for others, the choices they make in adolescence not only label them as delinquent but set them on a path embracing a way of life that will put them at risk for their entire lives.

Perhaps by better understanding these troubled kids, we can take steps to rectify the situation, to intervene early in their lives, and to assist in pointing out the errors of their ways. If we fail to accomplish this, then the morass that we as members of society seem now to find ourselves in can only deepen.

Society in the new millennium is held hostage by fear. We read with alarm about a 13-year-old girl getting snatched from the security of her own bedroom in the middle of a slumber party and then killed. We hear about a church youth group in prayer suddenly gunned down by a crazed gunman. But perhaps what shocks and alarms us the most is the increasingly violent turn that our youngsters seem to be taking. It involves more than the senseless and unending drive-by shootings of urban ethnic gang warfare. And it is more than the mounting body count of runaway youths strung out and overdosed on drugs. It is the perception that society is no longer in control of its destiny—that this next generation of youths is not just dazed and confused, not just those renegade kids; rather, they are armed and dangerous as well—the more unsettling suburban outlaws.

The term *at-risk* youth has traditionally described inner-city adolescents who are on the verge of choosing a life in gangs or the drug trade. The school shootings in places such as West Paducah, Kentucky, and Littleton, Colorado, show us that it is not just urban minority youths who are at risk. The recent explosion of school shootings caught most Americans off guard. *Time* magazine called the Columbine shooters, "the Monsters Next Door," leaving many to believe that street kids shooting each other is understandable, but upper-class suburban kids doing the same thing is beyond explanation (1). These suburban youths are also at risk of many of the same social ills. Only after repeated bloodbaths had occured in nonurban schools did this point enter the general public discourse.

The main reason for embarking on this book was to try to make some sense out of these alarming trends. This study attempts to serve several purposes. For one, the case studies and examples of different types of suburban youths can provide the sociology and criminal justice student with a clearer understanding of the various theories on juveniles and delinquent behavior put forth over the past several decades by sociologists and criminologists. Second, the variety of methodologies used in gathering the data for the study— from questionnaires to participant-observation to content analysis—offer examples to students who also intend to do studies of their own on certain aspects of modern youth culture.

Most of the youth in this book are male. Although some girls are active in deviant groups, most delinquent subcultures are overwhelmingly made up of boys. For example, one characteristic that the suburban school shooters of the 1990s had in common was their maleness. The challenge then is to understand the connection between masculinity and extreme deviance and violence. To do this we consider feminist theories and explanations that explore the social construction of gender.

For the layperson, this book can perhaps serve as a "Guide to Troubled Teens." It is hoped that the youths examined in this study will provide parents and concerned citizens with the tools to examine their own relationships with their children. They may also provide others—from youth counselors and social workers to correctional, probation, and parole officers— with important clues and behavioral indicators to look for when working with at-risk young people.

A GENERATION IN CRISIS?

In the 1990s research began revealing what those who had survived the 1980s already knew: The safe cocoon of middle-class youth was eroding. In late 1993 a poll that questioned 758 children between the ages of 10 and 17, along with their parents, found a generation living in fear. No longer sharing an optimistic view of the future or sharing the American Dream that their parents still believed in, this new generation seemed to be "growing up fast and frightened" (2).

Many of the juveniles expressed concerns about guns, drugs, poverty, and divorce issues that their parents could not have imagined when they were youngsters. The study also noted that the fears transcended locale, for it was no longer just children of the inner cities that were worried. Rural as well as suburban youths feared "coming of age in a rough world."

When specifically asked to identify their own and their families' primary concerns, the juveniles responded: violent crime against a family member (56 percent); an adult losing a job (53 percent); inability to afford shelter (47 percent); a family member developing a drug problem (38 percent); and the fear that their family would not stay together (38 percent), among other concerns.

Another national study also reported dire findings. In 1990 the commission formed by the National Association of State Boards of Education and the American Medical Association announced the results of their long-term study, noting with great alarm that the United States was raising a generation of adolescents plagued by pregnancies, illegal drug use, suicide, and violence (3). Although the rates appear to be dropping, the numbers are still shocking. More recent data show that 500,000 teen births occur each year, 42 percent of twelfth graders have used illicit drugs (4), one in ten young people has attempted suicide, and 1.5 million violent crimes against juveniles occur annually (5).

The commission's earlier report concluded that if immediate action was not soon undertaken to reverse these trends, American society would soon find itself with a failing economy and social unrest. Furthermore, according to the report, young people were less healthy and less prepared to take their places in society than their parents had been at their age. The report concluded that inattention to these problems has left thousands of youngsters doomed to failure, which for many will be a precursor to an adult life of crime, unemployment, or welfare dependency.

To remedy some of these concerns, the commission recommended that teenagers be guaranteed access to health services and that communities set up adolescent health centers in schools or other convenient places. Schools were also urged to play a larger role in the health and sex education of these youngsters.

In *Youth Crisis: Growing Up in a High-Risk Society,* Nanette J. Davis (1999) points out that adolescence is a period of transition from childhood to adulthood. Each of the institutions of this transition (the family, education, employment, and so on) is in a state of turmoil, causing youth to be in a state of crisis. Davis contends the condition of youth crisis is precipitated by three factors: (1) the high crisis conditions of both local and global institutions, (2) a society that encourages risk-taking behavior, and (3) a low value on social justice. She points out that the 30 percent of the growth of violent crimes between 1988 and 1992 was due to juveniles who live in an era of declining societal responsiveness to their needs (6).

Renegade Kids, Suburban Outlaws shares the concerns of these studies and documents the extent of the problem facing young people today. As previously stated, focusing primarily on white, suburban, middle-class, teenage males, the book differentiates youth behaviors that are merely styles, fads, or displays of youth culture from those that warrant broader societal responses because of their delinquent and deviant character.

WHAT IS YOUTH CULTURE?

Youth culture is a nebulous term. Do the activities of kindergartners count? What about weekend gatherings of yuppies? Usually, when we discuss youth culture, we are referring to a specific subculture or subset of the larger culture that is transitioning from childhood to adulthood. Sarah Thorton differentiates subculture from the terms *community* and *society*. A community is a more permanent population tied to a place, and a society is more a macroabstraction. Subcultures, in contrast, are fairly transient small groups of people united by a common interest (7).

The focus on youth culture as a specific social problem became a primary concern of sociologists, and society in general, in the 1950s. As the baby-boom children were liberated from the requirements of agriculture, the factory, and the military by the postwar economic boom, the children of the new suburbs discovered the freedom of a leisure-oriented society. Without a clear transition to adulthood, rebellion became institutionalized as a way of expressing this normlessness. David Matza (1964) suggested that the most common forms of rebelliousness are delinquency, radicalism, and bohemianism (8).

The second half of the twentieth century saw an explosion of youth subcultures as young people explored this new social role, or lack of role. From beatniks to Yippies to punkers to Goths, young people looked to each other for solidarity and a sense of meaning. Michael Brake argues that these subcultures provide five vital functions for young people: (1) They are problem-solving groups, even if those problems are existential in nature, (2) they provide a cultural experience on a manageable level, (3) they create an alternative reality of unique symbols, (4) they give meaning to leisure time, and (5) they give young people a place to work out personal issues (9).

These youth cultures receive attention from parents, authorities, and the news media and often become diffused into the larger culture. The slang of the hip-hoppers, the sneer of bikers, the tie-dyed shirts of Dead Heads, or the Doc Marten boots of skinheads all become part of the pantheon of mainstream American culture, leading youth to search out new forms of rebellion. Places such as the suburbs of Southern California become the repository of the diffusing subcultural styles of the media spotlight.

In several instances the youth cultures that played out in suburbia, such as the punk rocker and heavy metaler scene, were ones that came late to the inland communities. Youths elsewhere in the country (such as Los Angeles and

New York City) and abroad (such as London) had long embraced those particular styles. But in other aspects, the youth styles of these Southern California suburban neighborhoods have led the way, ushering in new teen fads—such as rave parties and tagger crews. This book examines all of these various trends.

Alienated youths in their various guises have long fascinated observers. Concerned parents and family members, peers, school officials, police, social workers, journalists, the mass media, and scholars alike have attempted to understand and work with these troubled youngsters in a concerted effort to reintegrate them into society. In this regard this book follows a long line of other works that have examined the "youth scene" of the day.

Albert K. Cohen, in his classic study (1955) *Delinquent Boys: The Culture of the Gang,* employed categories differentiating the corner boy, the collegiate boy, and the delinquent boy nearly half a century ago (10). Similar categories are used here to differentiate their counterparts of today. However, today the categories include the mall rats, punkers, and metalers (in place of the corner boy); the preppies and conformists (rather than the collegiate boy); and the taggers, skinheads, stoners, and satanists (as examples of the delinquent boy).

HOW DOES ONE STUDY YOUTH CULTURE?

Studying deviant youth subcultures is an inherently difficult endeavor. Most young people who are rebelling against adult society are not willing to sit down with adult researchers and clearly articulate their feelings about their lives. Young people who are involved in illegal activities such as tagging, drugs, or violence may be even less trusting of the academic investigator. For example, youths in correctional facilities are notoriously nice to adult visitors if they believe that person can help their situation.

If deviant youth are not forthcoming with their parents or authorities, how can researchers expect to obtain useful information about their world? Fortunately, social research has some tried-and-true tricks for getting at the truth. Social scientists have two approaches they can take to study youth: quantitative research and qualitative research.

Quantitative researchers look at large data sets and find patterns. The data usually come from anonymous surveys of large numbers of young people, often while in school. National surveys, such as Monitoring the Future, Youth in Transition, and the General Social Survey, regularly poll high school kids on a wide variety of topics. Criminologist Robert Agnew used Monitoring the Future surveys to find a relationship between delinquency and youths' stress levels (11).

The surveyed sample is assumed to be representative of the general youth population. But quantitative research can present some problems. Kids who drop out of school might not be represented on the school-administered surveys. Youths might forget or lie on the survey because they do not trust their anonymity. Or researchers may miscalculate or misinterpret the statistics.

Another approach is qualitative research, which attempts to understand the meanings of subjects' actions and views. Sometimes these researchers analyze their subjects' writings or music. More typically, researchers spend long periods of time with their subjects to try to see the world through their eyes. The idea is that, after a period of time, the subjects will come to trust the researcher and drop pretenses, acting more "naturally." Howard Becker did just that in his pioneering study of pot-smoking jazz musicians (12), and gang-researcher Malcolm Klein even managed to win the confidence of hard-core gang-bangers (13). But this research may also have flaws. For instance, subjects may still be "performing" for the researcher. Because of the time involved, sample sizes are usually quite small, unlike the big surveys. And because researchers are observing a local sample, the data may not be comparable to groups in other communities.

The research presented in this book represents both quantitative and qualitative methods. The idea for the research originated in Wayne S. Wooden's 1986 senior seminar class at California State Polytechnic University, Pomona, entitled, "Youth Culture and Social Deviance." The students wanted to explore the youth styles that their younger brothers and sisters were embracing. Several spoke of the "sibling gap" that existed between themselves and others in their families who were merely three or four years their junior.

Collectively the class developed and field tested a questionnaire of one hundred items that became known as the "Youth Survey" (see Appendix B). Armed with the questionnaires, the students fanned out to five shopping malls in the local area because malls had become—apart from junior and senior high schools—the "hangout" for suburban youths. There they administered the study, paying close attention to youth who self-identified as punk rockers and heavy metalers. The youth surveys were also administered in Christchurch, New Zealand, for a cross-cultural perspective. There Wooden received data from punk rockers and heavy metalers living "on the rough" (i.e., on the streets) as well as from students in several suburban high schools.

Along with quantitative data collection, qualitative research was also conducted. Sociology students analyzed their high school year books to delineate the hierarchy of various cliques. Wooden personally examined one middle-class school in the Inland Empire (an area in Southern California) in some detail, a school referred to in this book as "Raging High." For several days he studied the campus, interviewing the school psychologist who had been hired to work with troubled teenagers and coordinate programs that involved the local police department's gang-detail specialist as well as the counselors at the school. He also got to know the various cliques at the school as they staked out their turf or "corners" in the center of campus along one wall each lunch period.

Qualitative methods were also employed in the analysis of boxloads of letters received by the group, Parents of Punkers, in an attempt to explore another perspective on youth culture.

The research on more serious delinquents was done primarily by studying case files in the juvenile correctional system. Following his analysis of young arsonists in the California Youth Authority (CYA) (14), Wooden researched the files of white juvenile offenders who self-identified as punk rockers or heavy metalers to learn what kinds of criminal offenses they had committed that got them institutionalized. In addition to attending community-based workshops on juvenile crime and studying newspaper clippings, Wooden studied the case files (provided by the CYA) of fifty-two of these white stoner gang members.

On field trips to the Youth Authority's Youth Correctional Facility, Wooden administered questionnaires to several incarcerated racist teenagers. He conducted additional interviews with nonracist skinheads in local high schools. Using students as contacts, he was also able to interview members of tagger posses as well.

Additionally, Blazak used qualitative interviews to research suburban teens in a variety of settings. For several years he and his students observed and interviewed gutter-punks in Portland, Oregon. Volunteering as a group discussion leader in a juvenile correctional facility in Oregon as well, Blazak interviewed several suburban offenders who had been imprisoned by Oregon's tough mandatory minimum sentencing guidelines.

Since 1986 Blazak has been using ethnographic research methods, such as participant observation and guided conversations, to understand the motivations of racist and antiracist skinheads. He spent thirteen months with one group of skinheads in Orlando, Florida, slam dancing and going to Klan meetings with young skinheads. He also interviewed skins in urban areas such as Chicago in smaller cities such as Memphis, and in suburban, metropolitan areas such as Cobb County, outside of Atlanta (15).

Through an organization called Oregon Spotlight, which helps young people resist or leave hate groups, Blazak was able to interview a large number of youths about the issue of hate crimes. This included suburban high school students who were being actively recruited by hate groups as well as racist skinheads who actively recruited teenagers and who had personally committed hate crimes themselves.

Like past researchers who have explored earlier youth scenes, Wooden and Blazak made every attempt to get to know these kids, to interview them, to analyze their case files (for those who were incarcerated), and to try to understand these often troubled teens. In an ethnographic technique often used in studies of this sort, they let these youths speak for themselves. Through questionnaires and interviews they tried to provide these teenagers with a means to express their points of view.

This approach was most successful with the punk rockers, heavy metalers, tagger crew members, and both racist and nonracist teenage skinheads who consented to be interviewed for this study or who completed the extensive questionnaires. Several university students assisted with these sometime difficult interviews. Many students, when they themselves were in high school, had been involved in some of the youth cultures analyzed, and their observations and insights were invaluable.

What follows, therefore, is a work that examines the youth cultures and delinquencies of assorted suburban male youths who, for a variety of reasons that we hope to make clear, chose to deviate from the paths of conformity and respectability that most of their peers followed.

OUTLINE OF THE BOOK

This book is divided into three sections. After a discussion of the range of theories used to explain subcultural activity (Chapter 2), we examine, in the first section, youths whose rebellious nature has taken the form of sampling one or more of the youth styles and youth cultures of the moment. These teens are referred to as renegade kids because they abandoned the established norms of society, joining other youths in opposition to rules, defying—often through dress and demeanor—the status quo.

Their more delinquent counterparts—youths who are referred to as suburban outlaws—are examined in the second section of the book. Selecting a different path—one that seems to have led them into increasing despair and deviance—these often recidivist offenders are distinguished by a variety of offensive behaviors. They include youths who have joined a delinquent gang or a satanic cult or become a racist skinhead. By their actions they have placed themselves outside the norms of acceptable behavior, and society has had to intervene. By embracing a life of crime they have in effect become bandits or outlaws!

The third section explores parental and societal responses as well as future trends. How have various institutions responded to youthful offenders? From the local high school to the Office of Juvenile Justice and Delinquency Prevention have come numerous proposals. Finally, what can we expect of youth culture in the new millennium? Building on the findings in this book about the experiences of Generation X, we attempt to project the trends of suburban youthful deviance for the next cohort that we dub "Generation Why?"

RENEGADE KIDS

Part 1, "Renegade Kids," includes four chapters that examine contemporary youths in several settings. First is a general discussion of the meeting ground for modern youths, namely the suburban shopping mall. This is where we first encountered the array of youth cultures studied.

Chapter 3, "Mall Rats and Life in the Mall," explores the role that the modern mall plays in contemporary society, particularly as it pertains to middle-class teenagers. For those youths who spend most, if not all, of their available time in the mall, the shopping center serves as an arena in which they compete with each other, staking out their "turf" in much the same way as inner-city, ethnic gang members claim certain streets and neighborhoods as their own areas. In fact, in one of the malls examined for this study—after the mall had gone through a complete renovation—the first customers to arrive on the morning of the grand reopening were teenage punkers and metalers who quickly claimed the public area near the record stores and video arcades as their social space.

The discussion shifts in Chapter 4 to an examination of as many as thirteen distinctive youth identities that are present on suburban high school campuses. In the chapter, titled "Kicking Back at 'Raging High,' " current teenage clique structures at four suburban high schools are analyzed, noting how uniformly teenage groups are stratified. Most apparent is how the common bond of social activities, athletics, dress, musical tastes, and so on differentiate teenage groups from one another.

Of particular note is the emergence of "star athletes" as the privileged class—a distinction that for one high school in Southern California led to the rise of a clique of athletes named the "Spur Posse." Capitalizing on their athletic prowess, fame, and social position, they abused this special privilege by instituting morally offensive competitions of sexual conquest and engaging in antisocial and delinquent acts.

Noted in each of the high schools studied is the presence of youth groups that are viewed as less desirable and less popular by other youths. These teens were treated by others as social outcasts or misfits and included punk rockers, heavy metalers, taggers, racist skinheads, stoners, and satanists. And it is these socially disenfranchised youths that later (in Part II) become the central focus of this book. Additionally, the experiences of gay youth and their position in the high school clique structure is examined.

The discussion turns in Chapter 5 to an examination of the array of youth styles and youth cultures that have emerged over the past several years. "Punk and Anarchy: Changes in the Youth Scene" explores the punk and postpunk scenes. Although the lingo may have mutated—from "slamming" to "moshing," for instance—the teen scene has remained basically the same. Like fireflies to bright lights, these youths are still attracted to loud music and thrashing dance styles, throwing themselves with abandon into "the pit."

An analysis of letters written to a self-help organization for teenagers involved in the earlier years of the punk scene—as well as letters from their concerned parents and other citizens alarmed at what has been happening to American youths in general—provides insight into the issues that so upset the modern teenager. Excerpts from these sad, often desperate letters, as well as those from the irate public, demonstrate how confusing and frustrating it has been for parents and teenagers alike to understand each other, to bridge the gap, and to open up lines of communication.

The concluding chapter of the first section, "Gutter-Punks and the Lure of the Street," looks at a segment of the two million homeless youth in America, the gutter-punks. These are the most chronically homeless kids who cling to the punk rock identity. Gutter-punks in Portland, Oregon, were interviewed about their lifestyle and values and about what punk means to them. Through our ethnographic research, the homeless youths tell their story in their own words.

Additionally, we discuss the role of tattooing and body piercing among the punk subculture and its relationship to the larger youth culture.

The international appeal of punk and heavy metal is explored through the analysis of over six hundred questionnaires completed by youths in Southern California and Christchurch, New Zealand. We examine similarities between those youths who self-identified as punk rockers and those who self-identified as heavy metalers in both countries. Further, both of these two groups are contrasted with other teenagers who completed the questionnaire but did not identify themselves as punk rockers or heavy metalers.

The concerns of both punk rockers and heavy metalers in such areas as estrangement from family, alienation, and patterns of juvenile delinquency are discussed in this cross-cultural focus. The findings show that punk rockers in both countries were the *most* alienated, compared to heavy metalers and to the control group of teenagers not involved in either of these two other youth styles.

SUBURBAN OUTLAWS

Not all teenage behavior can be characterized as groups of youths struggling to differentiate themselves from previous generations by adapting distinctive music, hairstyles, dress, and fads and fashion. Some recent juvenile behavior has taken on a decidedly more sinister tone, warranting response and crackdowns by school authorities, public officials, and the juvenile justice system. This behavior has crossed the line from merely being part of a youth style or youth culture to activity that has broken the law and is clearly delinquent. The second section of the book, "Suburban Outlaws," examines these more criminal youth behaviors, studying those juveniles who have embraced a decidedly more deviant identity.

The examination of subcultures of suburban outlaws begins with "Suburban School Shooters" in an attempt to understand the Columbine massacre and place it in perspective. This is followed by an analysis of "Tagger Crews and Members of the Posse" who have "mapped the heavens," leaving their marks for all to see. Then the analysis shifts to an examination of teenage skinheads, both racist and nonracist. This is followed by a discussion of stoner gang members, heavy metalers, and some punkers who have defied society in ways that make them a danger to both themselves and others and who are now held behind bars for their crimes. Here we also analyze those youths who seem most extreme in their acting out and alienation—teenagers who embrace Satanism.

Chapter 7 begins this section with an exploration of school gun violence. The moral panic after the Columbine shootings allows us to compare the official statistics about school shootings to the media response. The climate after such events is usually filled with armchair theorizing that blames everything from video games to Marilyn Manson for the supposed increase in school violence.

The reality of school gun violence is discussed, contrasted to the moral panics. Based on recent government reports, school violence is actually decreasing. However, other research shows that students are more fearful now than in the past and many are bringing guns to school out of that fear.

Some possible explanations for the late 1990s trend of multiple-victim school shootings also are explored. Among these are the problem of psychopathic youth, the connections between gun violence and masculinity, and the problem of disengaged parents.

Our discussion then turns, in Chapter 8, to tagger crews, the newest form of delinquent patterns to emerge in suburban communities during the past decade. Tagger crews involve bands of youths—armed with anything from spray cans and felt pens to chiseled knives and guns—who mark the landscape with their tags. According to police officials, more than 600 such crews now roam Los Angeles County streets, competing with other posses on their "bombing" runs. Interviews with several members of one such tagger crew are presented in Chapter 8.

Chapter 9, "Skinheads: Teenagers and Hate Crimes," takes a detailed look at modern skinhead youth styles. Noting the alarming rapid increase, begun in the late 1980s, of teenagers who are identifying with such groups, the study differentiates between several types of skinheads, including both the racist, often delinquent, skinhead teenagers, as well as their nonracist counterparts.

Results of questionnaires completed by both types of skinheads are presented. As expected, racist skinheads express their bias and rage toward minorities. Often shunned at high school by their more popular peers, mistreated and abused at home, teenage racist skinheads bully ethnic minorities, immigrants, and gays whom they perceive to be "weaker" than themselves. Also, the role that multiculturalism plays in schools in the 1990s is shown to be a factor in the success of skinhead recruiting.

Chapter 10, "Stoner Gangs and Satanic Youths," continues the discussion of delinquents who embrace an even stronger, more defiant, and collective youth identity. Frequently referred to by the police and law enforcement personnel as "stoners," these troubled youths have a history of violent affiliations with the punk rocker, heavy metaler, and/or satanic youth styles. Typically involved with white juvenile gangs, these stoners engage in a variety of antisocial behaviors, often under the influence of drugs or alcohol.

A detailed analysis of the case files of all teenage stoner gang members housed within the institutions of the California Youth Authority reveals common patterns. Not surprisingly, many of these juvenile stoner gang members had traumatic childhood experiences and have abused drugs and alcohol since they were youngsters. Likewise, their parents have a history of substance abuse. A composite profile of the stoner gang members documents their deeply troubled and alienated nature. This chapter also includes a discussion of youth that embrace Satanism and practice satanic rituals and sacrifice. Several case studies are presented from the California Youth Authority's files of adolescents who were self-proclaimed Satanists. In this section satanic rituals are discussed— often in the youngsters' own words—and reasons are given for the increased interest by some of our nation's youths in these types of activities.

SOCIETAL RESPONSES AND TRENDS

Part III, "Societal Responses and Trends," concludes the analysis with two chapters. Chapter 11, "Reactions to Youthful Offenders," looks at the range of societal reactions to these contemporary youth styles. From programs such as Back in Control—which employs a "Tough Love" approach to "depunking" and "demetaling" delinquent youngsters—to the treatment approaches used in the adolescent treatment hospitals and our nation's juvenile correctional facilities, a variety of approaches are explored that have been or are being used to treat, assist, and reunite these often lost, angry, and confused youngsters with their families and with society.

Finally, Chapter 12, "Generation Why? Crisis at the Millennium," builds on the research to predict what we can expect for the generations born in the 1980s, 1990s, and beyond. As the proportion of young people increases while the baby boom ages, new social relationships can be expected. How can we help the young people of the twenty-first century from falling into the same traps their twentieth-century predecessors did? This chapter uses demographic tools, such as birth rates, to chart how generations are defined. We also examine the broader social trends in society that pertain to youth. Viewing society in a cyclical fashion, we note the shifts in cultural values during the past decades and project into the new century.

In summary, *Renegade Kids, Suburban Outlaws: From Youth Culture to Delinquency* pinpoints several reasons why, and in what ways, some teenagers feel alienated. By examining a variety of youthful identities, we also note the common factors and differences in their varied expressions. It is important to listen to their pleas and try to understand their pain. Throughout the book their voices speak loudly and clearly regarding their alienation and their need to find alternative expression to what is troubling them. Furthermore, their voices inform us about the roles conformity and deviance play in their young lives. Finally, these troubled youths also have something to say about family, school, and modern life in suburban America.

In moving from the general to the particular, this book explores certain patterns that distinguish teenagers who share common youth styles and youth cultures—such as mall rats, high school cliques, punkers, and metalers, discussed in the first section from teenagers who share more delinquent identities—such as school shooters, tagger crews, racist skinheads, stoners, and Satanists, discussed in the second section. By examining juveniles who embrace one of these youth identities or delinquencies, we hope that society will gain greater insight into the complexity of these often rebellious adolescents.

NOTES

1. "The Monsters Next Door," cover story, *Time* (3 May 1999).

2. Michele Ingrassia, "Growing Up Fast and Frightened," *Newsweek* (22 November 1993), p. 52.

3. "Study of Youths' Problems Finds a Generation at Risk," *The Los Angeles Times* (9 June 1990), p. A-3.

4. Nanette Davis, *Youth Crisis: Growing Up in the High-Risk Society* (New York: Greenwood, 1999).

5. Larry Siegel and Joseph Senna, *Juvenile Delinquency: Theory Practice, and Law.* (Belmont, Calif.: Wadsworth, 2000).

6. Davis.

7. Sarah Thorton, "General Introduction," in *The Subcultures Reader,* ed. Ken Gelder and Sarah Thorton (New York: Routledge, 1997), pp. 1–7.

8. David Matza, *Delinquency and Drift* (New York: Wiley, 1964).

9. Michael Brake, *Comparative Youth Culture* (New York: Routledge, 1985).

10. Albert K. Cohen, *Delinquent Boys: The Culture of the Gang* (New York: Free Press, 1955).

11. Robert Agnew, "Foundations for a General Strain Theory of Crime and Delinquency," *Criminology* 30 (1992), pp. 47–87.

12. Howard Becker, *The Outsiders* (New York: Free Press, 1963).

13. Malcolm Klein, *American Street Gang, Its Nature, Prevalence and Control* (New York: Oxford University Press, 1995).

14. Wayne S. Wooden and Martha Lou Berkey, *Children and Arson: America's Middle-Class Nightmare* (New York: Plenum Press, 1984).

15. Randy Blazak, "Hate in the Suburbs: The Rise of the Skinhead Counterculture," in *The Practical Skeptic: Readings in Sociology,* ed. Lisa J. McIntyre (Mountain View, Calif.: Mayfield, 1999).

2

▼

Understanding Why Youth Become Deviant

Why did two teenagers from stable families in an upper-middle class neighborhood go on a murderous shooting spree in their high school—a rampage that ended in their own suicide? Why do the kids of liberal parents become Nazi skinheads? Why does a young person who has everything to gain risk it all to spray paint his or her tag on others' property?

Explanations of youth deviance are as diverse as the deviance itself. Before the Enlightenment, willful children were believed to have "the Devil" in them. The Enlightenment gave us a scientific rationale for studying criminal behavior. Nineteenth-century theorists, such as Cesare Lombroso, based their research on the idea that criminality was the product of certain biological traits. Other early theorists, such as William H. Sheldon, believed that certain body types were predisposed to delinquency. The first juvenile court was founded in 1899 and based on the theory that the cause of delinquency could be be isolated and cured.

Contemporary explanations are more likely to look at social causes of delinquency. Steven Messner and Richard Rosenfeld argue that America's high crime rates are a product of the cultural value that pushes people to succeed "at all costs" (1). Marxist criminologists would describe juvenile delinquency as a reflection of alienation in a capitalist society. Conservative criminologists focus on the breakdown of traditional institutions, such as the family, as a cause of crime.

The biological explanations of the first criminologists have also gained new life. Theorists are now exploring possible links between crime and food allergies, hormonal imbalances, learning disabilities, genetics, and intelligence. All of these theorists are concerned with answering the question, why do some people engage in criminal activities whereas others do not? With research to support a specific theory, they claim a policy can be developed to reduce the causes of crime.

CRIMINOLOGICAL AND SOCIOLOGICAL PERSPECTIVES

Most explanations of crimes, such as the Columbine High School shootings, are ad hoc. They are generated from the street or the arm chair by casual observers of society, who are sure that America's juvenile crime "explosion" is the result of baby boom parenting, video games, rap music, violent movies, lack of spirituality or a potato-chip-based diet. Although the correlations they draw may carry some weight in the popular media, they are not usually supported by research.

Criminologists and sociologists are no different in their arm-chair theorizing, except for the fact that they research their ideas. A century of study has found relationships between delinquency and issues such as a child's connection to nondelinquent institutions, goal orientation, and supervision. Social researchers try to make connections between microlevel (or individual) and macrolevel (or societal) patterns. It might be impossible to explain all the school shooters of the 1990s with a single theory—after all, each case is different. But by studying the situations of each crime and the backgrounds of the criminals, certain patterns may emerge.

Because crime is a form of social deviance, a good criminological theory will help to explain noncriminal deviance as well. One can assume that some of the motivation to be a punker or a satanist also applies to those who become shooters, taggers, or violent skinheads. Most social scientists see crime as a part of a continuum of antisocial behavior, some of which is illegal, and some of which is not.

This chapter provides an overview of criminological theories that use a sociological perspective as their basis. That means that these theories focus on the impact of environment on the decision to commit crime. Unlike biological theories, such as Lombroso's, or psychological theories (the work of Sigmund Freud, for example), sociological theories find external motivation for crime. These theories make the most sense with regard to our topic.

Crime rates are lower in suburban areas than in cities, and this must be due to the influence of environment. Then how do we explain the youth who fall through the cracks and choose deviant lifestyles? The explanations reflect four important schools of thought: (1) classic American delinquency theories, (2) British subcultural theories, (3) theories based on concepts of gender, and (4) postmodern theories about youth culture.

CLASSIC AMERICAN DELINQUENCY THEORIES

The attempt to explain suburban youth crime takes us back to the early part of the twentieth century, when social researchers were trying to understand rising rates of urban youth crime. It was a time when the United States was becoming a nation of bustling metropolises. Millions of immigrants, from places such as Ireland and Italy, were settling in these growing cities. The combination of urbanization and immigration also gave birth to another new American tradition: gangs.

In Chicago the work of Frederick Thrasher helped to demonstrate the impact of environment on delinquency (2). Thrasher's theory led to the research of fellow Chicagoans Clifford R. Shaw and Henry D. McKay (3). Shaw and McKay found that criminogenic neighborhoods produced high rates of delinquency and were characterized by high levels of displacement, ethnic and economic segregation, and social ills. They lacked healthy community networks to help guide children. Shaw and McKays' findings remain valid today, reflected in the observation of a gang-outreach worker who recently said, "The 'hood' is a neighborhood without the neighbor" (4). In these socially disorganized "hoods," youths are free to roam the streets and follow their youthful impulses.

Thrasher studied 1,300 youth groups and concluded that delinquency is frequently the end result of disorganized neighborhoods. Gangs were formed in what he called interstitial neighborhoods—in other words, communities that lacked social resources. These were places where the "fabric" of society had become torn. Families were poor and weak, and deviant and nondeviant values clashed. The gang, according to Thrasher, gave boys a way to interact for fun and excitement and became an alternative lifestyle that, over time, tended toward criminal behavior.

In 1938 another Chicago researcher, Robert Merton, used Émile Durkheim's notion of anomie to explain delinquency (5). *Anomie* is the sense of normlessness or rootlessness that is produced by shifting moral values. Where Durkheim used anomie to explain suicide rates, Merton used the concept to understand decisions to commit crime. The source of the normlessness came from the gap between goals and means. The goal orientation of American culture does not mean that everyone has the means to achieve those goals. This is especially true for the lower economic classes.

A poor person may want the same material item that a middle-class person wants but may not have a legitimate means to obtain it (such as a well-paying job, a savings account, or a bank loan). Thus the person becomes frustrated. Merton argued that these people will become "innovators"; that is, they will use illegitimate means (crime) to achieve their material goal.

Albert K. Cohen, who was a student of Merton's, demonstrated a connection between anomie and the formation of deviant subcultures (6). According to Cohen, lower-class boys cannot live up to the "middle-class measuring rods" of authority figures and therefore develop "status frustration." This stressful situation pushes the boys into gangs because there they can achieve a measure of autonomy. What Cohen calls "reaction formation" drives these frustrated gang boys to reject conventional values and become negativistic and hedonistic. The gang is a "problem solver" because it allows the lower-class boy to lash out in anger.

Sociologist Walter Miller helped to explain both lower-class and middle-class subcultural delinquency. Among the poor, low levels of adult supervision and the lure of the streets pull youth into single-sex peer groups. For boys, subcultures emerge that are based around certain values, called "focal concerns" (7). These focal concerns include autonomy, fate, excitement, smartness, toughness, and trouble. For these lower-class boys deviance is actually conformity to these subcultural values. The more a boy is involved with his peer group, the more likely following the focal concerns will lead him into delinquency.

Conformity also explained middle-class delinquency for Miller. Where the poor and rich are pushed into adulthood fairly early, the middle-class has no clear transition out of childhood. This situation, referred to as "youth," is filled with conflicting authorities, expectations, and messages. What is the role of a 17-year-old in our society? As a response, youths pull away from the adult culture that denies them access and form their own "youth culture." The focal concerns of this middle-class youth subculture are based on irresponsibility and hedonism. As with the lower-class kids, the more they conform to the subculture, the more likely they are to be deviant (8). Of course, the different focal concerns will lead to different types of delinquency.

Classic American Delinquency Theories and Suburban Youth Crime

These theories were created to explain traditional concepts of crime, primarily those committed by lower-class urban youth. But each offers insight into the explanation of suburban youth crime. The link lies in the connections between similar issues for both urban and suburban kids.

Thrasher's issue of interstitial youth could also apply to suburban kids who are at odds with society. In many ways the suburbs are also disorganized in that they are similarly segregated without strong social networks. The economic demands placed on working families prevents them from putting down many roots. The value of individualism mandates that families keep to themselves—behind their electric garage doors and in front of their television sets—instead of building strong communities. The result is a suburban "hood" in which kids roam the cul-de-sacs and malls in search of excitement.

Merton's use of anomie may also apply here. Although the suburban youth may have more economic means, goal blockage still exists. As Robert Agnew demonstrated in his "general strain theory," noneconomic goal blockage can be just as stress inducing (9). A teen who does not have legitimate means to achieve popularity, for example, may turn to deviant means and "innovate." There is also the general state of anomie associated with suburban youth in general, in which the expectations of each generation become less and less defined.

Suburban cliques, such as taggers and "Trench Coat Mafias," also reflect Cohen's notion of subcultures as problem solvers. It is not just lower-class youth who have difficulty living up to the expectations of the middle class. Those who cannot compete in the academic market may retreat to subcultures and become negativistic. The logic of reaction formation is "if I can't have it, then I don't want it." The destructive behavior of taggers, skinheads, and school shooters may be the frustrated expression of those who feel they have been denied full access to middle-class status and success.

Perhaps most useful are Miller's subcultural deviance theories. Conformity to male youth groups and the broader youth culture produces specific types of delinquency. If suburban youth are told to act like adults but are not given the privileges of adulthood, then they will retreat into the subcultural world with its delinquency-producing focal concerns. A young person pays adult ticket prices at the movies at age 12 but is denied entry into adult "R-rated" films until age 17. Youths who are permitted to vote at 18 are not allowed to drink alcohol until they are 21. With no rite of passage, the refuge for youths who are frustrated by these mixed messages becomes the subculture. For those who end up in trouble-oriented male groups, such as skinheads, conformity leads to violence. For more typically middle-class coed groups, such as mall rats, conformity includes petty theft and drug use.

BRITISH SUBCULTURAL THEORIES

Greatly influenced by the writings of Karl Marx, British theorists in the 1970s and 1980s put American criminological theory in a specific social class framework. The research, primarily from Birmingham University's Centre for Contemporary Cultural Studies, investigated the meaning embedded in youth subcultures. Why do so many different youth subcultures appear and then disappear? Why do some, such as punk rock, exhibit such longevity? How does a young person decide which subculture to join?

In 1979 Dick Hebdige asserted that the subcultural style of young people represents a "signifying practice" (10). Written in the middle of England's punk rock explosion, Hebdige saw punk and other subcultures as communicating a specific value set through fashion, music, and argot or slang. This "language" is a reflection of the power struggles of youth. For example, the surreal style of the original punks, which included bondage clothes, trash bags, and occasionally swastikas, communicated the sense of economic hopelessness in postwar England. The skinheads, on the other hand, chose a style that reflected the unity of tough working-class values.

Birmingham sociologist Stuart Hall focused on the creative power of youth subcultures. Subcultures, such as the punks, created a form of resistance to structural contradictions in society by creating their own rituals and culture (11). The "spontaneous" nature of subcultures is actually an attempt to not be subordinated by the dominant culture. This helps to explain the link between the deviant styles of youth and minority subcultures, both of which are expected to assimilate into the dominant culture. Each subculture reflects a specific moment in history and reflects that moment in its own lifestyle. For example, the "hustling" lifestyle of many urban black youths reflects a "wage-less" subculture, which occurs in a society that does not provide wages to many urban black youths.

Michael Brake would agree with Hebdige and Hall that "subcultures become meaningful statements about youth's existential position" (12). For Brake, youth subcultures were functional in providing space for people to explore the world outside of the home and work. The rebellious nature of youth subcultures creates for teenagers a safe zone in which to explore their identity. This new reference group allows young people to express the leisure values of culture outside of the watchful eyes of adults. Young people's "separateness" from the adult world is emphasized in their subcultural style. Without the requirements of work and the family, young people are free to experiment with the relationships institutionalized in the dominant culture. Their experimentation can include the manipulation of fashion, music, violence, concepts of property, and sexual relationships.

British Subcultural Theories and American Suburban Subcultures

The applications of the "Birmingham School" theories to American subcultures seem clear. A primary difference in the two societies is the class orientation of England and the "classlessness" of the United States. In the latter nearly everyone identifies as "middle class" in contrast to the strong working-class identification present in England. But if one takes the British theorists' notion of subcultural style as a form of communication, one can see that American youth, although perhaps not "class conscious," reflect their feelings about class in their subcultures and cliques.

The unique styles of suburban youth are also a form of language, Hebdige would contend. The lifestyle of skinheads may reflect a longing for class status in postindustrial America, a nation in which many hard working people routinely lose their jobs. The style of the taggers mimics sensibilities about urban youth culture. As is the tradition, here suburban youth adopt a culture borrowed from black urban America in recognition of a common bond of alienation. Satanists may be involved in an unspoken dialogue about hegemonic religions and the inherent hypocrisy built into Judeo-Christian institutions.

Suburban youth are also involved in forms of resistance—resistance to power structures as well as to the banality of suburban life. These young people are infinitely creative in their ability to invent styles or discover cultural forms that signify that they have not bowed to authority figures. Whether it is celebrating politically incorrect symbols such as guns, swastikas, or Satan or appropriating the already marginalized styles of ghetto youth, many middle-class youth latch on to anything that will set them apart from suburban conformity. As Hall asserted, this will reflect the larger structural relations of power in the society. It should not be surprising then to see how high school cliques' hierarchy reflects society, with the rich kids and the jocks at the top and poor kids and social outcasts at the bottom.

Ultimately these subcultures are functional. As we mentioned with regard to Miller's theory, middle-class kids experience even more normlessness, which pushes them into subcultures. As Brake argues, these suburban subcultures give young people a forum in which to work out their identity, manage status issues, and experience leisure. The primary activity of these groups thus is not "getting into trouble" but exploring the existential problems they share by just hanging out.

GENDER-BASED THEORIES

The feminist movement of the 1970s gave us a new way of looking at juvenile delinquency. The overwhelming maleness of crime had previously been attributed to physical and hormonal differences and even differences in intelligence. But the rising rates of female criminality forced mainstream social scientists to explore the environmental factors that contribute to the gendered nature of crime. Feminist theorists, by attempting to explain female delinquency, have also helped us to explain male delinquency.

A starting point is Freda Adler's 1975 book, *Sisters in Crime* (13). Adler argues that the increase in female arrests has to do with the changing roles of women in society. The traditional gender roles that had guided behavior in the past kept women away from opportunities to commit crime. Their lives in the home as daughters and mothers kept their focus on domestic matters. As women became more active in the workforce and in the men's world in general and as the restraints of gender roles loosened, women's opportunity for crime increased.

The new assertiveness helped to explain female involvement in gangs, robbery, and white-collar crime. Moreover, it gives us clues into male criminality as well. The assertiveness of masculinity has always been paired with the opportunity for crime. Boys' freedom from the constraints of the domestic realm gives them the chance to become exposed to criminal opportunities. If Adler's position (known as liberal feminist theory) is correct, one can expect male and female crime rates to become more similar as women gain equal access into the male world.

Of course, male criminality still outweighs female criminality. Ninety-six percent of those sent to prison are male (14). Radical feminists look deeper for an explanation of female criminality. According to their research, female crime is characteristically different from male crime. For example, female murderers generally kill people who have abused them for long periods of time, whereas men kill for a number of different reasons. Radical feminists point to the role of abuse in sparking female delinquency and deviance. Federle and Chesney-Lind found high rates of sexual abuse and neglect among female offenders as well as a double standard about the criminality of female sexuality (15).

A similar feminist perspective is that of James Messerschmidt. His book, *Masculinities and Crime,* outlined the way in which patriarchy constructs a version of masculinity that not only exploits women (pushing some into crime) but also makes crime more natural for men (16). American masculinity is built upon values of autonomy and financial provision. When the legitimate means to masculinity (such as a solid job) are taken away, men resort to crime as a way of "doing gender."

For Messerschmidt, this explains the difference in delinquency rates among poor minority boys and suburban white boys. The suburban boys surrender their masculinity during the school day and may seek to reclaim it after school through minor forms of delinquency. They are aware that, ultimately, the school will give them the where withal to ensure their financial autonomy in adulthood. The poor minority boys face a much wider array of emasculating forces. Not only do school teachers restrict autonomy, but the nonschool world offers little promise of economic power or social freedom. The authoritarian powers of a racist and classist society rob poor minority boys of legitimate means to assert their masculinity, so they resort to more serious forms of delinquency.

Gender-Based Theories and Suburban Delinquency

Like urban crime, suburban crime is overwhelmingly male. Some types of suburban delinquency are more male than others (such as skinheads), and some are less (such as mall rats). The feminist theories give one an insight into the dynamics of gender in suburban youth crime.

From the liberal feminist perspective, the dominance of male youth crime in the suburbs has been a product of opportunity. Young women were kept at home in a domestic apprenticeship with their mothers, whereas boys were allowed to "sow their oats." Research has shown that middle-class girls are supervised more than their male counterparts. Their curfews are earlier, and they are expected to be escorted by a male when away from home. Traditionally this has limited girls' opportunity for delinquency, but as gender roles change and parent supervision decreases in the face of working mothers and absent fathers, female delinquency increases.

From the radical feminist theorist perspective, patriarchy is as prevalent in the suburbs as in the cities, and so is the experience of sexual abuse. A 1993 study conducted by Wellesley College found that 90 percent of adolescent girls have been sexually harassed in school (17). Opportunities for abused females in the suburbs to commit crime may be structurally different from those in urban settings, but the root cause is the same.

For boys, Messerschmidt's theory posits various emasculating forces coercing boys to "do gender" through crime. This includes not only the standard authoritarian structure of high school but also declining job prospects, households, feminist groups, gay and lesbian groups, and antiviolence movements. Without legitimate means to perform traditional masculine behaviors, boys turn to crime to satisfy that need.

POSTMODERN THEORIES

In the 1980s and 1990s the field of cultural studies emerged as an interdisciplinary way of viewing culture. Postmodernists broke down the artificial barriers between sociology, psychology, women's studies, history, and other academic areas. The goal of postmodern theorists was to move away from looking at social phenomena through one lens, whether that was Marxist, feminist, conservative, or liberal. Modernists' dreams of human emancipation gave way to postmodern realizations that many social explanations can be true simultaneously; they just depend on the viewer's perspective.

Part of this multiple reading of texts by postmodernists is the realization of the social construction of reality. In a media-saturated environment reality becomes what Baudrillard called "hyper-reality" (18). The representations of culture become representations as loops of media images recycle and the definitions of things become contested. What is rebellion, for example? Is it an honest desire by youth to separate from adult culture? Or is it a pose contrived by manufacturers to sell leather jackets and CDs?

One of the premiere postmodern texts on American youth culture was Donna Gaines's 1992 book, *Teenage Wasteland* (19). Gaines used ethnographic research to uncover the meaning of a heavy metal subculture in Bergenfield, New Jersey. By looking at "rebellion" through the eyes and words of young people themselves, she found a group who resisted the mind-numbing boredom and economic hopelessness of suburbia that ultimately, for some of her subjects, ended in suicide. Her "border-crossing" technique took researchers out of the comfortable theoretical realm and plunged them into the youths' own stark social construction.

The work of Lawrence Grossberg, especially his 1992 book, *We Gotta Get Out of This Place,* advocates for youth and their culture (20). Grossberg argues that young people are constantly at odds with institutions of authority over control of their domain. He makes the case that rock music, the historical anthem of youth, is constantly coopted by everything from advertisers selling sneakers to the Republican Party. Similarly, the very concept of "youth" is disputed. Aging baby boomers claim the mantel of youth at one end of the age spectrum, whereas "cool" images of rock and rebellion are marketed to young children through products such as Mutant Ninja Turtles at the other end of that same spectrum (21). Young people's struggle is one to maintain the vitality of their own space.

Tricia Rose places the rebellion of hip-hop in the context of postindustrial America (22). What seems to be, on one level, an art form based on dancing, sexuality, and resistance to racism is actually much more complex. Rap music expresses coded messages about life in jobless America—messages that are designed to confuse mainstream America. For example, Rose argues that the loud booming car stereos of rap fans is a form of aural graffiti that contests the hegemony of white America.

Postmodern Theories and Suburban Deviance

One of the key themes of theorists such as Gaines, Grossberg, and Rose (as well as other cultural studies researchers, such as Deena Weinstein, Joseph A. Kotarba, and George Lipsitz) is the use of music to understand the meanings within youth subcultures. The application of ethnographic research methods that allow youths to construct their own meanings adds a new insight into the study. The experience of young people in the late twentieth and early twenty-first centuries is intrinsically different from that of previous generations. It is even difficult to apply one's own youth experiences to contemporary youth culture. The attempt to decode music is key to understanding that difference.

Gaines's work has focused on suburban youth for the past decade and has reinforced the postmodern position that specific events in young people's lives—such as suicides and homicides—can be interpreted in a number of different ways by different subjects. Her method of creating multiple voices within a singular subculture can be key to understanding the wide range of behaviors within one social group. Not all renegade kids and suburban outlaws are alike and may even be dealing with competing interpretations of their own.

The danger of making youth culture monolithic is also an insight offered by Grossberg. Youth culture and its definition are inherently political. Where does one draw the borders of suburbia? When does a boy in a clique become a youth in a subculture? The contest over control of youth cultural images will be even more intense because of high levels of commercialism. Everything distinctively youth ends up for sale at the mall or in a Gap fashion fad.

Finally, Rose's research on hip-hop culture informs ideas about white suburban culture. She writes about the natural affinity of white youth to aspects of black culture, such as rap music. But more important is her approach that looks for multiple levels of meaning in the cultural choices young people make. Why would a twenty-first century teenager subscribe to a music form such as punk, which is twenty-five years old?

The postmodernists ask us to deconstruct the meaning of cultural forms. Something as seemingly insipid as disco or the Spice Girls can hold deep meaning for young people who cling to it as a reflection of their world (23).

NOTES

1. Steven Messner and Richard Rosenfeld, *Crime and the American Dream* (Belmont, Calif.: Wadsworth, 1994).

2. Frederick Thrasher, *The Gang* (Chicago: University of Chicago Press, 1927).

3. Clifford R. Shaw and Henry D. McKay, *Juvenile Delinquency in Urban Areas* (Chicago: University of Chicago Press, 1942).

4. Halim Rassan, "Youth Gang Outreach," public address, 1997.

5. Robert Merton, "Social Structure and Anomie," *American Sociological Review* 3 (1938), pp. 672–82.

6. Albert K.Cohen, *Delinquent Boys: The Culture of the Gang* (New York: Free Press, 1955).

7. Walter Miller, "Lower Class Culture as a Generating Milieu of Gang Delinquency," *Journal of Social Issues* 14 (1958), pp. 5–19.

8. William Kvaraceus and Walter Miller, "Norm-Violating Behavior in Middle-Class Culture," in editor, *Middle-Class Juvenile Delinquency,* ed. Edmund W. Vaz (New York: Harper and Row, 1959).

9. Robert Agnew, "Foundations of General Strain Theory of Crime and Delinquency," *Criminology* 30 (1992), pp. 47—87.

10. Dick Hebdige, *Subculture: The Meaning of Style* (London: Methuen, 1979).

11. Stuart Hall, "Culture and the State," in *The State and Popular Culture* (Milton Keynes, UK: Open University Press, 1972).

12. Michael Brake, *Comparative Youth Culture* (New York: Routledge, 1985).

13. Freda Adler, *Sisters in Crime: The Rise of the New Female Criminal* (New York: McGraw Hill, 1975).

14. June Stephenson, *Men Are Not Cost-Effective* (New York: Harper Collins, 1996).

15. Katherine Hunt Federle and Meda Chesney-Lind, "Special Issues of Juvenile Justice: Gender, Race and Ethnicity," in *Juvenile Justice and Public Policy,* ed. Ira Schwarz (New York: Lexington Books, 1992).

16. James W. Messerschmidt, *Masculinities and Crime* (Lantham, Md.: Rowan and Littlefield, 1993).

17. Center for Research on Women, *Secrets in Public: Sexual Harrassment in Our Schools* (Wellesley College, 1993).

18. Jean Baudrillard, *Simulations* (New York: Foreign Agent Press, 1983).

19. Donna Gaines, *Teenage Wasteland: Suburbia's Deadend Kids* (New York: Harper Collins, 1993).

20. Lawrence Grossberg, *We Gotta Get Out of This Place: Popular Conservatism and Postmodern Culture* (New York: Routledge, 1992).

21. Ibid.

22. Tricia Rose, *Black Noise: Rap Music and Black Culture in Contemporary America* (New York: Routledge, 1994).

23. Randy Blazak, "Po-Mo Pop: Puff Daddy and the Spice Girls Explain Postmodernism to America" (paper presented at the 1998 annual meetings of the Pacific Sociological Association, San Francisco, 17 April 1998).

▼

Renegade Kids

3

Mall Rats and Life

in the Mall

"12 Hurt in Gang Gunfire at Mall in West Covina"

What began as a toe-to-toe argument between two groups of teenagers escalated into a wild shooting incident inside a West Covina (California) shopping mall Monday night, leaving one bystander and one gang member injured and sending more than 50 horrified shoppers ducking for cover.

The melee, one of a number of violent incidents that have plagued Los Angeles-area shopping malls and theaters, broke out between members of two warring gangs about 6:30 P.M., during peak shopping hours at The Plaza, police said.

Like other malls, The Plaza in the San Gabriel Valley has become a magnet for young people, some of them gang members who engage in occasional arguments and shoving matches. Until Monday night, it was mild violence that the mall's unarmed security guards could usually handle, merchants said" (1).

THE MALLING OF SUBURBIA

The opening of the Mall of America in August 1992 in a suburb of Minneapolis, Minnesota, follows more than three decades in which malls have transformed the way people shop and entertain themselves. At 4.2 million square feet, the nation's largest enclosed mall is not the world's biggest mall. That distinction belongs to the West Edmonton Mall in Alberta, Canada.

However, the new megamall has supplanted the Del Amo Mall in Torrance, California, for that distinction in the United States.

The Mall of America's retail and entertainment center boasted a $70 million, seven-acre version of a Southern California theme park, a golf course, a fourteen-screen movie theater, nine nightclubs, numerous comedy clubs, sports clubs, and forty restaurants. The mall could encompass five Red Squares, thirty-two Boeing 747 jumbo jets, or thirty-four average American shopping centers. As one observer noted, "The Mall of America was conceived in the consumption-is-king days of the mid-eighties, when many Americans professed to enjoy shopping more than sex" (2).

According to one consumer study, at least once a month 94 percent of all adults in the United States visit a mall to make a purchase, see a movie, browse, or even date. Since the first enclosed shopping mall opened in 1957 in Edina, Minnesota (also outside Minneapolis), malls have accounted for an increasing share of all retail sales, although there are recent signs that the popularity of such malls may have peaked (3).

Survey data for 1990 showed that in Southern California, shoppers averaged eleven trips to the mall every ninety days and spent $45 per visit. At the Glendale Galleria—long famous as a mall where teenage trends in clothes and hairstyles are first spotted—shoppers visited about nine times per quarter, spending $65 on each occasion (4).

Major suburban shopping malls number about 17,000 in the United States, and each attracts, on average, between 100,000 and 150,000 people on a typical weekend. The suburban shopping mall has long replaced the town square as the mecca for commerce. According to one figure, the average person spends 2.6 hours and $84 during a typical visit, compared with 55 minutes and $34 at other shopping centers. Further, 19 percent of visitors to a mall purchase something and nearly all (97 percent) state they plan to return (5).

The Mall of America opened to capitalize on such consumer patterns. Ten times the size of the malls most people are accustomed to shopping in, the initial phase of this megamall was big enough to hold seventy-eight football fields. Furthermore, eight hundred specialty shops line four indoor streets on three levels, and one must walk a quarter of a mile along one street to get from an anchor store in one corner of the complex to the next. Another distinctive feature is a 300,000-square-foot indoor amusement park that features a roller coaster, flume rides, and merry-go-rounds (6).

SHOPPING 'TILL YOU DROP

Sociologists have charged malls with everything from "draining downtowns to becoming new town centers to making trends," according to one observer (7). But in Southern California, malls clearly have transformed the social landscape for hundreds of thousands of people, including suburban youths.

Three of the nation's five largest shopping centers are located in Southern California: the Del Amo Fashion Center in Torrance with 3 million square feet;

South Coast Plaza in Costa Mesa with 2.6 million square feet (the fourth largest mall after The Galleria in Houston, Texas, with 2.8 million square feet); and Lakewood Center in Lakewood, California, with 2.5 million square feet (8).

In a detailed economic study of the South Coast Plaza shopping mall in 1992, on its twenty-fifth anniversary, several interesting patterns were noted. For one, between 1967 and 1992 the number of stores increased from 70 (including two anchor stores) to 250 (with eight anchor stores). The top name stores also changed, reflecting an up-scaling of the mall to fit its new higher-income shoppers, drawn from newer, higher-income residential areas built in Orange County during the intervening years. Sears, Woolworth, and the May Company anchored the mall in 1967. But by 1992 the presence of Chanel, Tiffany, Gucci, Cartier, and Emporio Armani had long booted the "riff-raff" in favor of stores that would attract the free-spending "trendies." The annual number of shoppers increased as well in that time period. In 1967, 500,000 shoppers were drawn to the mall; in 1992 that number had risen to 18 million (9).

DELINQUENCY IN THE MALL

Trouble in shopping malls—such as the 1992 account of shootings in the West Covina mall—has been much in the news of late. A front-page story in *The Wall Street Journal,* for instance, featured this headline: "Shoppers Beware: Malls May Look Very Safe, but Some Lure Crooks as Well as the Shoppers." In discussing crimes that can plague a mall, the *Journal* article examined police records of fourteen major crime incidents that occurred in just one North Miami Beach mall over a three-year period. Crimes reported included several incidences of shoplifting, armed robbery, indecent exposure, disorderly conduct, and attempted rape (10).

The article also went on to cite several other serious incidents at other suburban malls across the country, including the following two reports:

- In northern New Jersey, packs of teenage thieves carry how-to manuals for pillaging shopping malls. In one recent sweep, police arrested sixty-five youths aged 11 to 14 for allegedly stealing an estimated $250,000 in merchandise.

- In the Northland Mall outside Detroit, police tallied 2,083 crimes in 1985. Of these, 1,041 crimes were serious, including murders, assaults, rapes, robberies, and car thefts. It could have been worse, police say, had it not been for the mall management's tough approach: Northland's guards receive 240 hours of police training and have full arrest power, which eliminates any waiting for local police to arrive (11).

According to police officials, suburban malls—though not as crime-ridden as inner cities—are not as safe as one would expect. Besides being convenient for consumers, they also entice the criminal element as well, including muggers, rapists, car thieves, and shoplifters. Crime, it appears, is occurring more frequently in "nice places, like suburban malls" (12).

The actual numbers or rates of incidents of violence in malls are difficult to obtain. National crime statistics on mall crime (or on mall security litigation, the more technical term) are not tabulated, so the actual numbers are not available. Also, most police statistics are organized according to geographical areas that often do not isolate crime rates at a given locale such as a mall.

Furthermore, malls change over the years as the demographics of the surrounding community change, as with the South Coast Plaza. Officials note, however, that as crime in general spreads to the suburbs, malls—particularly older ones in formerly white-collar areas—are increasingly vulnerable.

One criminologist refers to malls as the new "Main Streets" of America, arguing that they get more crime per capita than the old main streets used to. Malls, in his opinion, have become a "no man's land" (13).

Other communities' crime statistics for malls are equally alarming. In the New Jersey community of Paramus, for example, 90 percent of crimes occur in the city's malls. A police study in the late-1980s showed 1,670 reported crimes at the malls—including 79 assaults and 346 stolen cars as well as shoplifting and robberies—in the first seven months of one year. The police chief attributed this 20 percent increase over the year before to an escalating drug problem (14).

In south Florida one upscale mall reported 10 sex offenses, 176 assaults, 64 holdups, 597 burglaries, 445 stolen cars, and about 2,000 larcenies, including shoplifting, within a two-year period in the late 1980s (15).

"Child Thieves Plague Malls"

A "charismatic" shoplifting mastermind organized about 75 New York City boys into a gang of thieves and gave them a manual that concentrates on expensive designer clothing at suburban malls in four states, authorities said. New Jersey and New York City police said children from a Brooklyn neighborhood made weekend trips to shoplift up to $800 worth of clothes apiece in exchange for money and drugs from the ringleader.

The latest arrests came when ten boys were nabbed at the Paramus Park mall, where forty-two children have been arrested, and at Willowbrook Mall in Wayne fifty boys have been arrested. The police chief described the boys as "streetwise and slick" and said they work in groups of ten on Saturdays, either taking a bus or being driven to New Jersey (16).

Such criminal patterns are not unique to the United States. During the Christmas holiday season in London, England, one recent year, fashionable department stores reported the occurrence of "streaming"—bands of juveniles racing through the aisles, grabbing what they could get their hands on, then tearing out of the stores before they could be apprehended.

The most common type of delinquency at malls is petty theft. Shoplifting costs consumers over 20 billion dollars a year (17). For the kids at the mall, "boosting" store items allows girls to be as criminal as boys. Females are as likely as males to be caught, although males are more likely to be convicted (18).

The presence of small items for sale in a mall and the traditional role of women as "shoppers" gives girls more opportunity to steal. But as young men flood the malls, the gender gap in shoplifting is closing (19). Male shoplifters tend to steal more expensive items and conceal them in their clothes. Women are more likely to take clothing, cosmetics, and food and conceal them in bags or purses (20).

Research about shoplifting helps one to understand how the kids in the mall commit their crimes. According to Baumer and Rosenbaum, 70 percent of juveniles apprehended for shoplifting were working in groups (21). Most were in their midteens. The shoplifting arrest rate declines after age 17 (only to creep up again after age 23). Baumer and Rosenbaum found that these young shoplifters shared certain characteristics—they were very nervous, walked up and down the isles aimlessly, looked around frequently, and left the store, returning on several occasions.

R. H. Moore studied 300 convicted shoplifters and found a common pattern (22). Young amateurs were the most common type (56 percent). They stole small personal items when they had the opportunity. These petty thieves admitted their behavior was morally wrong. They tended to be plagued with mild personality disorders or, most commonly for females, psychosocial stressors, such as family disruption. Other types included "impulse shoplifters" (15 percent), who would pick up an item and carry it around the store deciding whether to steal it, and "occasional offenders" (15 percent), who would steal for the thrill or because they were dared to. The occasional offenders would be embarrassed when caught and plead for a second chance.

At the beginning of the twentieth century, affluent women who shoplifted were diagnosed with "kleptomania" to protect them from the stigma of criminality (23). Today's kids in the mall who steal do not have that same luxury even though research shows that 80 percent of those who engage in "nonsensical shoplifting" show signs of clinical depression. Today's youth are more likely to be formally labeled as criminal (24).

An Inviolate Place

Although the original concept of the mall dates back to ancient Greece, the actual term *mall* started out in old England as nothing more than a strip of green grass where a croquetlike game called "pall mall" was played. Today malls in England are referred to as "retail markets" (25).

The inviolate feel of a mall—somewhere between a living room and a park—makes any violent disruption such as crime and assault seem all the more shocking. Malls are among the few common areas where people from different ethnic backgrounds, social classes, and neighborhoods cross paths willingly.

According to one urban anthropologist, violence is not what one expects to encounter in malls. "Their major design is safety, to provide strangers with a safe place to exchange goods. It's very much a symbolic ground for safe space, and a violent transgression on it is a collective violation" (26).

Violent incidents at malls shatter this sense of security. Although not all incidents involve youths, many mall operators see teenagers as a major problem. In a 1990 poll by the International Council of Shopping Centers, 37 percent agreed that large groups of teenagers were bothersome. Keeping the malls safe presents a paradox because, at the same time, the shopkeepers want teenagers around because they are frequent shoppers. There is a lot of "teen buying power" (27).

SOCIAL FUNCTIONS OF MALLS

Several excellent books and magazine articles have been published on the social phenomenon of teenagers and suburban shopping malls. William Kowinski, for instance, in his book *The Malling of America: An Inside Look at the Great Consumer Paradise,* describes the mall as the modern version of "Main Street USA." Devoting an entire chapter to youths, "Kids in the Mall: Growing Up Controlled," Kowinski contends that the majority of American youths today have probably been going to malls all of their lives, spending more time in the mall than anywhere else but home and school (28).

One could argue that just as lower-income youths get their "street smarts" from hanging out on inner-city street corners, their middle-class counterparts, hanging out in these suburban shopping meccas, get (more or less) exposed to the larger world and gain a sense of "mall (or consumer) smarts."

Kowinski sees the mall as a "university of suburban materialism," where youth from coast-to-coast are educated in material consumption. Noting the economic and social ramifications of suburban youths' buying power, Kowinski views this as but another reflection of the changes taking place in family life and social mores. Concurring with child psychologist David Elkind, Kowinski feels that the pressure on teens to buy the array of products presented in the mall probably exposes these youngsters to too much of the adult world too quickly, hurrying the child to become an adult (29).

In another important book, *The Mall: An Attempted Escape from Everyday Life,* Jerry Jacobs presents an ethnographic account of a mid-sized, enclosed suburban shopping center. Jacobs notes how the mall serves different age groups, including teenagers, and social classes in their search for meaning and as a "flight from boredom." The modern mall, Jacobs argues, provides three things for its participants. First, it offers people entertainment or just plain diversion. Second, it provides the public with convenient shopping. And, third, the mall offers public, social space—a place to meet and interact with others. In other words the modern shopping center has become an "indoor street corner society (30).

Karen Lansky contends that kids spend so much time in the mall partly because parents encourage it, assuming it is safe and that there is adult supervision. The structured and controlling environment of the mall is ideal for them. According to Lansky, "True mall rats lack structure in their home lives, and adolescents about to make the big leap into growing up crave more structure than our modern society cares to acknowledge "(31).

Lansky also believes that the mall has become *the* focus of these young people's lives.

Malls are easy. Food, drink, bathrooms, shops, movie theaters—every part of the life-support system a modern kid needs is in the mall. Instant gratification for body and senses—and all of it close at hand, because malls are designed to make life more comfortable by eliminating parking problems, long walks, heavy doors, hot sun, and depressing clouds. It is ironic, in fact, that the mall is becoming all that many kids know of the outside world. It is a placeless space whose primary virtue is that it is all inside. Kids come in from the cold (or heat) for a variety of reasons, of course. But the main reason they seek the mall, especially in the summer when school is out, seems to be because they cannot think of anything better to do (32).

Lansky sees mall rats as kids with nowhere else to go. Their parents may drink or take drugs, be violent or just gone. Whatever the situation, the mall becomes the home they don't otherwise have. For them, the mall is a rich, stimulating, warm, clean, organized, comfortable structure—the only structure in some of their lives (33).

In gathering material for her research, Lansky interviewed several adolescents. One male expressed the belief that the mall "belongs to the mall rats." Arguing that the mall is *his* property, his mission in life, he said, is to become "top mall rat," adding that without the mall he and his friends would become "street people." A female mall habitué Lansky interviewed complained that the only place in the mall that is "theirs" is the arcade because she and her friends get kicked out of the other places. Security warns them to keep moving if they are not buying anything. It is these kids, according to Lansky, that the mall owners do not like. The managers resent having to set limits for these kids—limits that should be the responsibility of the community or their family. The owners discourage these youth because they often do not have much money to spend, yet drain the mall's resources (34).

A DAY IN THE LIFE OF A MALL RAT

For the first edition of this book, a study was conducted in 1988. It was decided to contact teenage youths in suburban malls because they were so readily accessible there, easy to approach and to interview. A detailed questionnaire, titled the "Youth Survey" (see Appendix A), was developed.

Although teenagers in several suburban high schools would be approached as well, the vast majority of the interviews and surveys gathered for the Youth Survey portion of this study were completed by over four hundred youths in Southern California malls. The initial focus of this study, therefore, began with meeting and talking with these so-called teenage mall rats.

One of the first young men so contacted was "Bob Bogan," or "Skidd Marx," as he preferred to be called, who allowed Wooden to spend several afternoons with him as he wandered through the Brea Mall. Seventeen and

5'10" tall, Skidd struck a mean pose. With his black hair spiked all over with three separate one-foot tails in back, Skidd also sported eye makeup, a leather jacket studded with spikes, a white T-shirt with a punk band logo on it, black Levis rolled up high, and black Converse high tops. Skidd also sported four hanging earrings in each ear and a loop pierced into his right nostril. Decked out in full punk regalia, Skidd cut the swaggering image of the "young man about the mall."

Skidd, like all of the teenagers studied in this book, resided in suburbia. He came from a middle-class background, and both of his parents worked. He defined himself as "a suburban punk bordering on the punk funk." Skidd, in true mall rat fashion, spent much of his free time and social life in the Brea Mall.

Q: When did you first define yourself as being into punk or punk funk? How did the process occur?

A: It was in my third year of high school. I really wasn't feeling that good about myself at the time. I felt very self-conscious at school. I always kind of dressed differently. Being tall, people usually looked at me physically, and I used to be very insecure about that. So I kind of had the attitude, if I do something a little bit different, then that would be the reason why they're staring at me. I can't do anything about the fact that I'm tall.

Q: So it gave you a rationalization?

A: Right. The punk thing is when I just didn't care what I looked like. My parents were always saying, "You're such a nice looking young man. Why do you want to do that?" That really used to bother me. I remember that when I'd get depressed, I'd go into the bathroom, and I'd just start butchering my hair. I look back now on those days when I was "hard core punk" and kind of laugh at it. But I cut all my hair off, and I would just dress really crappy all the time. I didn't want anyone to know that I was from a middle-class family. My parents have a Mercedes, and I didn't even want to drive around in it.

Q: Who was the first person to label you as punk, or did you label yourself?

A: Yeah, I just labeled myself. I had some friends then that were punk, and I was really into skateboarding, and a lot of people that were into punk were into skateboarding. That's how we would come to the mall—on our skateboards.

Q: Did defining yourself as punk solve some issues for you?

A: I thought so at the time. But I don't really think it did. At the time I thought of these things very differently than I think of them now. That was three years ago when I was fourteen. At the time I thought, oh, this is great. I liked the attention, and another reason was that my girlfriend's parents were very middle-of-the-road. I never really liked them, and I kind of liked to piss them off.

Q: What does punk mean to you now?

A: I don't know because it's really lost its focus now, I think. To me, I still consider myself a punk on the inside, if we still go by the definition of punk as doing your own thing. I still go to a lot of the gigs (concerts), and I hang out with my punk friends here.

Q: Why is society threatened by, or indifferent to, youths like you?

A: I think a lot of it is that they don't have the balls to do it themselves. I heard a real interesting thing in a punk movie. This guy says—and he used to dye his hair a different color every other week—a lot of people don't like it because they look at him and wish they could dye their hair blue or orange or yellow or whatever, but they're in their jobs or locked in to certain things, and they're pissed at him because they can't do it themselves.

Q: The anger that you experience, where does it come from?

A: A large part of why I still insist on being a little bit different is because it really bugs me when people can't get past what people look like on the outside. That's one of the arguments I have with my parents. When I used to cut my hair up, I would say, "Look, I haven't changed on the inside any, so what should it matter what I look like on the outside?" And that's still one of my big battles with them. They say, "You're going to have to conform. You're going to have to do this if you want to get ahead in society, and first impressions are a big part of it."

Q: You don't have the same middle-class aspirations as your family?

A: No, I don't. They're into making money. My dad told me he was going to become a millionaire within the next year and a half. I believe he will because he's damn good at what he does. He's vice-president of investments at a major financial firm. You know, "Get a piece of the rock."

Q: Do you ever see yourself changing into something like that?

A: Sometimes I feel that I want more money. Like right now I do want more money. I need money to pay insurance on my car and fix it up. Whatever I can do to keep it running. It's a piece of shit. It's an old '73 Nova. But, you know, I want to have money so I can go see bands, so I can go party, so I can buy my girlfriend nice things, like take her out to dinner maybe once now and then, and buy her a gift on her birthday.

Q: Why do you spend so much time at the mall?

A: It's weird, this place, the Brea Mall. I've been coming here since I've been in sixth grade. I've lived in Brea for almost eight years now. I've always come here. Even when I was a kid. Whenever I don't have anything to do I come to this mall.

Q: You just come here to hang out?

A: Yeah, just because there's nothing else to do. You go to the arcade. You walk around. This is where all your friends hang out. Talk to people. I know everyone that works in this mall. I work in this mall. I know all the people that work in here. I know everyone that hangs out and stuff. We have a bad image now because there are people that come to this mall with an attitude like, "We're so great. If you don't hang out here, you're not cool." That's not the way I feel. I've never felt that way. It's just a place for me to go when I'm bored. There's nothing to do now. I've really no place to go. I've got school, I've got work, I've got band, and I've got a girlfriend. I'm always busy, but I always seem to be bored. There's really never anything exciting to do. "Nothing to do?" "Go hang out at the mall."

"What are you going to do today?" "Like hang out at the mall. Hang out with everybody else who's bored."

"I've got no money. Let's hang out at the mall."

A guy we know who comes from Boston came here about two years ago. Off the Greyhound from Boston. He left Boston because the scene was dead. In L.A. he said, "Where do all the punks hang out?" They go to the "Brea Mall." He got on a bus that said "Brea Mall," came here, and we met him. And he's been here ever since.

Q: Why are you at the mall today?

A: I got out of school at 12:20 P.M. I didn't feel like going home and doing my homework. Nothing else to do. I didn't want to sit home watching the TV set. It's stupid. TV sucks. So I come here. There's nothing to do. I come here and I talk to my friends. What the hell. Or I go to work. Or I have band practice. Or I go see my girlfriend. It's just something to do. And you can tell everybody this, "Punks are not all scumballs. A few of them are. And I'm graduating with honors from high school. I've always been a straight-A student, and I still am."

Q: What's it like working in the mall?

A: I don't dress totally punk while I'm at work. I work at May Company. I used to do a lot of little experiments on people. 'Cause when I used to have my hair cut really short, people can't tell if you're trying to be punk or you're just conservative. They can't tell. So I'd be waiting on them all along. Then we'd get up to the counter, and I'd go to sign their check or whatever, and I'd put my arm up on the counter and I'd have a dog chain for a bracelet. All of a sudden, all the rules changed. Their perceptions of me, all of a sudden— bingo—"punk" jumped into their mind. So I could have been the nicest guy in the world, but as soon as they thought I was a punk, then I was a piece of shit. Just like that.

Q: How would they express that change?

A: They were just really stand-offish. All of a sudden. You could just watch them recoil. A lot of times I would wear a safety pin for a lapel pin. A safety pin with a padlock hanging off of it. People would always ask me, "What does that signify? What is that?" People always want to know the rules, and I wouldn't give them to them.

Q: Isn't that what punk's about? Isn't that the statement you are making dressed today like you are and roaming the mall?

A: Oh, yeah, exactly. A lot of it is taking symbols that people are so accustomed to and distorting them. That's the way with the swastika. They'll take a swastika and put it next to a happy face. Just really destroy things. Just designify and resignify things so they don't mean anything anymore.

People want the rules so badly. That's another thing I noticed while working at May Company. People are basically cattle. They feel very comfortable in a line. Because they don't have to think. And they feel safe. So as a punk, when you question that, and you look them straight in their faces and say, "I'm not going to stand in line. And I'm not going to be afraid to think." That kind of scares them off.

Q: Are you very street wise?

A: I was never street wise at all until I got into punk. I was always so at home so sheltered. I never was even kicked out of my house. But being a punk, you always learned how to be streetwise. Spending time watching people here in the mall, I've learned the things of the street—how to act, what to do, what's a good move, and all that. 'Cause I've stayed a week on the street. I spent some time at this person's house, and you just go off and have fun. Live wherever. It was fun. I don't think I could do it though all the time. But I had a good time.

As this interview with Skidd Marx demonstrates, many of these young-sters in the mall suffer from boredom. Lansky noted this sad pattern as well:

Ask the kids in the malls, and they'll talk about boredom: great, yawning, empty stretches of boredom against which they don't know how to marshal their undirected energies. Boredom that neither their families nor their communities nor their schools are prepared to acknowledge and help them with (35).

Lansky also views sexual posturing as another element that attracts these kids to the mall. No one expects these youths to follow through on their sexual impulses, but this very absence of expectation provides the kids with the opportunity to indulge in their wildest fantasies. In the mall,

They cluster about like pigeons looking for a handout. They are a pastiche of multicolored bandannas tied around jeans and heads, earrings, leg warmers, flats and miniskirts, sheared sweatshirts, spiked haircuts, garish makeup, pirate shirts and juliette nails—symbols of the boredom and voyeurism that are a modern adolescent dilemma (36).

Malls have become our contemporary town squares. Not just the preferred place to shop, they are also popular teenage hangouts and rendezvous arenas for singles on the prowl. Shopping malls have become our fantasy cities.

The sociological and cultural ramifications of the shopping mall have been well documented. For some observers, young people's values have shifted away from the family. With parents taking a less active role in rearing their children, middle-class teens are looking outside the family for some form of structure. The malls are one place they find it. For some youths the mall helps to fill a void left by churches, schools, and families when they fail to provide centers of ritual and meaning.

For many teens this means a muddling of traditional middle-class values. Life in the mall with its endless array of material goods leads some of today's teens to become more materialistic, less realistic, and harder to motivate than teens of previous generations.

Sociologists also worry that malls help create kids' illusions that they will never have to suffer from want. Under one giant roof, malls demonstrate the same endless conspicuous consumption fed to these teenagers on television. Only two generations removed from the Great Depression, today's middle-class youths are generally ignorant of poverty or the potential for it, particularly due to the economic boom years of the late-1990s.

In 1999 a new trend developed—demalling (37). Although malls will continue to dominate retailing and serve as teenage suburban hang-outs, consumer tastes may have shifted away from enclosed complexes to more open-aired, streetlike facilities. In some areas previous mall space is being converted into large entertainment centers, office buildings, and even housing. Even with such changes, youth—though they may no longer be termed "mall rats"—will continue their quest to stake out territory, establish turf, and consume.

Youth at the Movies—at the Mall

In the teen films of the early 1980s, the mall was a central location. Movies such as *Weird Science (1985)* and *Valley Girl* (1983) reflected how the mall had become the town square for high school kids. The best of the era, *Fast Times at Ridgemont High (1982)*, based on Cameron Crowe's undercover study of teens, uses the mall as a metaphor for the dead-end economy of teendom. Jobs at the multiplex or the fast-food restaurant seem little different from the slacking done by Jeff Spicolli (Sean Penn) at the video arcade. It was not until Kevin Smith's *Mall Rats (1995)* that the dark side of the mall, as a temple of consumerism, was lampooned.

NOTES

1. Newspaper accounts are interspersed throughout this book in edited form. In several instances, identifying characteristics such as names and locations have been altered. The exact citation, however, is given. Vicki Torres, "Two Hurt in Gang Gunfire at Mall in West Covina," *Los Angeles Times* (26 February 1992), p. A-1.

2. Bernice Kanner, "Mall Madness," *New York* (29 March 1993), p. 18.

3. Isabel Wilkerson, "World's Biggest Mall to Have 800-Plus Shops," *San Francisco Chronicle* (14 June 1989), p. B-7.

4. Peter Bennet, "Malls Offer a Walk on the Mild Side," *Los Angeles Times* (20 December 1990), p. E-19.

5. Kanner.

6. Wilkerson.

7. Jennifer Lowe, "A Mirror of OC Life," *Orange County Register* (15 March 1992), p. B-1.

8. Ibid., p. B-4.

9. Ibid.

10. Ann Hagedorn, "Malls May Look Safe, but Some Lure Crooks as Well as the Crowds," *The Wall Street Journal* (10 September 1987), p. A-1.

11. Ibid.

12. Ibid.

13. Ibid.

14. Ibid.

15. Ibid.

16. "Child Thieves Plague Malls," *San Francisco Chronicle* (22 April 1989), p. A-2.

17. Larry Siegel, *Criminology* (Bellmont, CA: Wadsworth, 2000).

18. Curt R. Bartol, *Criminal Behavior: A Psychosocial Approach* (New Jersey: Prentice Hall, 1998) p. 327.

19. R. H. Moore, "Shoplifting in Middle-America: Patterns and Motivational Correlates," *International Journal of Offender Therapy and Comparative Criminology* 28 (1984), pp. 53–64.

20. Bartol.

21. T. L. Baumer and D. P. Rosenbaum, *Combatting Retail Theft: Programs and Strategies* (Boston, MA: Buterworth, 1984).

22. Moore.

23. Llod Klemke, *The Sociology of Shoplifting: Boosters and Snitches Today* (Westport, CT: Praeger, 1992).

24. E. Yates, "The Influence of Psychosocial Factors on Nonsensical Shoplifting," *International Journal of Offender Therapy and Comparative Criminology* 30 (1986), pp. 203–11.

25. L. M. Boyd, "The Grab Bag," *San Francisco Chronicle* (20 March 1988), p. F-7.

26. Pat Morrison, "Violence Mars Malls' Image as Safe Places to Shop, Relax," *Los Angeles Times* (1 March 1992), p. B-1.

27. Ibid., p. B-4.

28. William S. Kowinski, The *Malling of America: An Inside Look at the Great Consumer Paradise* (New York: William Morrow and Company, 1985), p. 351.

29. Ibid.

30. Jerry Jacobs, *The Mall: An Attempted Escape from Everyday Life* (Prospects Heights, IL: Waveland Press, 1984).

31. Karen Lansky, "Mall Rats," *Los Angeles Magazine* (August 1984), p. 250.

32. Ibid., p. 254.

33. Ibid., p. 257.

34. Ibid.

35. Ibid.

36. Ibid.

37. Morris Newman, "In Rise and Fall of Malls, Weaker Ones Get 'Demalled,'" *Los Angeles Times* (14 December 1999), p. A-1.

4

Kicking Back
at "Raging High"

"Truancy Soaring: Why Go to Class When Mall Beckons?"

On a typical day last month, nearly one of every three Sacramento County high school students—more than 10,000—missed one or more academic classes. The problem is reaching crisis proportions at some schools, where nearly half the students skip class each day, the Sacramento Bee learned by examining attendance records in the county's five largest school districts.

"It's easy enough—you just walk out," said Rachel, a 15-year-old sophomore at McClatchy High School. "They have hall monitors, but if you skip every day, you know what you're doing. It's easy to get away with it." Rachel said most of her classmates skip about ten periods a week. Typically, they forge their parents' signatures on notes to get back into class, she said (1).

"Campus Styles Rekindle Debate on School Codes"

Shawn Peters, a 16-year-old junior at South Whittier High School, hardly thought twice about wearing a gold stud earring on his left ear.

"It's a form of identification and I like the way it looks on me," he said.

But school officials were chagrined when Peters, who favors Judas Priest T-shirts and a leather jacket, appeared on campus last December wearing the earring. Saying earrings on boys are not appropriate for campus, school officials gave Peters an ultimatum: Take it off or be suspended.

He refused, touching off a battle between school officials and the American Civil Liberties Union. Shawn missed three days of school but was allowed back on campus—

with the earrings—after the South Whittier school board decided that it could not afford a costly court fight to uphold its position (2).

"Where 'Boys Will Be Boys,' and Adults Are Befuddled"

It was lunchtime at Lakewood High School, and the big men on campus were strutting their stuff at the local Taco Bell.

Eric Richardson, a 17-year-old football star, swaggered in, a T-shirt reading "No Crybabies" stretched taut across his pectorals.

"I got the power! I got the finesse! I got everything!" Eric declaimed to no one in particular.

Eric and eight of his friends, members of a group called the Spur Posse, had spent the last few days in jail, accused of molesting and raping girls as young as 10.

Now all but one had been released, while investigations continued. And the boys returned to school this week to a heroes' welcome, their status enhanced and their scrapbooks thicker by several press clippings. The tale of the Spur Posse in some ways sounds like an old story about bad boys and fast girls, about athletes who can do no wrong and the people who fawn over them. But it comes as codes of sexual conduct are colliding with boys-will-be-boys mores and as unemployment and broken marriages are troubling the still waters of this piece of suburbia southeast of Los Angeles (3).

THE FOSTERING OF LOW SELF-ESTEEM

Although it often smacks of cliché, America's teenagers have serious self-esteem issues. According to material collected by a gang prevention and intervention project located in Southern California, Turning Point, the major key to resolving the "social ills" of our junior high and high school campuses is to focus on how to improve and bolster each student's self-esteem.

This view is supported by the findings of the "Report of the California Commission for Reform of Intermediate and Secondary Education," which contends that a person's education should contribute to self-understanding and self-esteem. Both of these organizations and other groups agree that by teaching self-esteem, our public schools will help students overcome their negative ideas about themselves and discover their unique potential (4).

According to one study, two out of three Americans suffer from low self-esteem. Although 80 percent of children entering school in kindergarten or the first grade feel good about themselves, by the time they have reached the fifth grade, the number has dropped to 20 percent. And by the time they become seniors in high school, the number has dropped to 5 percent! (5)

Furthermore, according to this report, students endure the equivalent of sixty days each year of reprimanding, nagging, and punishment. During twelve years of schooling, a student is subjected to 15,000 negative statements. That is three times the number of positive statements received.

In a recent National Institute of Education study, 1,000 30-year-olds were asked whether they felt that their high school education had taught them the skills they needed in the real world. Over four-fifths answered, "Absolutely not." When asked about the skills they wished they had been taught in high school, they answered:

> Relationship skills—such as how to get along better with the people they live with; how to find and keep a job; how to handle conflict; how to be a good parent; how to understand the normal development of a child; skills in financial management; and the "meaning of life" (6).

In a related study, 2,000 youths in 120 high schools were asked the following two questions: If you were to develop a program for your high school to help you cope with what you're needing now, and what you think you will need in the future, what would the program include? And list the top ten problems in your life that you wish were dealt with better at home and at school (7).

The respondents listed the same skills as the 30-year-olds in the National Institute of Education study. They further suggested that the skills training would have to include assuming responsibility for one's actions; respecting one's self and others; gaining a better sense of reality; and improving relationship skills. The two top problems they listed were *loneliness,* with even the most popular kids stating that they felt lonely, and *not liking themselves.*

The Consequences of Low Self-Esteem

Esteem issues were raised in the school shootings in Springfield, Oregon, and Littleton, Colorado, and, based on the research, should not be quickly dismissed. Students who hold themselves in low self-esteem frequently resort to antisocial and delinquent behavior. When such behaviors are expressed within the school context, as they often are, they can take many forms. On the personal level, these frustrated students frequently engage in acts of truancy; experience despondency or depression; resort to drug and/or alcohol abuse; attempt or commit suicide; show disrespect for their parents, teachers, and authorities; become disruptive and inattentive in class; and/or fail to perform up to their academic potential.

According to the National Center of Health, one adolescent attempts suicide every seventy seconds. Furthermore, over 6,000 students per year take their own lives. Nationwide, one of every ten adolescents will make a serious attempt at suicide before graduating from high school (8).

Other alarming statistics from the National Center of Health include the following:

- Every twenty minutes an adolescent is killed in an automobile accident. Over 50 percent of these accidents are attributed to alcohol or drug abuse.
- Every thirty seconds an adolescent becomes pregnant. Fourteen adolescents per day have their *third* child.
- One-half of all high school seniors have used illegal drugs; 90 percent have used alcohol.

- One-fourth of the current high school population is judged to have a serious problem with alcohol or drugs. (Serious drinking is defined as going on a binge once every three weeks and drinking away from the family on a regular basis.)
- Dropping out of school is now considered seriously by 50 percent of *all* high school youths in the United States. The dropout rate is now 27 percent nationally and 50 percent in urban settings (9).

These teenagers' frustrations may not end with acts of self-destruction. Some students who are unable to cope with the pressures of home and school may take out their hostility on the teaching faculty, administrators, and staff of the schools they attend; on other students; or on school property. Such delinquent behavior may include committing acts of violence against teachers and staff; bullying or intimidating fellow students; participating in acts of vandalism against school property, including arson (as Wooden and Berkey's book, *Children and Arson: America's Middle-Class Nightmare,* conclusively documented (10); and/or joining gangs and participating in "gang-banging" activity.

HIGH SCHOOL BULLIES

Surely affecting the self-esteem of teens is the ongoing problem of bullying. Bullying peaks between fifth and ninth grade but is still prevalent in high schools (11). A study of 207 junior and senior high school students found that 88 percent had observed bullying and 77 percent claimed to have been bullied (12). The traditional bully is physically or verbally violent, but under the watchful eye of school officials, bullies may use psychological tactics, such as exclusion, ridicule, and shame.

The impact is significant. For anyone who has survived the trauma of repeated harassment and victimization by a handful of bullies, the issue raises a host of emotions. An estimated 160,000 kids miss school everyday in the United States for fear of being bullied, according to the National Association of School Psychologists (13). Victims tend to have chronic physical and psychological problems, including low self-esteem, depression, and the tendency to become chronic victims. Their problems can reach into adulthood, leading to fearfulness and schizophrenia (14).

The issue of the victimization of young males and their responses to it began to get national attention when the school shootings began in the mid-1990s. William Pollack, author of *Real Boys: Rescuing Our Sons from the Myth of Boyhood,* observed, "When enough shame collects inside him—when he feels disconnected, unpopular, less than 'masculine,' maybe even hated—the boy tries to master his feelings and reconnect with others through violence" (15).

The web sites that popped up to praise Kip Kinkel and the Columbine shooters were the disparate voices of bully victims who saw an end to bullying in the equalizing power of the gun.

The outlook for the bullies themselves is not bright either, even if they survive the rage of their victims. They are more likely to drop of school (16) and suffer from abuse at home (17). A Scandinavian study found that bullies experienced a lifetime of problems. Those who were violent at eight were still aggressive at thirty. They were more likely to commit antisocial acts than non-bullies, including vandalism, truancy, fighting, theft, and drunkenness and to experience higher arrest rates(18).

The days when the bully was just another character in the world of students are now being challenged. Teachers are learning to tell where rough-housing becomes bullying, and administrators are no longer assuming that parents, who may be bullies themselves, are best suited to solve the problem. Successful programs that reduce school bullying are discussed in Chapter 11.

SOCIAL CLIQUES AND YOUTH CULTURE

The modern high school campus is frequently the locale where teenagers are most critically judged by their peers. In high school, students establish a social hierarchy. One's position within this hierarchy plays a major role in shaping one's self-esteem. Popular students who are placed high in the status hierarchy frequently express high self-esteem, whereas less popular students who are placed lower on the scale often express lower self-esteem.

The positioning of one's clique, or social group, relative to the other cliques and students on campus also affects self-esteem. Not fitting in with any clique is bound to produce unpleasant experiences. Being identified with a less popular clique is apt to negatively affect a youngster who may have a fragile ego.

Several researchers have looked at the impact of cliques on adolescent behavior. Cliques—defined as small, exclusive groups made up of three or more individuals who share similar interests and strong loyalties toward one another—provide their members with a refuge from the pressures of home and school (19).

As early as age 8, same-sex, close-knit groups or cliques take shape. During the teens, almost all of both sexes become involved in cliques, whose members are usually of similar social status, although someone of a different background may be included if they share attributes (for example, attractiveness, personality traits, or athletic prowess) that are highly valued by that particular clique (20).

All adolescent groups, including cliques, constitute the so-called peer or youth culture, which presumably possesses a distinct social identity. One observer views the youth culture as not always explicitly antiadult but as belligerently nonadult. This peer culture is usually independent of the larger society and has its own distinctive values and behaviors (21).

Youth culture in general serves several functions. It helps adolescents define their values and behaviors. Most youths today do not follow in the footsteps of their parents but face a vast array of alternatives concerning career choices, moral codes, and lifestyles. As a result, they find refuge in their own culture until they have developed their own identity. They use their peer group to sort themselves out.

One sociologist sees cultural differences in this pattern, with adolescent peer groups assuming more importance in some societies than in others. Such groups are most important in nations, such as the United States, where the family unit fails to adequately meet youths' social needs due, in part, to parents and other family members having their own set of priorities (22). Although not all sociologists agree about whether such a thing as a "common" youth culture exists, most observers of contemporary youths would concur that distinctive youth styles differentiate the various peer groups. They would also agree that youth cultures share values that distinguish them from adult culture. One observer of youth cultures noted, "[They] can be defined only in terms of distinctive life styles which are to a great extent self-generated and autonomous" (23).

Several people have commented on the various factors that encourage the growth of youth cultures. One has argued that the affluence of Western society accounts for these distinctive youth styles:

> Only a wealthy society can afford a large leisure class of teenagers not yet in the labor force but already consumers on a large scale. What adolescents earn, besides what they succeed in wresting from their elders, they spend chiefly on themselves, for such items as records, cars, travel, clothes, cosmetics, and recreational paraphernalia. Meanwhile, this same affluence demands, for its support, a high level of training which itself prolongs the transitional period to adulthood (24).

Up to age 12, and after age 19, parents generally have more influence on their offspring than peers do. But from ages 12 through 18, what peers say often matters more than what parents say.

Not all teenagers participate equally in the youth culture. In fact, the vast majority of youths are basically "conformist-oriented," to apply one of the five cultural adaptations that Robert K. Merton (25) observed. Such youths shy away from assuming a "total identity" or "master status" of any particular youth style—whether that is the identity of a punk rocker, a heavy metaler, or a racist skinhead. Instead, conformists opt to be just typical, average teenagers who, although affiliating with the general youth culture because of their age, choose not to affiliate with any one distinctive youth culture.

The other adaptations, according to Merton, include innovators, ritualists, retreatists, and rebels. Such a typology is useful in examining the array of youth styles that this book discusses. In fact, punk rockers, for instance, can be categorized as innovators in that, from their perspective, they see themselves as trying to change and improve their social environment. On the other hand, others might categorize their behavior as one of the other three groups: ritualists in that they mimic the behavior and dress of other youths like themselves; retreatists because many seem to have dropped out of society; or rebels in that some espouse anarchy and civil disobedience.

Studies on High School Campuses

Several sociologists have studied the teen status hierarchy and teen life in high schools. Schwartz and Merten, studying an upper-middle-class high school in 1967, found two distinctive youth styles—the *socies* and the *hoods*—as well as a third, residual category composed of students who identified with neither of the other two types (26).

The socies represented the top stratum of the prestige system and established the values that determined high or popular school status. The hoods, on the other hand, were from a lower socioeconomic status than the socies and included the "out-of-its," such as students who had a mental handicap and slow learners; the rebels; the intellectuals; and those who somehow deviated from the prestige group. Schwartz and Merten described "the others" as just ordinary students who did not fit into the other two cliques.

Gary Schwartz, in *Beyond Conformity or Rebellion: Youth and Authority in America,* analyzed the distinctive youth cultures present in six different communities throughout the United States. In one of these communities, which he named Patusa—a small, conventional, midwestern American town— Schwartz noted that the teenage clique structure in the high school closely reflected the socioeconomic status and prestige of the students' parents (27). These patterns were similar to the findings of the classic *Elmstown's Youth* study done by A. B. Hollingshead on a community in Indiana in the late 1940s (28).

Schwartz, in examining the "peer group world" of Patusa High School, observed four broad categories. In descending order in terms of popularity and prestige, they were *youth elites, religious youths, fashionable freaks,* and *greasers.*

The youth elites comprised three distinct subgroups: the student politicos, the athletes, and the "brains" of the high school. Each of these groups had different bases for high status. As Schwartz noted, "Seen from below, they are all beneficiaries of official privileges. Seen from within their own ranks, they are three separate groups who do not associate with and do not even particularly like one another" (29).

Due to the rural character of the small town, the religious youths in Patusa High School had the second highest level of prestige. The town Christian church, for instance, with 2,000 members, had the largest youth club, and this social contact carried over into the high school campus. Although the youth members were generally passive, according to Schwartz, they did accept authority and were average students at school.

The fashionable freaks, on the other hand, had as their reference point the larger youth culture from the outside world. As Schwartz observed, "The social sources of [their] form of peer sociability are rooted in cosmopolitan culture." These youths, who dressed in the latest urban fashion and listened to the newest recording artists, merely were marking time until they graduated from high school and could move to more cosmopolitan areas.

Finally, the greasers, a term synonymous with working- and lower-class youths, clustered heavily in the remedial classes. They frequently socialized in public meeting areas such as the local pool halls, behind the welding shop at school, and the bowling alley in town. Although alcohol and drugs such as marijuana would be used by some of the youth elites and fashionable freaks, the greasers were the ones most suspected of substance abuse.

The heavy drug users, known in Patusa as "freaks" or "burn-outs," were highly visible due to their demeanor, appearance, and group activities. Although such heavy drug use did cross socioeconomic and clique lines, in general, according to Schwartz, the greasers were the ones most frequently apprehended and expelled from school for possession and drug usage (30).

CLIQUE STRUCTURES IN FOUR SUBURBAN HIGH SCHOOLS

Patusa High School was located in a small-town, middle-America, rural setting. For the purposes of this study, it was decided to examine the teenage clique structures of several suburban high schools located in Southern California. Of particular interest in this analysis would be the following five issues:

1. Were the teenage status hierarchies similar in each of these Southern California high schools, including the terminology used to distinguish one social clique from another?

2. Were the status hierarchies in the Southern California schools similar to those found in Patusa High School, or were there differences in the rank ordering of the different youth groups because of differences in geographic region or locale?

3. What was the demeanor of some of those youths at the top of the clique structure in terms of how they handled their special status and how they treated some female students?

4. How did those students who were part of less popular cliques feel about their position, and how were they treated by the other social cliques in their school?

5. Could the various youth cultures found in these Southern California suburban high schools be grouped according to the four-subculture typology based on a study of collegiate subcultures?

Four "typical" suburban high schools, based on university student suggestions, were selected for comparative analysis with the Patusa study. With the assistance of several students who had attended these particular high schools as recently as three years preceding the analysis, the clique structures and status hierarchies of the four high schools were examined. The study analyzed the senior yearbooks of each of these four schools. For purposes of discussion, each graduating senior was classified into his or her respective social clique and group.

Table 4.1   Southern California High School Clique Structures

1	2	3	4
Jocks	Jocks	Jocks	Jocks
Cheerleaders	Socs	Partiers	Surfers
Tweakies	Cheerleaders	Cheerleaders/ Barbie dolls	Trendies/preppies
Trendies	Death rockers	Preppies	Punks/metalers
Drama freaks	Cha-chas	Burners	Death rockers/ Dance clubbers
Bandos	Brains	Band members	
Smacks	Metal heads	Geeks/nerds	Cholos
Dirt-bags	Asians	Brains	Brains
Sluts			
Punks			
Loners			

All four of the high schools examined shared similar characteristics. They were large, cosmopolitan, and located in the suburban areas that served as "feeder schools" to California State Polytechnic University (Cal Poly) in Pomona. The students who attended these high schools were predominantly Caucasian and from middle- to upper-middle-class socioeconomic backgrounds. As part of the research, each of the four schools was visited, and the clique structure was discussed with representatives of the school administration such as senior counselors who commented on and validated the findings.

Similarity of Status Hierarchies

As the summary table, "Southern California High School Clique Structures," depicts, the status hierarchy of cliques was generally similar in each of the four high schools analyzed, although the students in the schools often used different names or terminology to distinguish one social clique from another. Each group is listed in *descending* order of popularity.

High School Case Study 1

Jocks   The jocks at this school consisted of boys who actively participated in many of the sports on campus. They strutted around the campus in letter jackets to broadcast to all other students their athletic ability. Most were self-centered and egotistical. At parties jocks could be seen participating in beer-drinking contests and smoking marijuana. They had no problems finding dates and tended to choose cheerleaders as their girlfriends. For jocks, high school was fun—a positive part of life that increased their self-image.

Cheerleaders The cheerleaders were attractive, school-spirited, and popular. They were constantly being elected homecoming and prom queens. Unlike the jocks, the cheerleaders acknowledged other students who were not as popular, wanting to be everyone's idol and friend. They had high self-esteem and confidence.

Tweakies The tweakies were boys who had an extremely "laid back" attitude toward school. They often skipped class to go to the beach and consumed alcohol whenever they had the chance. Surfboards and girls were more important than school. They had their own slang, including words such as "bogus" (terrible), "righteous" (out of sight, the best), "gnarly" (cool), and "sweet" (perfect). They wore baggy clothing and sandals.

Trendies The trendies were desperate to fit in and spent their time shopping for the latest trends in clothing. They constantly changed their looks in hopes of finding a style that would make them popular. To be labeled a "trendie" was not good. It meant that you were "hard-up" for friends and would do anything, other than be yourself, to become popular.

Drama Freaks The drama freaks were students who were completely engrossed in acting. Constantly practicing for upcoming plays and musicals, they were viewed by others as an extremely loud and obnoxious group. The majority of students considered "drama freaks" to be fake. They dressed in high fashion, and the girls wore brightly colored makeup. Many of them were excellent actors, but they could never draw a distinct line between fantasy and reality.

Bandos The bandos were similar to the drama freaks, but instead of being centered on acting, they were centered on band. Students viewed them as "nerds" and thought of them as "uncool." Bandos spent the majority of their time practicing their instruments and were never seen at any of the weekend parties. They were very conservative in dress.

Smacks The smacks were students who had extremely high GPA's. They were overly friendly to all teachers and always had their hands up in class. They spent many hours studying while their peers were shopping, partying, or playing sports. Only those students who were not popular were labeled smacks. A few students in the popular cliques who received high grades were not labeled as smacks.

Dirt-Bags The dirt-bags came from middle-class families but were considered the "lowlifes" of the campus. They roamed around school constantly brushing long hair out of their eyes. They frequently skipped school to smoke marijuana or party at a friend's house. Many of the dirt-bags were enrolled in remedial-level classes, and many were held back from graduating or dropped out because of failing grades. Their typical dress consisted of heavy-metal-band T-shirts and jeans.

Sluts Some girls were labeled sluts because of their provocative clothing, such as tight jeans, high heels, and no undergarments. They usually had bleached hair and wore a lot of makeup. They were popular merely for sexual purposes. They loved to party and had sex with many fellow male students.

Punks The punks dressed in torn jeans, combat boots, and wore Mohawks. They were harmless, merely making a statement about their individuality. Many of them were intelligent and enrolled in honors classes. They could be found on the outskirts of campus. Fellow students did not see them as a threat and respected their uniqueness.

Loners The loners had no peer group to socialize with and were always in a corner eating lunch or studying. Everyone tended to ignore them, and the loners avoided contact with any of the cliques. They were very introverted and never talked in the classroom.

High School Case Study 2

Jocks Similar to the status hierarchy of high school 1, the jocks in this second high school were also the most popular students. The jocks were bonded by their sports and Friday night parties. They always ended the week with a huge party and five kegs of beer. The jocks were very cocky and obnoxious and were not very successful with grades. In this high school there were no African-American or Asian jocks; they were mainly Anglo with some Hispanics.

Socs The socs were rich, white students and the metal heads' worst enemy. The typical "soc" always wore the latest fashion—Guess jeans, Gennera shirts, and Reebok tennis shoes—and their hair was always neat and clean with a salon look. The soc community was very exclusive.

Cheerleaders The cheerleaders were usually part of the soc clique. They were involved in student government, and many were scholastically intelligent. They did use drugs but often tried to hide their addiction from parents and teachers.

Death Rockers The death rockers were bonded by music, which was generally an alternative Hollywood underground type, bordering on punk rock. Their clique was entirely open and nondiscriminatory. They wore black clothing, black makeup, and dyed black hair. Their appearance challenged, "Like me for who I am, not for where I live or what I wear." They were seldom athletic or extracurricular, but they were very scholastic.

Cha-Chas The cha-chas were mostly Hispanic and wore "GQ"-type outfits. The boys styled their hair in pompadours, and the girls teased theirs to resemble a lion's mane. They drove lowered minitrucks with huge speakers that created loud bass sounds and listened mainly to rap music. The only sport they played was soccer. Most cha-chas dropped out of school or failed to earn enough credits to graduate.

Brains This group was bound by the classes they took: math, biology, chemistry, physics, computer programming, and honors courses. They never were invited to parties and had a reputation for never touching alcohol or drugs. They did not thrive on fashion and had no set dress code or hairstyle. They ate lunch in the cafeteria and studied in the library when finished. Tennis was the only sport that a brain would consider playing. They belonged to the science club and the California Scholastic Federation.

Metal Heads They were the students who idolized Van Halen, bonded in their clique by hard rock music from the 1970s and heavy metal music from the 1980s. Their dress consisted of old Levi jeans, concert T-shirts, cowboy boots, and long hair. They never denied their use of drugs and in fact often flaunted it. They did not participate in sports and were not involved in student government. The metal heads usually did not excel scholastically, and the only thing they considered as a potential career was stardom in the music industry.

Asians This clique included groups of Vietnamese, Chinese, and Filipinos. Anybody who could not speak their language was automatically rejected by them. They rarely spoke English except to teachers. Asians excelled in math and computer classes but lacked the verbal ability to excel in English and social science classes. Because they were different, the jocks and socs ridiculed them relentlessly.

High School Case Study 3

Jocks They were the most predominant clique, and they ran the school. They always knew what was going on and were always at the center of attention. Underclassmen stayed away from jocks because they had the power to force them to do what they wanted. Jocks wore their letter jackets to remind everyone of their status. They also sometimes received preferential treatment from teachers after intervention by their coach.

Partiers The partiers were mostly in the average track, able to party without jeopardizing their grades, thus avoiding being placed into remedial classes. The partiers included a group called the "Lunch Club," who met at lunchtime every Thursday to drink heavily at the home of a student whose parents were working. To be accepted into this group, a student was required to play an assortment of drinking games that usually made them sick. They frequented parties on weekends and always brought alcohol into the football games.

Cheerleaders or Barbie Dolls They were the girls that all the boys desired. When they were not in their cheerleading uniforms, they wore all the fashionable clothes. They partied and hung out with the athletes. If a student was seen with a cheerleader, the student was considered popular as well.

Preppies The preppies arrived at school in flashy new sports cars that their parents bought for them soon after they turned 16. They wore plaid pants or shorts, along with an Izod or Polo shirt, penny loafers, and matching argyle socks.

Burners Often placed into the remedial track, burners appeared to be stoned most of the time. This group included the rocker crowd, along with some punkers. Their territory was the school-provided smoking area and a park across the street from school called "Toke" Grove, instead of Oak Grove, because of the constant drug activity there.

Band Members On the surface they were perceived as squares who enjoyed playing music, except at sporting events, when their playing abilities focused positive attention on them. In actuality, they were the rowdiest group. They had privileges others did not have, such as marching in parades or going to special events, but they often partied and got into trouble more often than any other group.

Geeks or Nerds These students were not accepted into any group, so they formed their own. They were often the target of practical jokes. Geeks retaliated by throwing soda, water balloons, or rotten fruit from the third floor onto students in the quad below. They were avid members of the Science Fiction Club and were also among the few people who actually ate lunch in the cafeteria.

Brains These were the people who threw the GPA of every class off the scale. Brains usually spent their lunch in one of the labs or in the library working on their homework. They preferred not to socialize with anyone.

High School Case Study 4

Jocks They were the most influential group on this campus as well. Unfortunately, there were numerous instances in which jocks beat up people at parties or in public places for no apparent reason. The assaults were committed gang-style, with three or four jocks beating up on one person. A few were convicted and sent to jail or juvenile hall. Their aggressive behavior was later attributed to steroid use.

However, most of the jocks were "all-American" boys who dated cheerleaders—but were not especially intelligent. Another group of jocks were labeled the "502 Crew." They prided themselves on their drinking ability. Still another group of jocks, the "TKE" (Tappa Kegga Encinitas), were the rivals of the 502 Crew.

Surfers The second largest group on campus, surfers tended to keep to themselves merely because their lifestyle was so different. They had their own lingo and a laid-back attitude: "Smoke some pot, drink some beer, kick back, eat some Mexican food, and catch a wave." They were hardly ever at school because they were at the beach.

Trendies or Preppies These were the mainstream kids. They were the homecoming and prom queens, the student body officers, and the student leaders. On the surface, they were every parent's dream, but they used drugs just as much as everyone else.

Punks and Metalers They were the devils and did whatever they wanted, not caring who knew. They got wasted before, during, and after school. They sold drugs on campus and were often kicked out of their classes and put on detention. In reality, they were not any worse than anyone else. They just chose not to hide their beliefs and attitudes or drug use.

Death Rockers or Dance Clubbers They were known as the "wall people" because they hung out at the wall in the center of campus. They had a "holier than thou" attitude that turned people off. They were too soft-core for the punk, yet too strange for the mainstream kids. Everyone usually ignored them or teased them.

Cholos No one really knew much about the cholos because there were so few of them at school. Because the school was white, middle-class, and suburban, these lower-class Mexican-Americans did not fit in. They had their gangs, who occasionally fought rival gangs. Usually the only sign of their existence was some occasional graffiti on the outside school walls or in the bathrooms.

Brains Although they occasionally drank, they were the only group on campus who did not do drugs. They were not respected for their high intelligence and grades because they felt they were superior to everyone else and formed an elite. Usually brains are considered nerds and ostracized, but these students ostracized everyone else. They were the most isolated group because they felt they had no need to socialize with others.

Beyond these four "typical" high school clique structures, our study found even more groups, often with derogatory names, some of which included the following:

- *Black cockroaches:* kids who wore all black (such as the death rockers)
- *BAs:* students of Native-American ancestry ("bows and arrows")
- *Skanks:* girlfriends of the heavy metal groups
- *Motorheads:* guys who drove old Mustangs or Camaros
- *Waterjockeys:* swimmers and water polo players
- *Kickers:* cowboys and sons of cowboys
- *The tuna barge:* fast girls

- *Daddy's girls:* spoiled rich girls
- *Puppy power:* freshmen and sophomore males who were popular partly due to athletic prowess
- *The shadows:* students who were into death rock
- *Disco biscuits:* youths who liked to party and drink and disliked school
- *Dog squad:* girls on the drill team that wanted to be cheerleaders but were less attractive and less coordinated and came from lower socioeconomic backgrounds

One of the students, looking at the entire clique structure at her high school, summed up the various groups in this fashion: "The first clique was the trendy, the second was the 'worker bees,' the third was intelligent, and the last was simply lost." Finally, many college students indicated that they failed to fall into any one specific category while attending high school. Instead, they maintained a role of "floater," drifting among several of the cliques while maintaining their independence.

Gender and High School Cliques

As the clique summaries indicate, the teenage status hierarchies in these four Southern California suburban high schools were generally similar. However, each high school—apart from the categories for jocks, cheerleaders, and brains—used different terminology to describe the other campus cliques. Furthermore, in two of the high schools (1 and 3), the terms used to refer to some of the less popular cliques were downright cruel. In the first school, derogatory terms for females included "smacks," "dirt-bags," and "sluts"; and in the third high school, the derogatory terms for other students were "burners," "geeks," or "nerds."

One of the clearest patterns is the way in which the rankings reflect traditional notions of gender. The archetypal image of teen masculinity—the jock—trumped all four school lists. Not surprising is the evidence that jocks often do double duty as bullies (31). The female subordinate to the jock—the cheerleader—ranked second or third at the schools. The cheerleader's role is to support the activities of the jocks on the field, at pep rallies, and at parties. It is the quintessential female role in the traditional gender-hierarchy of high school. The aggressive male and the pretty, supportive female are rewarded with popularity. The autonomous male tweakies and surfers also ranked high.

Those at the bottom of the rankings were the cliques that break the macho jock and peppy cheerleader gender roles. Asexual geeks, nerds, and band members are removed from the dating scene as are asocial loners and ostracized minority groups. Border crossing, long-haired dirt-bags and metal heads, androgynous punks, and sexually powerful sluts threatened the gender status quo. At the very bottom were the brains, perceived to be the least masculine males and often the targets of bullies.

Of particular interest to this book (and the topic of chapters to follow) are some of these latter two groups at the bottom of the suburban high school clique hierarchies: the fashionable freaks who engaged in the popular youth cultures of the day (such as punkers and metalers) and the modern equivalent of the greasers or teen rebels: taggers, racist skinheads, stoners, and Satanists. But first let us examine the rowdy and immoral behavior of some of those youths at the top of the high school clique hierarchy: the jocks.

THE LEADERS OF THE PACK

As this analysis denotes, there is no doubt that the high school athlete—particularly those males who letter in such prestigious sports as football and basketball —are given special privileges in high school. But what happens when such status goes to their heads and they begin to act indifferently and insensitively toward others in their school and community?

This issue reached national debate with the shocking case of the Spur Posse that unfolded in spring 1993 at Lakewood High School in Southern California, a suburban community located just thirty miles from Los Angeles and the Cal Poly, Pomona, campus. The nation's news media were quick to focus on this alarming incident as the excerpt from the front page of the *New York Times* at the beginning of this chapter demonstrates.

Perhaps one of the leads from the *Los Angeles Times* best delineates the scope of the problem: "A Stain Spreads in Suburbia: Issues of teen promiscuity, forced sex and parental neglect rock Lakewood, once a bastion of morality. Many see the town and its unrepentant Spur Posse as symbols of a declining America" (32). This comment from an article in *Newsweek* further laments the problem: "Mixed Messages: California's 'Spur Posse' scandal underscores the varying signals society sends teens about sex" (33).

As the *Los Angeles Times* article pointed out:

> All of a sudden, in a glaring media spotlight, Lakewood stands as a reluctant symbol of declining America. Sex sprees, violence and turmoil were about the last things many residents might have expected in the mostly white middle-class community—the prototype of the modern California suburb when it was laid out on nine square miles of sugar beet fields in the early 1950s. What the founders created—a verdant sprawl of parks, ball diamonds and quiet streets—seemed all but immune to today's spreading plague of gang warfare. If any city could make the claim, Lakewood remained Norman Rockwell's America, a family place, as solid a bastion of traditional ethical values as might be found.

> But no more. The innocence has given way to hard questions and self-searching. Residents talk fearfully, and some escort their teenagers to school because of recent street fights and alleged threats of retribution—all involving mostly white youths raised without financial hardship, the products of fine schools. Issues of promiscuity, forced sex and parental neglect are out in the open (34).

What concerned this community (and the country as a whole) was the disclosure that a clique called the Spur Posse, most of them top athletes at the local high school, told investigators that they had kept a tally of the number of young girls they had bedded. Founded in 1989 as a sort of high school fraternity, many juveniles of the Spur Posse, which counted twenty to thirty boys as members and was named for the San Antonio Spurs professional basketball team, brashly claimed they had sex with as many as sixty girls.

It appears as if one of their main activities was "hooking up," or having sex, with as many girls as possible. Furthermore, because of their local hero status as athletes, the boys took turns having sex with the same girls and later boasted about their conquests, labeling some of the girls as "sluts" for "putting out" for them and their friends.

Eight members of this high school boys' clique were arrested on charges of lewd conduct, unlawful intercourse, and rape allegedly involving seven girls from 10 to 16 years of age. Other charges filed by the authorities included burglary, assault, intimidation of witnesses, and other crimes.

But what also shocked the community was the staunch support these athletes received from other students who denounced the Spurs' accusers as "whores" and "promiscuous girls who got what they asked for." Furthermore, many of the parents of those accused were equally unrepentant. The "boys will be boys" attitude of some of the parents was particularly bothersome. One father *boasted* to reporters about the virility of his three sons, one of whom had been a founder of the Spur Posse.

Teenage sex without responsibility—and without precaution in this time of AIDS and other sexually transmitted diseases—is serious business and foolhardy, to say the least. But in truth, the most striking thing about the Spur Posse, as one reporter noted, was that these juveniles' actions appeared to be more about "scoring" than about sex, about conquest rather than intimacy. Sex, like the athletic field, had become yet another arena in which these teenagers competed (35).

Such alarming behavior is not found just in Southern California. In October 1993, in Rockville, Maryland, a 16-year-old son of a Washington-area school superintendent was one of five juveniles charged with rape in connection with a gang named the Chronics, whose objective was also to have sex with as many girls as possible (36).

Sex and sexual promiscuity have become another fact of adolescent life. And over the past few decades, the age of initial sexual experience has been declining. According to a 1990 survey by the Centers for Disease Control and Prevention, seven out of ten high school seniors and over half (54 percent) of ninth through twelfth graders have had intercourse at least once (37).

The extraordinary attention given the Spur Posse, according to one commentator in the Los Angeles area, was partly due to the increased interest in sexual harassment on campus. Citing figures from a recent magazine survey that found that almost 90 percent of 2,002 high school-age girls had been sexually harassed, the reporter notes that the Lakewood High School incident has been but another case in which girls continue to submit to sexual aggression when they do not want to. And if these girls complain afterward, they are told they wanted it and are mocked by unsympathetic peers (38).

Sadly, the community of Lakewood was left with many unanswered questions in the wake of the sex scandal and the negative publicity it generated. But as our previous discussion of four other Southern California suburban high schools pointed out, Lakewood High is obviously not alone in these matters.

The Byrds

One former student in one of the other schools examined for this study spoke about the top group at her high school, a group known as the "The Byrds," of which she was a member:

> The group consisted of approximately twelve guys and eight girls. "The Byrds" were established when we were juniors by four of my guy friends. When I look back now at what The Byrds stood for, it really sickens me. Only the guys could be a "Byrd." It was formed by them, but as they got more and more recognition, the name just became applied to the rest of the group.
>
> The guys in my clique were all drop-dead beautiful. I guess you could say that they were the big men on campus. They were desired by every girl. Well, of course, they knew it, and The Byrds were born.
>
> They were like a nonviolent gang. They had a full initiation ceremony to become a Byrd, and the quest was sex. It was by no means forced sex, and they did not keep tabs either. To become a Byrd, a guy must first be accepted by the rest of the guys. Then the "pledge" would have to find a girl that was willing to have sex with him. The actual initiation ceremony consisted of a Byrd and a pledge having sexual intercourse with two girls at the same time, in the same room. They called this "going side by side." This, of course, was the one aspect of our group that the other girls and I were not proud of. We thought they were so disrespectful.
>
> The girls in the clique were never used in the initiations. We were like their sisters and were completely off limits to any kind of activities like that. Our clique was special. We were like one big family. We differed from the other cliques in school because ours was not based on superficial friendships and egoism. We looked out for one another and took care of each other. We loved to drive into Los Angeles and the club scene. That was our way of life outside of campus. We were always aware of the latest trends and fashions and were one of the first to sport them at school.

Obviously, the behavior exhibited by certain males of the Lakewood Spur Posse and The Byrds is reprehensible. With the prestige that comes with being a star athlete or a popular student should come the responsibility of setting a good example and of showing respect and restraint. But these students were acting out the dominant messages about gender in the United States, that male sexuality is unrestrained and powerful and that females are rewarded for playing the game.

Comments by Students Who Have Been Ostracized

Another issue our analysis of the four suburban high school clique structures raised was the impact on the student of being placed in a less prestigious position or social clique. What pressures were placed on the student to be selected or accepted into, and remain within, a particular social clique?

As the following statements of university students who were ostracized by their high school peers indicate, being taunted and experiencing ridicule and discrimination were not pleasant experiences.

One male Asian student recalls his high school days and explains why he chose to become a punk rocker:

> Like many other Vietnamese teenagers, I began to question my identity. Although I had made some American friends in school, they did not treat me the same as others. I was often made fun of because of my slanted eyes and my accent. Feeling left out from everybody, I started to go out frequently and was introduced to other Vietnamese teenagers who were having the same problem. A community of Oriental punkers was formed, and they fought and stole as a daily practice. I joined these teenagers and became a punker. Being one of them gave me a sense of belonging and security. It gave me an identity. In school and at home I paid little attention to anybody.

One of the so-called fashionable freaks in high school recalls her experience:

> We were shunned and made fun of. We were called freaks. We were different and not well liked. We were harassed. We had food thrown at us and we were spit upon. The attackers were primarily the jocks. We were treated worse as a group than as individuals. An example of this is how I was treated by my former "friends."
>
> When I was with my fashionable freak friends, my former friends and other cliques ignored me, but if I were alone, they would talk to me as if I was still their friend. This angered me, and I eventually cut off all ties with those types of people. I think the reason we were treated so badly is because people were jealous and envious of our individuality, and they felt threatened by us because we were different.

A female student recalls the process of becoming a member of the punk social clique during high school, as well as the attending consequences this decision had for her:

> Being new in school was hard, and I started to hang around with the "weird" kids. I had always been a straight "A" student, but suddenly

grades became unimportant to me. I began to slowly get into more and more trouble. I had no curfew and stayed out all night. I met a lot of new people who introduced me to crystal, coke, acid, and other various drugs. I ditched all of my classes, and for the first time in life, I began failing in school.

I had also turned punk, and my appearance was strange. I wore all black, including my makeup. My hair was short in some places, long in others, and ranged from white to orange to pink to black. I wore chains, crosses, and skulls. After getting arrested for possession of cocaine, I soon became tired of the whole punk scene—tired of people laughing at the way I looked, staring at me, and making fun of me.

Another Cal Poly, Pomona, student remembers his high school experience and his heavy involvement with drugs and alcohol:

Upon entering high school, I was exposed to many new people. In order to maintain my status of being a leader and high achiever, I strived (sic) to be the biggest drug addict on campus. All that was required of me to be in this drug group was to experiment with different drugs. It is just amazing what one will do in such a group situation. One example is drinking tequila every day for a couple of months in order to be with your friends. Another example is burglarizing houses, including neighbors and family friends, in order to obtain money and alcohol to party with. I know that these decisions would never have been made by myself, but with the help of "friends," the answer didn't seem to be very hard to come by.

During the time span from freshman to junior year in high school, I had become a complete idiot. My education assumed the lowest space on my priority list, and selling drugs and having a good time were at the top.

One college student recalls his rambunctious high school days as a "stoner":

Like many presumptuous teenagers, I was thoroughly convinced that I knew what life was all about, and anyone who didn't see reality as I did was a fool. I was basically a loner, ostracized by my peers, but I did have a handful of friends; most were in one faction of the "stoner" clique.

Stoners at my school cultivated the reputation of being wild, self-destructive, party animals. Our motto was SFB—Shoot for a Buzz. Most of us would snort some coke or drop acid on occasion, but for the most part, pot was the drug of choice, followed closely by beer. Stoners were, in my judgment, second in the social hierarchy.

Although the occasional drug bust would occur, a good percentage of us—myself included—would get stoned nearly every day. What was taking place in the parking lots and in the field by the gym was common knowledge. I remember one particularly brash incident: Two students actually lit up a joint (in class) while a film was being shown by a substitute teacher. As I recall, the only penalty they suffered was not being able to finish the whole cigarette.

Another college student recalls his high school days and the "punk phase" he went through in this way, as he describes a typical high school punk party scene:

> The people gathered were of various ages and interests. Several people, for the most part fellow high school students, were present who didn't display punk dress or hairstyle. Although not directly associated with the punk movement, they seemed to enjoy the social aspects of punk music or had friends who were punkers. The true high school punks made up the largest part of the crowd. Appearing in similar style and dress, they constituted the most visible and active of all present.
>
> Many people, especially high schoolers, embrace the social, stylistic, and musical aspects of the punk culture without abandoning traditional forms of livelihood. They gain financial support from their families and in most cases continue their education and pursue a career. They seem to find in punk an identification with a cause, a quality which may be lacking in their lives. They seem to find refuge in the adoption of a style of dress and taste which provides an identity and enables them to stand out. This type of punk—which I was—is apt to look back at their affiliation with the movement as their "punk phase."

Still another college senior majoring in psychology examines what punk has meant to him:

> I was a "hard-core" punker throughout high school. I was the typical stereotype of a punker. I became a punker for individualistic reasons. I wanted to form my own identity and be different. Now that I am in college I have "grown up" after being a punk. In many of my thoughts and ideals, I still think along those terms. Instead of exploiting myself externally, I have tried to internalize my youthful rebellion and transform it into positive and helpful actions. I think that's one reason why I want to counsel people.

And, finally, one college student summed up her experience in high school and its relentless pressure to conform:

> Would I relive my high school years if I could? No, thanks!
> I really had a hard time in high school. The courses were interesting, but the peer pressure was just too much. High school in America is not really about academics. It's pretty much learning social skills. How someone interacts in a social setting is the main focus of secondary education. I feel this needs no further explanation because any high school graduate probably understands my point of view.

Queer Youth in High Schools

One group that did not even register in the Southern California study was sexual minority students. In the 1990s students who were open about their gay, lesbian, or bisexual status were more "out" on high school campuses. Although it is still more common for students to become public about their sexuality at college, away from their families and home towns, changing social climates have given many teenagers enough security to be gay in high school, even forming school groups (39).

Gay youth are still among the most ostracized kids in the United States. Gay and lesbian youth are six times more likely to attempt suicide than straight kids (40). Due to harassment, gay, lesbian, and bisexual youth have a 28-percent dropout rate, according to the U.S. Department of Health and Human Resources (41). They are more likely to become homeless and the victims of violence by family members, bullies, and homophobes. Their cliques and subcultures, then, become ways to navigate the minefield of high school that is populated with messages about the normality of heterosexuality: jocks and cheerleaders, prom queens and kings, dances, sex education classes, the harassment of nonmasculine boys and unfeminine girls, and the outing of gay teachers.

Gay or queer student groups (as many now choose to be called) have met with varying success. With names like the Lambda Youth Group, Out Proud, and Rainbow Pride, they have struggled for tolerance in high schools. One of the more well-known cases is the Gay/Straight Student Alliance (GSA) at East High School in Salt Lake City, Utah. The club was founded in 1995 and quickly received harassment from homophobic students, the school, and the justice system itself. Some students formed a counter group, called S.A.F.E.— Students Against Faggots Everywhere. East High banned the GSA group, and in February 1996, the Salt Lake City Board of Education banned all noncurricular clubs. Shortly after that, state lawmakers passed a bill outlawing school clubs that promote illegal activity or sexual activity of any kind (42).

Jacob Orosco, student president of the GSA, posted on his web site in 1996, "To me taking clubs from us is like putting a gun in our hands and waiting for the trigger to be pulled. How many times do we have to walk out of our schools before we are heard? In high school 'our community' clubs give us the feeling of belonging. We need to take a stand and get our clubs back."

After repeated harassment from both students and adults, 17-year-old Orosco hung himself in his family's home on September 3, 1997. After much protest and legal wrangling, the East High GSA was allowed to meet on campus as a noncurricular club with an outside sponsor. But how many queer youths took the events in Utah as a sign that high school was a place to stay in the closet?

The Clustering of High School Cliques

There were similarities between the high school youth cultures in our study and those uncovered by Trow and Clark in a study of collegiate subcultures (43).

High school cliques in Southern California—based on this small sample of four suburban high schools—could be grouped or clustered in ways comparable to the four distinctive groups of collegiate, vocational, academic, and nonconformist subcultures found to exist among college students in the Trow and Clark study.

The first group is the *collegiate* student. These high school cliques would include the jocks, cheerleaders, socs, partiers, surfers, tweakies (laid back), and Barbie dolls. These students attend high school not just for academic reasons—most plan to or hope to attend college—but for athletic and social reasons as well. Their activities accord them popularity. This group also includes the "wannabes" or "poseurs" who try to gain popularity by associating with more popular students.

The second category is the *vocational* student. They include the cholos, cha-chas, dirt-bags, burners, beaners (Mexicans), rap groups, and sluts. In high school, moreover, these students are frequently tracked into the noncollege preparatory vocational classes such as woodshop, auto mechanics, and other vocational and agricultural programs for males; and typing, homemaking skills, and general secretarial programs for females. Vocational students also include those from traditional ethnic backgrounds who dress according to their (sub)culture's expectations. This group includes many of the ethnic gang members as well (although few gang members were present in the more affluent high schools analyzed for this study) and females who have reputations for being sexually active and available.

The third group found in high school is the *academic* students. These include a wide variety of high school cliques, including the brains, geeks or nerds, "ugly pets," smacks, drama freaks, and bandos. The academic group affiliate strongly with the high school in terms of academics as well as specialized group activities or interests. These students generally excelled in some aspect of school life but were not in the mainstream, popular high school cliques. These students would eventually go on to college, often getting admitted to prestigious public and private universities because of their top scholastic records.

Finally, the *nonconformists* were present in high school but differed from the nonconformist of the college setting in important ways. In high school, the nonconformists, located often near the bottom of the school hierarchy, include the punk rockers, heavy metalers, death rockers, loners, and skinheads.

Although many of the punk rockers and heavy metalers in high school could be compared to the radicals, intellectuals, and alienated students of college, other high school youths in the nonconformist category would not be college bound. These include the more delinquent punkers, metalers, taggers, skinheads, stoners, and Satanists. Furthermore, often their exploits as teenagers, both in and out of high school, would eventually bring them to the attention of the authorities and the juvenile justice system.

These nonconformist youths are the main focus of this book. But for now, the discussion turns to a more in-depth analysis of teenage youths that embraced some aspect of the changing punk youth culture.

Youth at the Movies—High School Cliques

The power of high school cliques may never have been dealt with as powerfully as James Dean's *Rebel Without a Cause* (1955). The darkly sarcastic *Heathers* (1989) may have been more of a model for Columbine than *The Basketball Diaries* (1995). In it, a charming misfit played by Christian Slater, along with the typically alienated Winona Ryder, concocts a scheme to kill the jocks and the popular girls and then blow up the school. Slater later battled with suburban cliques in *Pump Up the Volume* (1990). More recently, *Ten Things I Hate about You* (1999) diagrammed the status hierarchy of the high school clique structure in a modern version of Shakespeare's *Taming of the Shrew.*

NOTES

1. Jim Sanders and Patrick Hoge, "Truancy Soaring: Why Go to Class When Mall Beckons?" *Sacramento Bee* (11 June 1989), p. A-1.

2. George Ramos, "Campus Styles Rekindle Debate on School Codes," *Los Angeles Times* (25 December 1984), p. B-1.

3. Jane Gross, "Where 'Boys Will Be Boys,' and Adults Are Befuddled," *New York Times* (29 March 1993), p. A-1.

4. *Turning Point: Gang Prevention and Intervention Project* pamphlet (12912 Brookhurst Street, Suite 385, Garden Grove, CA 92640).

5. *For Instructors Only* 9 (July 1987) (Emerson, NJ: Performance Learning Systems).

6. *Turning Point,* pamphlet, p. 4.

7. Ibid., p. 5.

8. Ibid., p. 6.

9. Ibid.

10. Wayne S. Wooden and Martha Lou Berkey, *Children and Arson: America's Middle-Class Nightmare* (New York: Plenum Press, 1984).

11. Nanette Davis, *Youth Crisis: Growing Up in the High-Risk Society* (New York: Greenwood, 1999).

12. Rolf Loeber and Magda Stouthamer-Loeber, "Juvenile Aggression at Home and at School," in *Violence in American Schools,* ed. Delbert S. Elliot, Beatrix A. Hamburg, and Kirk R. Williams (New York: Cambridge, 1998), p. 99.

13. Larry Siegel and Joseph Senna, *Juvenile Delinquency: Theory, Practice, and Law.* (Belmont, CA: Wadsworth, 2000), p. 376.

14. William Pollack, *Real Boys: Rescuing Our Sons from the Myth of Boyhood* (New York: Random House, 1998), p. 344.

15. Susan P. Limber and Maury M. Nation, "Bullying among Children and Youth," in *Combating Fear and Restoring Safety in Schools,* ed. June Arnette and Marjorie Walsleben (Washington, D.C.: Office of Juvenile Justice & Delinquency Prevention, 1998).

16. Pollack, p. 346.

17. Susan P. Limber and Maury M. Nation.

18. David Farrington, "Understanding and Preventing Bullying," in *Crime and Justice,* Vol. 17, ed. Michael Tonry (Chicago, IL: University of Chicago Press, 1993), pp. 381–457.

19. D. C. Dunphy, "The Social Structure of Urban Adolescent Peer Groups," *Sociometry* 26 (1963), pp. 230–46.

20. Ibid.

21. Ibid.

22. Peter L. Berger, *Invitation to Sociology: A Humanistic Perspective* (Garden City, NY: Doubleday/Anchor, 1963).

23. Ibid., p. 396.

24. R. E. Grinder, "Distinctiveness and Thrust in the American Youth Culture," *Journal of Social Issues* 25:2 (1969), pp. 7–19.

25. Robert K. Merton, *Social Theory and Social Structure* (New York: Free Press, 1957).

26. Gary Schwartz and Don Merten, "The Language of Adolescence: An Anthropological Approach to the Youth Culture," *American Journal of Sociology* 72, (1987), pp. 453–468.

27. Gary Schwartz, *Beyond Conformity or Rebellion: Youth and Authority in America* (Chicago, IL: University of Chicago Press, 1987).

28. A. B. Hollingshead, *Elmstown's Youth* (New York: Wiley and Sons, 1949).

29. Schwartz, p. 101.

30. Ibid., pp. 71–105.

31. Limber and Nation.

32. David Ferrell and Somini Sengupta, "A Stain Spreads in Suburbia: Issues of teen promiscuity, forced sex and parental neglect rock Lakewood, once a bastion of morality. Many see the town and its unrepentant Spur Posse as symbols of a declining America," *Los Angeles Times* (6 April 1993), p. A-1.

33. David Gelman and Patrick Rogers, "Mixed Signals: California's 'Spur Posse' scandal underscores the varying signals society sends teens about sex," *Newsweek* (12 April 1993), pp. 28–29.

34. Ferrell and Sengupta.

35. Gelman and Rogers.

36. "School Chief's Son in Sex Scandal," *The Arizona Republic* (30 October 1993), p. A-21.

37. Gelman and Rogers, p. 28.

38. Robin Abcarian, "Spur Posse Case—the Same Old (Sad) Story," *Los Angeles Times* (7 April 1993), p. E-1.

39. Ritc C. Savin-Williams, "The Disclosure to Families of Same-Sex Attractions by Lesbian, Gay and Bisexual Youths," in *Journal of Research on Adolescence* 8:1 (1998), pp. 49–68.

40. P. Gibson, "Gay Male and Lesbian Suicide," in *Report of the Secretary's Task Force on Youth Suicide* (U.S. Department of Health and Human Services, 1996).

41. Eric Gutierez, "TV's Gay Teenagers Get Real," *Los Angeles Times* (10 May 1999), pp. F1–F10.

42. Hilary Groutage, "East High Alliance a Haven in a Hostile World" in *Salt Lake Tribune* (12 July 1998), p. A-1.

43. L. S. Lewis, "The Value of College to Different Subcultures," *School Review,* 77:1 (1969), pp. 32–40.

5

▼

Punks and Anarchy: Changes in the Youth Scene

There is something special about punk rock. As it enters the new century as the preeminent posture of youth rebellion, it has managed to cling to its original values. In the face of attempts to use punk to sell everything from cars to banking services, punkers have been able to resist cooptation. Since the summer of 1976, punk has expressed one consistent message: Youth is a time of emotional anarchy.

In its twenty-five year history, punk and its various children, including riot grrrl, hard-core, grunge, rave, and indy rock, have given inarticulate young people a creative form of expression. Dick Hebdige identified the importance of punk as a form of communication in his 1979 book, *Subculture: The Meaning of Style* (1). The alienation working-class youth felt in England in the 1970s manifested in a sort of "signifying practice" in which punks used their fashion to make a statement.

According to Hebdige, "The punks wore clothes which were the sartorial equivalent of swear words, and they swore as they dressed—with calculated effect, lacing obscenities into record notes and publicity releases, interviews, and love songs. Clothed in chaos, they produced Noise in the calmly orchestrated Crisis of everyday life in the late 1970s (2).

For Americans the original punk movement had a slightly more middle-class "new wave" spin to it, but little has changed from the original posturing (3).

The 2000 gutter-punk of Haight Street in San Francisco looks strikingly similar to the 1981 punk of London's Kings Road, when the band, the Exploited, were singing, "Punks Not Dead." Contemporary punk bands, like California's Rancid, look as if they stepped out of a time machine. Even aging punk founders, such as Johnny Rotten of the Sex Pistols and Joe Strummer of the Clash, "spit" on the notion of becoming "legitimate."

Simon Frith argued that punk immediately caught the attention of social theorists and jaded critics because of its attack on formalism (4). On three levels punk challenged the subcultural status quo. First, punk broke down the barriers between artists and audiences, becoming a type of folk music as well as a form of youth working-class consciousness. Second, it challenged standard commodity production with a "do-it-yourself" ethic. The 1980 Bow Wow Wow song, "C30 C60 C90 Go," urged kids to tape their favorite songs off of the radio instead of buying the records. In punk, "small is beautiful" and multinational record companies are evil. Finally, punk raised issues about the meaning of music. It was activism that crossed musical borders and political spectrums. It was, as Hebdige referred to it, "collision."

Punk stumbled onto something that gave it a longevity that hippies and break dancers lacked—institutionalized rebellion. The primary value of punk is anarchy. From the founding songs of the Ramones and Sex Pistols to the twenty-first-century punk of the Offspring, the subculture is designed to provoke. Chaos is preferable to any order, whether right, left, or boring center. The punk style is a weapon to distance the adult generation. As the comments of parents of punkers and punks themselves will show, the friction between adults and kids is just what the punks want. This is their route to liberation.

A BRIEF HISTORY OF PUNK

Punks are very conscious of their history. A young punker might have a patch of a band, (such as D.O.A., that recorded before they were born) safety-pinned to their leather jacket. They might get some of the dates or facts wrong, but they can clearly articulate value themes.

Where does any subculture begin? The early rumblings of punk are most often traced to the underground music scene of Lower East Side New York City in the mid-1970s. In clubs such as Max's Kansas City and CBGB's, artists including Lou Reed, Patti Smith, Iggy Pop, the New York Dolls, and the Ramones experimented with noise, gender-bending, and the nihilism that characterized the decade. After a British tour by the New York Dolls and the Ramones, rock promoter and sex-boutique owner Malcolm McLaren hit upon the idea of crafting a youth movement based on one of the Ramones' favorite self-descriptors, "punk" (5).

London in the summer of 1976 is generally seen as the crucible of the punk explosion. It was summer of the first Concorde, the first Apple computer, and Britain's "Silver Jubilee" for their queen. McLaren's greatest project, the band the Sex Pistols, shocked with their single, "God Save the Queen" (with its chorus "She ain't no human being"). The hot weather and economic drought drove scores of kids away from their ABBA and Eagles records into the punk subculture. They chopped their hair off and made their own clothes. You did not really buy punk fashion as much as you created it. "Individuality was the key, with hand-sprayed clothes, ripped trousers, and extravagant hairstyles" (6). The first punks pogo-danced to the abrasive clanging of their music and delighted in horrifying aging hippies and adults.

Back in the United States, New York's punk scene developed, with bands like the Tuff Darts and the Talking Heads. Soon Los Angeles had its own punk scene with the even harder sounds of bands such as Black Flag and the Circle Jerks. The early punk subculture was essentially a rebellion against patriarchal structures. Women in early punk bands, such as Siouxise and the Banshees (London), Blondie (New York), and X (Los Angeles) were free to be as aggressive as their male counterparts. The androgyny of punk helped to keep the subculture out of the male-dominated production of other youth scenes, such as mods or campus radicalism.

Despite the break-up of the Sex Pistols in 1978 and the 1979 death of their bass player, Sid Vicious, punk survived into the 1980s. The critical acclaim of the 1980 album *London Calling* by the Clash helped punk to seep into every small-town high school world. Ronald Reagan and Margaret Thatcher's Cold War arms race with the Soviets forced punk rock and punks to become more political. Bands such as the Dead Kennedys in the United States and Anti-Pasti in the United Kingdom wrote political anarchy anthems that were adopted by various splinters of the movement, such as peace-punks and straight-edgers. The late 1980s saw punk lose ground to the burgeoning heavy metal scene that seemed not only to capture the energy of the original punk scene but was also characterized by misogyny, which punk rejected.

The year 1991 is often referred to as "the year that punk broke" into the mainstream (7). One Seattle band, Nirvana, and one song, "Smells Like Teen Spirit," managed to capture the youthful angst of the new decade. The video, complete with anarchist cheerleaders, featured singer Kurt Cobain expressing the alienation of living in a consumer-driven culture. "I feel stupid and contagious. Here we are—now entertain us" (8).

The song struck a chord and managed to reignite punk under the media-manufactured label, "grunge." The supposed grunge scene in Seattle—starring bands such as Pearl Jam and Soundgarden (featured in the 1992 grunge movie *Singles*)—was actually similar to youth scenes all over the United States, where kids were combining elements of punk and heavy metal and trying to make sense of life in the early years of the Clinton era.

The suicide of Kurt Cobain on April 8, 1994, gave punk its first martyr since the heroin overdose by Sid Vicious in 1979. But Cobain was more of a gentle poet of youth culture than a punk clown. His death had mainstream media, from *Newsweek* to CNN, discussing Emile Durkheim and the "anomie of Generation X."

As the century ended, the kids who still clung to the punk identity were the core of the over two million homeless youths, the gutter-punks. Gutter-punks are visible in every major U.S. city. They are the kids with purple hair, tattered Army jackets, wallet chains, and combat boots. They are "punker than punk" in their rejection of mainstream society. Occasionally their desire to shock gets in the way of their daily quest for spare change and shelter, but they have made the ideal of anarchy a reality in their lives on the streets.

This chapter begins with a discussion of the power of punks to provoke by examining some of the teenage punk rockers and their families who became involved with a self-help organization, Parents of Punkers, in the early to mid-1980s. This is followed by an analysis of selected letters written by youth and other citizens who responded to the appearances by these punk rockers on several nationally syndicated television shows. Then we discuss a few of the letters that teenagers have written over the years to *Flipside,* a prominent Southern California-based "fanzine," or magazine devoted to followers of the contemporary punk and postpunk scene.

The chapter that follows this one continues the discussion of punk, concluding with interviews with gutter-punks and focusing on runaway youth who cling to the punk identity. We will also examine punk identities in cross-cultural perspectives.

PARENTS OF PUNKERS

Serena Dank, a community counselor in the greater Los Angeles area, first became aware of the problem of teenagers turning to the punk movement while she was working in the early 1980s with violent youths and youth gangs in the city of Norwalk. School counselors had referred young punkers to her at the nonprofit Community Counseling Associates she and a colleague had formed.

From 1981 through 1986 Dank met with over four hundred families in Southern California. She also conferred with numerous other families across the country who were concerned about their rebellious offspring and had sought her out for advice.

Parents of Punkers was formed to help both punkers and parents whose children were involved in the punk style. The organization took no position on what should be the appropriate public policy toward punk although Parents of Punkers believed that many of the values and behaviors promoted by punk ran against the grain of almost all concerned parents.

According to Dank, when punk rock came to the United States from England in the late 1970s, punk rock's raw, aggressive sound "caught the ears of youth on the west coast" (9). Overnight, punk groups were formed in the Los Angeles area, appearing in a variety of teenage nightspots such as the Stardust Ballroom, the Starwood Nightclub, Vex, Club 88, Cathay De Grande, the Whisky-A-Go-Go, and Madame Wong's.

From the very beginning, the philosophy of hard-core punk rock appeared to be one of total anarchy. Youths were quick to "hold a beef against anybody and anything that reeked of the establishment." The words of punk music often summed up the violence-oriented, uncaring feelings of many hard-core punkers. One such song of this early period, "No Values," proclaimed that one should not insist that everything in society is all right. Otherwise youths might resort to violence and "start destroying" everything in sight and "blow(ing) you away" (10).

According to Dank, not everyone who associated with punk fit the aggressive mold. Many punkers, including the poseurs or wannabes, were on the periphery of the main punk culture and enjoyed the music and the dress without embracing the total philosophy. For these youngsters punk was "dressing up" on the weekends to attend the club gigs.

It was the hard-core punkers (and their families) who were "totally into" the punk sound and philosophy that went along with it that Dank treated. In interviews with the news media at the time, Dank gave examples of the violence and senseless aggression that were the trademarks of the hard-core punker:

> They'll go to great extremes to do anything that offends and defies society. I know of one girl who wore Rosary beads around her neck with a skull attached to offend Catholics. The friends of another girl I knew celebrated her 21st birthday party by slamming twenty-one holes in the wall (11).

Early critics of the violent aspect of the punk style drew attention to the "slamming" that took place on the dance floor of the gigs. When serious punkers got down and danced to their music, they slam danced. Much of the aggressive behavior observed at concerts occurred in the slam pits close to the stage where rockers would get tossed around.

Such rituals continue today, but the names have changed. Now, instead of slamming, teenagers engage in "moshing"—jumping up on stage, being thrown off onto the crowd, and passed around the tight band of fans close to the stage (where the dance pit is located).

Moshing, like slamming, starts off with bouncing lightly on one's feet. The dancer begins moving to the left and right, then smashing—hard—into the person next to him. Usually the dance amounts to nothing more than playful pushing and shoving. But at other times, fists are thrown, fights break out, and people get hurt. Some bands even pride themselves on the fights and ensuing violence created at their gigs.

In the United States punk by the early 1980s had become the general banner under which everything from "Christian punk" to "devil music" and "art music" was lumped, spreading philosophies of anarchism and nihilism, along with a million different "isms" along the way. From the very beginning the punk rock scene appealed to the young. Both the bands and their followers were frequently juveniles barely into their teens. Even today, alternative rock concerts have fans in attendance who are 13 and 14 years old, if not younger. Some of the members of the bands are little older.

As Dank noted at the time, "The abundance of crazy-colored hair cut in bizarre shapes, death shades of makeup, and the outlandish punkers' dress—along with the reported violence and self-abuse incited by the music—had many parents at a loss. Parents and kids were unbelievably alienated. Many kids had virtually no relationship with their parents, while the parents couldn't relate to punk at all and didn't know where to turn (12).

As with most youth cultures, their music was the "glue" that held the entire group together. Commenting during the early years of the punk rock movement, one observer noted that the "music brings a lot of turmoil at home. It's almost like subliminal advertising. It has such an undercurrent of hate—it can be playing and you get bombarded with it. You read the words, and it's all negative. It upsets your entire life (13).

For Dank an early concern with punk music was the potentially negative effects it had upon younger children who internalized the lyrics and embraced the punk philosophy without understanding the irony or parody in much of the music.

Kids were initially attracted to punk because of its music and clothing, but they stayed in it because they liked the attention, even if it was negative. The hardcore punk—in contrast to the poseurs—was the type that parents were afraid (all) their children would become. The hard-corers were the ones made infamous on television and in newspapers. The only rule they lived by was that there were *no* rules.

Some punks fell in between the hard-corers and poseurs. In full regalia this middle-type, nevertheless, aroused concern since they frequently appeared harsher than the simple statement they were trying to deliver: "It's all right to be yourself and do what you want" (14).

For some parents punk was merely a phase their children were going through. According to one mother who was involved with Parents of Punkers for several months, "I did not mind when my 16-year-old son first started looking punk, although I questioned his Mohawk hairstyle. Punk is part of the maturing process for some kids. Kids in the 1930s wore long fur coats. I'm sure those parents went crazy, too, but it goes away (15).

Some of the adolescents, however, involved with Parents of Punkers did not agree that punk was merely a phase. One punk rocker, interviewed while she was still involved with the movement, claimed: "I don't picture myself dressing like this at 30. It's a phase, but not one that I'm going to grow out of. It's more a phase that I'll grow with (16).

Through the Parents of Punkers organization, Dank acted as a facilitator, educating parents on punk and eventually helping them to form support groups or networks of knowledgeable mothers and fathers others could turn to for assistance. She also conducted parenting workshops.

Dank's advice for parents of punkers is also appropriate today for families that are confused by other youth styles that their children may be involved with:

Parents should know what their kids are into. To start off, read the words from one of your son's or daughter's record albums. Discuss what the words mean with your child. Hear what he has to say and don't condemn him. Try to get to know your kid. Many children do things because of a need for attention or a cry for help. To gain a clearer understanding into the world of punk, parents should visit a punk club or at least stand outside to see what is going on and what it's all about. Parents need most, however, to learn to set limits that are compatible with the values they feel should be instilled in their children. Parents still have the right to set limits on their children. Love and limits convey security. And love will allow the limits to spread out (17).

VOICES FROM THE FRINGE

Parents of Punkers received much publicity during the years of its operation. Besides being the subject of countless interviews by the press, Serena Dank and her group were the focus of an extended article in *US* magazine. The novelty and success of her program also brought her to the attention of television producers. On two occasions she and several of the punkers she was counseling appeared on "The Phil Donahue Show" to discuss the punk youth culture. And Dank—along with both the parents and their punk offspring—were the subjects on national and local network shows such as the "Today" show on NBC; "Hour Magazine," a nationally syndicated special features show; and three segments of "Eye on LA," an ABC locally affiliated show aimed at the Los Angeles market.

Whenever the group appeared on television, the program and the topic elicited a great deal of response from the viewing public. Teenage punk rockers responded either in support of Parents of Punkers' efforts or in opposition to Dank's views on dangers of the hard-core punk scene. Furthermore, other concerned citizens wrote in, voicing their opinions on both the topic and the punkers themselves. In all, Dank estimated she received close to one thousand letters from people who had seen one or more of the television shows and who felt strongly enough about the subject to take the time to write to her.

Copies of 105 of these letters were made available for our analysis. As the following edited excerpts from 20 of these letters indicate, the American public held wide-ranging views and attitudes concerning the entire punk youth culture.

Letters from Punk Rockers

Forty-five of the letters (43 percent) analyzed were written by punk rockers themselves. Thirty-six of these (80 percent) were supportive of the punk movement and youth style. The rest discussed parental problems. One letter from a male punk rocker discussed his efforts to escape the punk scene. One female punk high-school student wrote to denounce the stereotyping of punkers:

> I wish to criticize you for your generalizations and grotesque stereotypes of "punk" teenagers. I find it appalling to see that in our supposed modern thinking world, prejudices would still be based on a person's taste in music and clothing. Have you people any sense of originality in style? In these desperate times, we teenagers are searching for some way to hold on to our "selfs."

> I attend a school in an upper-middle-class area. I am enrolled in advanced academic courses, am an honor student, and am a representative in the junior Class Council. I am heavily involved with the marching band, track, and *I am a punk*. From the shoes, to the hair, to the polk-a-dot leotards, I am punk. Most of the punks at school are on an unusually creative mode. Many are top athletes, musicians, valedictorians, artists, and cheerleaders. And most have a high academic standing. We are creative, fun-loving, and mentally and physically healthy people. And I resent the implication that we are bizarre, warped cult-members. I hope you reevaluate your position.

A 16-year-old male punker defended his lifestyle:

> I am a "punker." I love life. I love my girlfriend, and I want to see my children grow up to be free from peer groups, death and many other things that face me today. I want you to understand something. I didn't become a punker to make friends. I became a punker to be free from trying to be someone I'm not. When I was a "rocker," I did drugs and alcohol. I fought my parents a heck of a lot more than I do now. And from listening to the music, I was depressed. Now I'm free from all of that. But one thing that makes me mad is that people won't accept me for what I am, and I mean "normal" people like the clones who run this world today. People stare at me because my hair is shaved on the sides.

One older teenager expressed concerns for the evils of a campaign against the punk youth culture:

> I have been listening to punk for five years, and I attend punk concerts at the local clubs regularly. Admittedly, punk has grown more violent in the last few years as "pogoing" has gradually been replaced with "slamming," but I never heard of, or saw, violence at a punk concert until it began to receive massive media exposure. In fact, I have yet to actually see a fight at a punk concert. It seems to me that punk is the least violent of all musical movements.
> Alcohol and drugs are sometimes present in these halls. But the pressure to imbibe is not stressed among punks as it is among businessmen and football players. Young people should be allowed to express distaste for the values and mediocrity of modern America.

The violence associated with punk rock is the direct result of media exposure which draws thrill seekers to concerts. You are creating mayhem by attracting jocks, red-necks, and plain idiots to our clubs. Please, in the name of sanity, Stop! Please stop your media campaign which is destroying the good intentions of a once self-respecting movement. Punk is passe, but you are making it dangerous.

Many letters from punks, however, were written by teenagers who were crying out for help, as the following excerpt from a 16-year-old female indicates.

I am a punk. I cut my arms and recut the cuts to make scars. When I get angry or upset I have these urges to hurt myself. I love playing with fire and seeing how much pain I can bear. I guess I punish myself by hitting walls and digging into my arms with glass. I guess I like pain or something. I mean I don't but I do. Do you understand?

I picture myself doing all kinds of destructive even suicidal things. Like running red lights into cars, taking a .22 and shooting myself in the head, opening the car door and jumping out while it's moving. The thing is, I'm afraid maybe I'll do it sometime.

A year ago I started a new high school. I had a hard time fitting in basically because I'm shy and don't have much—none really—self-confidence. Well, the punks accepted me. I could become a part of something. I cut my hair, wore the clothes, and listened to the music. All my friends were punks. I was sort of into the self-mutilation before and I fit right in. A year before that I was into a lot of drugs.

Another 14-year-old female, who signed her letter "Vomit," also discussed inflicting pain upon herself.

I am a so-called punker. I enjoy listening to the music I listen to, believing in what I believe in, and even self-inflicting pain. When I see the first drop of blood I actually feel a sense of relief and definitely no regret for what I am doing. Maybe it is not the best solution to my problems, but as of right now I have nothing to stop me from doing it except myself, and I don't want to stop.

I have a set goal for when I am a mature adult which is to be a psychiatrist (I bet I didn't even spell it right). It is probably a stupid thing for a person in my position to want to become because I probably need one myself but my mom and dad think it's a start.

Another teenage female wrote in to discuss how becoming part of the punk youth culture assisted her by providing her with a social group:

All of my life I've been a bit of a social outcast, with few friends. I have always dressed unusual, always been a brain, and always asked questions when others acquiesced. My depression and isolation hit a peak at the end of my fourteenth year and I started to cut up my arms with razor blades, and even burn my wrist to a pulp with cigarettes. This was all *before* I became involved with the punk scene. While I was trying to stop, or at least decrease my self-mutilation, I made good friends with punks at my school, and thanks to them and the other friends I met at the local punk club, I have managed to keep my suicidal and self-deprecating feelings in check most of the time.

Other youths requested assistance in dealing with their parents, who did not understand the punk youth scene. One male wrote:

> I would like some more information about how to relate to my parents better and tell them I am not throwing my life away. I actually am not a bad kid. I get good grades, am straight-edge, and yet my folks are scared that I am becoming a derelict of society just because of my choices in music and clothing. I am so afraid of what my parents would think that I can't even bring my friends over to my house without the thought of giving my parents cardiac arrest.

Likewise, a female wished her mom would support her more:

> Can you help me get my mom to understand me? She doesn't know why I "have to do this" to myself and doesn't get why I "haven't outgrown this stage yet." She doesn't understand that this is how I am. During these "discussions," I'm the one keeping my voice down and making sensible statements. But that doesn't matter because she doesn't even hear me. I have friends whose parents accept and even support them. I'd settle for being able to leave the house without my mom having an ill look on her face!

One high school junior wrote in to complain about his parents' indifference:

> My parents have decided that ignorance is bliss. If they ignore their kids' problems, things will be great again on middle-class "Respectable Street" (my dad's a doctor). Let me tell you this. I have been a follower of John Lennon's ever since I was a little kid. He was like a modern Christ to me. When he was assassinated, my parents didn't care—my dad even expected me to go to school the next day! They acted as if nothing happened, and they knew it was a turning point in my life. I tried to commit suicide but they didn't notice. My mom is an invalid, at home all the time, but she was too busy watching TV to care. I doubt if she would have even taken it seriously if she did find out.

Another 16-year-old female punk rocker wrote about her parents' failure to listen to her:

> My parents don't seem to care. They say that people like me are sick and that we need to be put in mental institutions. They have not thrown me out of the house yet, but they are ready to. I had decided to try to leave punk after being in it for two years. I went to my mother and told her that I wanted to talk about getting out. You know what she said? She said, "Well, I am glad you finally came to your senses. I

hope that you're fed up with that trash." I tried to tell her what was causing me to turn to punk. She said, "Never mind. I don't want to hear anything else about it. At least I don't have to send you to a mental hospital." That really did it. It did not help me one bit. It only pushed me deeper into punk.

Letters from Parents, Other Family Members, and Friends

Nearly all of the thirty letters that were written by parents, other family members, or friends of punkers were quite critical of the entire punk movement.

One mother wrote a lengthy letter, pleading for help with her delinquent son:

> We have a son that's been getting into trouble since he was 6 years old. Nothing serious at first, just his behavior in school. Without help it got serious. He was finally kicked out. We couldn't get him into any local schools, so we had to send him away to schools for kids with behavior problems, where he was supposed to get help, but he never did.
>
> Anyway, the older he got, the more of a punk he became. The way he dressed, earring in the ear, the whole bit. We argued a lot. I tried to reason. I punished. Nothing helped. I remember when he was about 8 years old, I spanked him, and he ran away. Oh, he came back the next day.
>
> My husband is a minister. We have prayed. He's gone to church with us. Our son was never interested. My husband has counseled numerous children and teens and was able to get through to most of them. We both are really hurt because nothing we've said or done has helped our son.
>
> We took him to a psychiatrist, against our son's wishes. He said he didn't need a shrink. There was a big argument, but he went, after his dad insisted. The doctor's finding was that he couldn't tell the difference between right and wrong all the time. That he was so very angry inside. When he could tell the difference, he was not able to stop himself from doing wrong.
>
> He soon started getting in trouble with the law. It started with him stealing a bike. He joined a gang of boys later on in his life, boys that stole bikes. The guys were glad to have our son because he's very good with his hands. He can fix almost anything.
>
> He seemed to get into trouble after each argument. We felt he was doing it to get even or to hurt us. He never realized that he was hurting himself. You see, he had gotten to the place where he didn't love himself, and yet he didn't know it. He still doesn't know it.
>
> From the behavior schools, he finally went to jail, a detention school for boys and girls. He served 1 1/2 years without getting any help from a doctor. He came home after serving time. For a while he was alright. Then he started going out looking for his old buddies.
>
> Our son smokes pot, drinks, steals, sleeps with girls, the works. Only 16 years old—you name it and he's done it. We have raised 12 children. He's the only one we never could reach.

Would you believe me if I told you that he and his friends went out and stole a car. Well, he's in jail. His friends ran. He couldn't get out of the car so easy as he was driving. It was his turn to drive. When the police stopped them, he wouldn't name his friends.

I have a guilty feeling for feeling glad that he's in jail. My husband is always in court with him, and he's pastoring a church. I feel guilty because when he's out and the phone rings, I think it's the hospital to say he's been shot.

You're doing a very fine job. I sure wish there had been an organization like yours that could have helped our son. He used to be so nice. His trial is tomorrow. I hope you don't mind my writing. I needed to talk some way, so writing really helped.

One concerned father of a 12-year-old boy wrote the following:

Our son got into punk rock about a year ago. At first, my wife and I didn't mind it because all he did was listen to punk music. The only thing we did mind was the lyrics to some of that music.

One day he shocked us both by coming home with blue hair and a pierced ear. I didn't like it and I expressed my disapproval to him. He told me not to worry about it. Now he has both his ears pierced (one of them is pierced three times) and he wears trashy clothes. He pierced his ears without our knowledge because he knew that we wouldn't have allowed it, and no matter how much we plead with him, he refuses to change his style of dress. My wife and I are pretty liberal and therefore do not force him to change his appearance, but we do wish that he would listen to us.

He is a good boy, but we are getting worried. He has started breaking his curfew, and his grades have slipped from straight As to Bs and Cs. We are also very worried that he may be getting into drugs. We are hoping and praying that he hasn't taken any drugs and never will, but still, the anxiety is there. Our relationship with him has diminished quite a bit since he has become a punker, and I'm afraid. Afraid that he will start doing things that are bad and wrong. Afraid that we'll grow farther apart. I don't want that to happen. I want us to be close. Help us, please.

A concerned mother wrote the following:

My son has taken to spending his time with a rather unappealing group of fellows. They claim to be "into" the punk scene and have embraced what I define as clearly antisocial behavior. My son is a good boy, but he appears to have become carried away in his attempt to be a full-fledged member of the movement of the day. He looks and acts as if he were raised in a subway and has never seen the light of day. His music even exudes the monophonic drone readily found in a subway tunnel. Needless to say, I am concerned about his well being.

One parent wrote about how his son's punk behavior might be misinterpreted as a reflection of how poorly they, as his parents, had raised him.

> Our son's involvement in punk rock has put a lot of strain on my wife, essentially because many of her friends have noticed his change in character. One of them even asked if he was using drugs. We feel positive that he would not misuse drugs. We are more concerned with how his behavior reflects upon my wife and I. His obvious change in behavior puts us in an awkward position when we try to explain it to friends. We are afraid that our friends may interpret his radical behavior as the result of the way we brought him up.

One mother wrote of her fear of her own son:

> I have been having trouble with my fourteen-year-old since his father died two years ago. I first thought he was just going through the regular teenage rebel stage, but then he turned very cold toward me. I can't talk to him anymore without him swearing at me and threatening me. I'm afraid of my own son! I don't even dare talk to him about counseling anymore. I had mentioned it one night after finding pot in his room. He just blew up. I was actually afraid he was going to kill me or something. It was a terrible scene.
>
> I just don't know whom to turn to. I don't belong to a parish and don't have any real close friends who I can talk to. I come home at night and just cry. I don't know my son anymore. He never speaks to me.

Letters from Other Concerned Viewers

Many people wrote in to express their concern about the punk rock movement and the punks that had appeared on the television shows. Thirty such letters were analyzed.

One self-proclaimed, born-again Christian wrote the following:

> Punk rock is no good at all. Punk rock is of the devil. It is the parents' fault the way the kids act. The parents are out in some bar with some other man or woman, and their kids are on the street getting into trouble.

A woman wrote in, "greatly appalled" at what she had seen on the television show.

> The punks! Those rejects of society and no wonder. What a bunch of uglies. What a decay of our society they represent. They claim that they are dressed and made up as they are because they feel comfortable that way. I feel comfortable in my nightgown, too, but that does not mean that I wear it for work or play.
>
> Their outside betrays their sick and evil inside. I denounce the "Donahue Show" for even putting those "uglies" on his show where

youngsters can easily watch them and may follow their misguided attitude.

Not all the letters were from people critical of punk youths. One elderly couple in their sixties wrote to say they were in "partial sympathy with the crazy kids" they had seen on television.

> Many young people are confused (to say the least) when people tell them "things are great—times will be better"—when they know they are not better and won't be better. I think patriotism is difficult to muster when you see that governments turn their backs on the needy and are more interested in building a great army and beautiful warships and a fascinating defense force than in their people.
>
> Maybe it helps to dye your hair purple, wear arm bands, or fantasize. Maybe then you can feel like you are protesting the bad things you see, hear or feel.

A supportive grandfather declared, "If I were 17 instead of 77, I would be a 'punkie,'" and made these observations:

> I know a woman who kicked her son out of their house because of his long hair and beard. She was ashamed of what neighbors would think. However, she did not mind that her husband cheated on his income tax, broke speed laws or took towels from hotel rooms. She does not mind that her church accepts money from a Mafia member. She is an anti-abortionist while favoring war. I prefer any punker to her.
>
> My son's two children are punkers. Both graduated from high school in three years with honors. They are both welcome in their parents' home and in our home.

Finally, one letter voiced a concern of a different sort:

> I have a problem like the "Parents of Punkers" have except that it's my mom that's the punker. I'm embarrassed to go to town with my mom because she colors her hair all weird. My mom tries to be with the "in" crowd, and it's embarrassing if some of my friends come over. Is there anything that you can send me so that I can show my friends that my mom isn't crazy?

LETTERS TO THE FANZINES

Fanzines are magazines that began in the early 1980s by catering to the punk youth culture. They continue to be published in several different countries around the world. Today, the magazines' appeal has broadened to youths involved in the postpunk scene as well.

In the United States alone, there are over 150 such magazines, published either bimonthly or quarterly. The most famous of the fanzines, at least on the West Coast, include *Flipside, Ink Disease, Maximum Rock N Roll,* and *Propaganda.*

Other fanzines that have been published throughout the United States include *Animal 'Zine* (St. Lawrence, Kansas), *Bad Meat* (Bartlesville, Oklahoma), *Basket Case* (Staten Island, New York), *Bloody Mess* (Peoria, Illinois), *Choose Your Fate* (Etters, Pennsylvania), *United Underground* (Houston, Texas), and *Punk Planet* (Olympia, Washington).

Fanzines are also popular in other countries. For instance, *Alternative Punk* is published in Quebec, Canada; *Antrim Alternative* in Belfast, Ireland; *Pig Paper* in Ontario, Canada; *One World* in Auckland, New Zealand; and *Sub* in Skannege, Sweden.

A typical issue in the magazines includes letters to the editor, advertisements for rock or punk bands soon to play in the area, comic strips depicting punk characters, advertisements for albums or record stores, feature articles on new or popular bands along with interviews, a pen pal section, a lengthy classified section, and many pictures of band members or fans standing in line at gigs or slam dancing or moshing in the pit.

One of the most long-lasting and consistently popular fanzines, *Flipside* (from Whittier, California), began publication in 1977 and is still in publication, with January/February 2000 marking its 122nd issue. Anywhere from 80 to 170 pages in length, each issue is crammed with articles and letters from punk and rock fans involved with the current scene. Topics raised in the fanzine are often well crafted and reflect the concerns of the day.

All of the following quotations are taken from one early issue of *Flipside,* published in 1982. One young writer, for instance, bemoans the way the media have "ruined the movement":

> It really is a shame that punk has been so exploited by the media. I think that is where the whole violence bit started. The news was always saying it (punk) was "weird" and "bizarre." They treated it as if it was a Devil's cult or something. They flat out lied about it, saying that the people involved were violent, sadomasochists, who only wanted to riot all the time.
>
> Such a thing couldn't have been further from the truth. We only wanted to be left alone and free to listen to the music we loved and what was wrong with that? They had to keep nosing around until they were sure they had it all analyzed in their little black books. Only what they didn't realize is that by that time there was a new generation of punks who were never into it until they read about it in the papers. So, thinking that it was all violence, (they) acted accordingly. Brainwashed, the media had won again.

Frequently teenagers write in to *Flipside* trying to explain what punk is or what it means to them. One young male fan described his affiliation with punk in this way:

> Punk is people. People tired of shit getting shoved in their head. Conform. It's a fucking attitude, a lifestyle that allows (for) individuality and creativity. So I don't want to wear an alligator on my tit and prefer green lipstick to red or pink. That's my trip. I'm happy and my appearance reflects why, who and what I am.

People like to reassure themselves I'm going thru the rebellion my youth entitles me to. I went through my rebellion last year. I was a partyer (sic), took all sorts of drugs, and screwed up my head and life. Well now I'm 15 and got my shit together good, got a job, moved out, and still get myself to school. No, this is no fuck'en rebellion. There's no one to rebel at, except society in general. This is a lifestyle I've acquired, that relates to me, and caters to my individual needs.

Other youths write in voicing their disappointment with the direction the punk movement has taken:

This whole movement started with youth sick of what society had to offer. Now it's not that. It's changed to how many gigs have you been to? How many symbols do you know? Did you slam at that gig? Well, I think that's bullshit!

Another youth is critical of the punk scene as it manifested itself in California:

I'm beginning to think that California is like another country, all that bullshit about the "Cal Lifestyle" is almost true. Kids here seem to be affected by peer pressure more than other places. Being cool is the most important thing. Right now it's cool to be a punk in high school, so all the otherwise "loadies" and "too hip" people are "into" the punk scene. They're not punks and they blow the whole image.

Some youths see the punk culture as a continuation of earlier rebellious youth movements:

The revolution didn't start with punk. It didn't start with the hippies. And it didn't start with the beatniks. It started with the Pilgrims feeling the oppression of their countries and coming to the "New World." All the movements since then have just added to the momentum.

Another youth describes his involvement more succinctly:

I'm a punk rocker 'cause there's nothing left in American culture to conform to and we're all bored.

Or punk has been described by another youth in this manner:

Punk is chip on the shoulder, burden on the back, boil under the armpit music—indulgent, sniveling and essentially youth-obsessed.

Some youths use the fanzines to discuss what some of the components of the punk culture mean to them. One male discussed his first experiences "slamming in the pit":

I was shocked to see the slam dance. So I thought, well I'll try slamming. I went there with a couple of my friends and we did it and it was so cool. It was so totally different than anything that the media had said. I can see how they (the media) have exploited what it looked like, but it was totally different.

That's what the media does. Unless they experience it, they don't know what it's like. They think that when you go in there and you're bumped real hard, that it hurts. It really doesn't hurt because you're on such a rush. You're just bouncing around.

Another explains his views as to why punk is primarily a male phenomenon and how females are treated at the gigs:

There is a lot of macho kind of things to do along with punk. The slam dance is kind of a macho thing. Even girls that participate in the slam usually do so by creating their own maleness. They are not out there in their spiked heels slamming. They give up their femininity and take on all the masculine characteristics.

I don't see a lot of the things that go on at gigs, so my girlfriend points them out to me. They are playing the same old games. The girls are there to pick up guys and the guys are there to pick up the girls. It's a lot more forward, I would imagine. I've been at gigs where guys would just ask when they walked by if they would give them "head."

In summary, the fanzines like *Flipside* have provided youths with the opportunity to express their feelings on a wide range of subjects of concern to them (as we have seen with just this small sampling). Over the years these magazines have come to serve as a rallying cry for the entire youth culture.

Youth continue to express their take on current events through *Flipside*. Responding to the Columbine shooting incident, one sophomore high school student from Kentucky noted in a 1999 piece titled "Class War":

The majority of the people and media all think that the involved gunmen in these shootings are just a bunch of crazy teenagers who can't handle their anger in any other way. I believe there is a lot more to it. First, I want to say that I don't in any way fully justify what these students have done.

A lot of the media believes that these students were just ridiculed every now and then, and that it's not that serious. But the media does not notice that when these outcast kids are told that they are worthless everyday of their life, it could make them more mentally unstable than they already are. My friends and I get treated unfairly in the same way but we can ignore it a lot easier. Basically what happens is that these kids are sick of seeing high school athletes getting away with whatever they want. I get sick of it too but once again I just ignore it.

Fortunately I will not let (them) get to me by listening to punk rock and playing in a band, but a lot of other teenagers can't do the same. We have to teach kids at an early age that discrimination is wrong and you can't just ridicule someone because they are different (18).

> ### Youth at the Movies—Punk Rockers
>
> The specter of violent punks has been used as a film device from *The Class of 1984* (1982) to *Freeway* (1996). The best of the "bad punk" movies is not *The Doom Generation* (1995) but *Repo Man* (1984). In it a "hard core" Emilio Estevez is surrounded by a wild cast of characters, including a band of punk vandals who blame society for their criminality. The best portrayal of real punks is either Penelope Spheeris's 1981 documentary, *Decline of Western Civilization,* or her 1983 drama, *Suburbia.* In *Decline* the punks speak for themselves, but in *Suburbia* the viewer gets to see the punks defending their ideological terrain against local rednecks.

NOTES

1. Dick Hebdige, *Subculture: The Meaning of Style* (Methuen: London, 1979).

2. Ibid, p. 114

3. Michael Brake, *Comparative Youth Culture* (New York: Routledge, 1985), p. 77

4. Simon Frith, "Formalism, Realism and Leisure: The Case of Punk (1980)," in *The Subcultures Reader,* ed. Ken Gelder and Sarah Thorton (London: Routledge, 1997)

5. Adrain Boot and Chris Salewicz, *Punk: The Illustrated History of a Music Revolution* (New York: Penguin, 1996).

6. Martin Roach, *Dr. Martens* (AirWair Limited, 1999), p. 32.

7. *The Year That Punk Broke* (Geffen Video, 1991).

8. Kurt Cobain, "Smells Like Teen Spirit," on Nirvana's *Nevermind* (Geffen Records, 1991).

9. Ina Avonow, "Parents of Punkers Learning to Cope with Problems," *Los Angeles Times* (12 March 1982), p. V-2.

10. Jeff Goldthorpe, *Intoxicated Culture: A Political History of the California Punk Scene* (San Francisco State University, San Francisco, CA: Ph.D. diss., 1990), p. 205.

11. Nicole Yorkin, "Where to Turn When Your Son Dyes His Hair Green and Blue: Parents of Punkers Attempt to Bridge the Gap," *Los Angeles Herald Examiner* (28 December 1981), p. A-7.

12. Ibid.

13. Faye Zuckerman, "Punk Rock Sparks This Era's Generation Gap," *Daily News* (22 November 1981), p. A-8.

14. David Figura, "Group Advocates Parental Limits on 'Punker' Children," *Huntington Park Daily Signal* (24 September 1981), p. B-1.

15. Aronow.

16. Ibid.

17. Figura.

18. Anonymous, "Class War," *Flipside* (May/June 1999) (119) (P.O. Box 363, Whittier, CA), p. 13.

6

Gutter-Punks and the Lure of the Street

In late 1999 a U.S. Conference of Mayors' report noted the increase in homeless youth during the 1990s (1). At the depths of the economic downturn in 1991, children and teens accounted for 27 percent of the nation's homeless population. By the end of the decade, such youth made up a third, according to the report, which based their findings on surveys from government and private agencies in twenty-six states.

Furthermore, acccording to the report, national prosperity is the culprit, often putting children and their parents onto the streets due to the higher cost of housing while, at the same time, the government was decreasing—if not eliminating—assistance. In another recent study, 80 percent of the parents and children serviced by the Union Rescue Mission in downtown Los Angeles blamed poverty; eight years ago most blamed drugs and alcohol (2).

Approximately 16 percent of America's two million homeless youth have run away more than five times (3). These 320,000 "chronically homeless" young people are the new Skid Row. They have chosen a life on the streets over life at home. Some are running away from sexually or physically abusive parents. Some are "push outs," pushed out by parents who did not approve of their child's sexual orientation or other lifestyle choices or who could not reconcile the responsibilities of parenting with their own consumptive lifestyle. And some youth are just troublemakers who responded to their parents' desperate attempt to "create more structure" by hitting the streets.

The proportions of each vary depending on the data source, but all share several things in common: Sleeping under damp highway overpasses, begging for spare change, and selling their bodies for pizza money are preferable to life at home.

The most hard-core of the homeless subculture are the gutter-punks. These refugees from suburbia are the most chronically homeless. Following the trend back into the cities, these kids have used the downwardly mobile style of punk rock as both a shocking fashion statement and a commentary about the chaos of contemporary society.

YOUNG AND ADRIFT

Portland, Oregon, has about two thousand homeless youth on the streets and in various shelters. About fifty gutter-punks congregate daily in urban parks, dry street corners, and Pioneer Square (Portland's town square). They look menacing with multiple body-piercings, homemade tattoos, ripped clothing, and unwashed hair. But most are teenagers, scrambling to survive from day to day. Portland police officer commander Ed May commented, "They're the 1990s' version of the countercultural movement" (4).

Interviews with a dozen gutter-punks were conducted on a number of topics, including their interpretations of punk value themes. Most were between 16 and 18 and had been on the street for about a year. They knew how to work the system, including which shelters would let them shower and use the phone. Many chose not to take advantage of available beds in shelters because of restrictions placed on "clients."

Certain value themes emerged in these interviews that were consistent with those identified by Kathryn Joan Fox (5). Fox found that the structure of the punk subculture followed commitment to punk values. The hard-core punks had a strong belief in, and concern for, the punk scene, and their values were based on a "distinctly anti-establishment, anarchistic sentiment." Being punk was of utmost importance to them.

The soft core punks were less serious about the scene but still espoused punk values and styles, such as mohawk haircuts. "Preppie" punks were attracted to the subculture only for the fashion and did not care about the countercultural scene or punk values. They only "dressed punk." A fourth group, called "spectators," was the largest. These nonpunks interacted with the punks in their world of clubs and parties. They are the voyeurs of the scene who may one day become hard-core punks.

The gutter-punk scene in Portland (and elsewhere) follows a similar structure. Like the hard-core punks, the core of the gutter-punk population identifies itself through its extreme styles: Lip piercings, neck tattoos, colored hair, and rats for pets are all signifiers.

PIERCED AND TATTOOED: CONTEMPORARY YOUTH STYLES

Although punks have managed to keep their lifestyle from being coopted into the hegemonic culture, much of their style has been borrowed by the mainstream. Much like the pop trend of New Wave music in the early 1980s, "alternative rock" of today mimics much of the anger and posing of punk rock. Popular bands like the Foo Fighters and Sugar Ray are closer to Fox's "preppie punks," whose styles are far removed from the values and culture of punk.

Similarly, body modification in the forms of tattooing and piercing has been appropriated by the larger youth culture. Tongue piercing, once the act of the most hard-core gutter-punk, was brought to the masses by Mel C of the Spice Girls and is now as common among sorority women as among punk women.

In a sense punkers have given youth culture another style for mainstream consumption. Tattoos were once the domain of convicts, sailors, and skinheads. The spread of their popularity has been linked to different processes. For some, body modification is a way of regaining ownership of the self, away from market-driven definitions of identity. Another explanation sees tattoos and piercings as a form of social protest, guaranteed to get a reaction. Finally, body modification is explained as a cultural trend, a fad that will pass (6). Any viewing of MTV will demonstrate how strong the socialization to tattoo is.

Like tribal societies, punks see body modification as a rite of passage, a symbol of commitment to the group. In James Myers's 1992 study, "Nonmainstream Body Modification," women modified their bodies to represent a transition in their lives, whether it was a divorce or coming to terms with their incest victimization (7).

For many youths body adornments are a way to symbolize their independence from their parents. Body modification is now being used by young people to signify their "coming out." Some youths have used piercings to publicly identify their sexual orientation, and others have used tattoos to express their religious or spiritual beliefs (8).

Of course, as frat boys and pro athletes become more pierced and tattooed, punks have to work harder to create shock. In addition to more tattoos and bigger (and more random) piercings, punks have pioneered the arts of branding, burning, and scarification. Partially out of frustration with the cultural diffusion of their styles, punks have gone to greater extremes to prove their loyalty to their values and to express their alienation from society. One group of gutter-punks in San Francisco, angry that body piercing had become a fad, cut off their little fingers. Unfortunately for them, this may become a fad in the twenty-first century.

Comments by the Gutter-Punks

Statements by the gutter-punks of Portland delineate these fashion trends. They care about differentiating themselves from mainstream culture. One boy named Kurt, 17, said, "I look like this because society is so screwed up. It's like they want you to buy a different fashion each week. I'm anti-fashion. You'll never see this look at Meier and Frank [a department store]. They'd have to fumigate the place."

Roxy, a 15-year-old girl with pierced eyebrows, said, "Oh, I did this just because it scares people. It's like a big "fuck you" to all those people like my parents."

Like the hard-core punks, the core gutter-punks cared about their scene. They depended on each other, often sharing information about squats, shelters, and services. They regularly divided up the money collected from begging, or "spaynging," for food and beer (*spaynging* is gutter-punk for *collecting spare change.*). The gutter-punk lifestyle was important to them.

As Dean, 18, noted, "We're like a family out here. We're the last vagabonds. People think we're just dirty, but we're righteous. We prove every day that you can live free on what this fat country throws away. We are political even if we aren't actually 'political.' Yeah, there are some fake gutter-punks, but we know the real ones because the real ones 'get it.'"

Throughout the interviews the values of the gutter-punks were best articulated by the core members of the group. They followed the themes found by Fox and others in more traditional punk subcultures and were best summed up by Scabby, a 16-year-old male: "We're punk because punk is the only way to say that you don't approve of society. The punks in the '70s talked about anarchy, but we live it. Everything is fucked, our parents, the cops, education, it's all bullshit. We're all punks because we want out of that world. We want to create our own world."

The nihilism was further expressed by Lucy, 19: "Yeah, being on the street might suck, but it's better than being at home. The world is a big mess because of all the mindless rule-followers who don't question anything. We make our own rules out here."

Beyond the core gutter-punks were bands of soft-core—other homeless kids who adopted some of the punk fashion but without the commitment to the subculture. Additionally, a version of Fox's preppie punks were a part of the Oregon street world. Referred to as "grommets" or "weekend warriors," these kids were not actually homeless but spent days or weekends "slumming" with the core group to obtain a thrill of safe rebellion. Many youths were from stable homes that were just hoping to frighten their parents.

One such youth, Snake, 17, explained:

> We're like the main people in this scene. We're always here. There are some kids from the shelters who hang out with us sometimes, fellow travelers. But then there's these total poseurs. They show up here at Starbucks and want to pretend they're with us. It sucks, because they spaynge and it cuts into our survival money. But sometimes the girls are cute and the guys bring dope. But they're just total wannabes. They could care less about what we believe in.

The values of the gutter-punks are in line with the core values Linda Andes found in her study, "Growing Up Punk" (9). Using Andes's model, the gutter-punks move through four stages of identity: *predisposition, rebellion, affiliation, and transcendence.*

In the predisposition phase, the punks value themselves as different from "normal" others. In the rebellion stage, the value is placed on offensiveness and shock. In the affiliation stage, the punks value being a member of the in-group and not being a grommet. Finally, in the transcendence stage, the values include personal integrity, honesty, and individualism.

As ideological as these youths can wax, life as a gutter-punk is hard. Rain, the police, thieves, addicts, older vagrants, and trouble-seeking "party boys" are all potential threats. Most keep themselves numb with beer or the drug of choice, methamphetamines. "Meth" allows them to survive the boredom and gives them the energy to scrounge for survival.

Many turn to the sex trade. The United States has half-a-million juvenile prostitutes (10). Both male and female members of the Portland sample had used prostitution as a way to gain cash. Their punk ideals gave them the ability not to bond with anyone too long because, ultimately, anarchy is an individual action.

What comes across from the gutter-punks—as well as from the letters written by punkers, along with Dank's reflections on the youths she treated (discussed in the preceding chapter)—is the loneliness, sadness, and frustration these youngsters experienced. As discussed earlier, these juveniles are classic examples of anomic individuals almost broken in spirit by their sense of hope-lessness and pain. It is truly a tragedy that so many people, including our youths, feel this level of despair. For many of these youngsters, being involved in punk at least provides them with a focus and a support group even if, as we have seen, such a group in certain ways merely exacerbated their problems.

Like homeless youth in the Portland area, those interviewed in Los Ange-les by one reporter guarded their privacy. Whether they had run away or had been forced out of their homes because of conflict or abuse, street kids are hesitant to seek assistance because they fear being captured by authorities. Ac-cording to a director of a homeless shelter, Jacob House, twice as many youth in 1999 than the previous year were using their services. Many of the youths, the director claimed, felt that life on the street was better than at home (11).

PUNK AS UNIVERSAL REBELLION

"Punks in Christchurch"

It was mid-afternoon and getting chilly as I approached a group of punks and skin-heads sitting on steps in front of Christchurch Cathedral. With their spiky hairstyles, frayed clothing and lace-up boots, they were a harsh contrast to the towering holy place.

Would they mind if I had a chat with them?

"I wish more people would stop and talk to us," said one of the group. "Usually they insult us, stare at us, and try to cause trouble."

"We are just people," piped up one of the men in ripped mohawk haircut and as-sorted badges.

Some of the group had held jobs, but lost them when they went to work with un-usual hairstyles or wearing their particular style of clothing. Some still had jobs, and all wanted to work. None gave me any aggro [aggravation].

"We are just the same as everyone else, but we just have different appearances," said one young woman. "We like listening to rock and roll music with a message, doing what we want, but boredom is a big thing. We just want to be accepted for what we are." (12)

During the past three decades both punk and heavy metal have become global youth subcultures. Teens in the foothills of the Andes wear Kurt Cobain T-shirts. Youth in western Russia mosh to the music of Korn. Italian youth bang their heads to the death metal of Sepultura. Australian teens spike their hair in classic punk style. Are all these youths responding to the same sense of alienation?

To explore to what extent such youth identities create such problems for teenagers, a detailed study of youths in two countries was undertaken. Some 623 teenagers between the ages of 15 and 18 participated, completing an extensive three-page, 100-item questionnaire. (See Appendix A for a copy of "Youth Survey 1.")

Youths were contacted in both Southern California, where 419 teenagers completed the questionnaire in 1986 and 1987, and in Christchurch, New Zealand, where 204 teenagers participated in the study in 1988. A comparative, cross-cultural focus was selected in order to determine the degree of significant differences that might exist between punk rockers and heavy metalers in the two countries.

Further, the comparative analysis was undertaken to determine whether major differences within categories existed between the two countries. That is, did punk rockers share similar attitudes regardless of locale? Likewise, did heavy metalers share comparable views regardless of whether they lived in Southern California or New Zealand?

New Zealand was selected as the comparative country because it was English-speaking, and, more important, the country also had teenagers who were highly visible—at least in the Christchurch area—in both the punk rock and heavy-metal youth scene. (See Appendix B for a discussion of the methodology, the subjects' background information, and their family relations.)

Alienation and Isolation

Not dramatically different from the comments of the Parents of Punkers' founder, the levels of alienation in both groups in each country was high. Family estrangement was a form of conflict expressed by the punkers and metalers in these surveyed groups (reported in Appendix B). Patterns of alienation from one's self, from one's significant others, and from society in general were also noted, as Table 6.1 shows.

Self Addressing attitudes about one's self, the punk rockers in both locales were twice as likely to agree with the statement that they sometimes felt like committing suicide. One-third of the California punkers and two-fifths of the

Table 6.1 Punk Rockers and Heavy Metalers in Cross-Cultural Perspective: Youths in Southern California and New Zealand

Alienation and Isolation	CP	CHM	CC	NZP	NZM	NZC
I do not want to get involved in society.	18%	13%	14%[9]	24%	23%	16%
I would not fight in a war to protect my country.	48%	16%	26%[1]	47%	43%	25%
It is good for people to be rebellious.	55%	43%	54%	47%	43%	25%
Females are equal to males.	71%	55%	57%[8]	71%	80%	70%
It is not important to me that I fit in with some group.	74%	56%	57%	53%	53%	32%
I am a loner.	20%	17%	17%[5]	6%	37%	27%
Sometimes I feel like committing suicide.	34%	14%	14%[1]	41%	20%	16%
Basically life is rather boring.	29%	26%	14%[2]	40%	32%	20%
I am not happy with my life	15%	12%	8%	18%	7%	7%
I do not have many close friends.	29%	33%	27%	24%	17%	19%
I only get along with people in my own group.	25%	16%	17%	31%	13%	5%[6]
There will be a nuclear war in my lifetime.	36%	34%	27%[5]	24%	17%	19%

Code: CP = California Punk Rockers; CHM = California Heavy Metalers; CC = California Controls; NZP = New Zealand Punk Rockers; NZM = New Zealand Heavy Metalers; NZC = New Zealand Controls

[1]sig. <.001
[2]sig. <.002
[3]sig. <.003
[4]sig. <.004
[5]sig. <.01
[6]sig. <.02
[7]sig. <.03
[8]sig. <.04
[9]sig. <.05

New Zealand punk rockers reported that they had felt suicidal (compared to 14 percent of the California metalers and 20 percent of the New Zealand metalers).

Punkers were also slightly more likely to agree with the view that life was rather boring and that they were not happy with their lives, compared to the metalers and the control group. In New Zealand a greater percentage of youths expressed feelings of boredom. When questioned further, they said that there was nothing to do in New Zealand. These feelings perhaps reflected the lack of youth cultural diversity available within their slower-paced, traditional culture (compared to Southern California at least).

There were fewer opportunities in New Zealand for punkers or metalers to participate in their chosen youth culture because there were fewer people involved in it and fewer public places such as concerts and gigs to attend. In contrast, in Southern California one's weekends could be filled with activities catering to the punk rocker and heavy-metaler youth cultures.

Others Reflecting their attitudes toward others, youths in the California sample, in general, had fewer close friends than did youths in the New Zealand group. One-third of the California metalers, for instance (which was twice the percentage of the New Zealand group), reported they did not have many close friends. One-fourth of the punkers in both locales also reported few close friends. Further, one-fourth of the punkers in both countries expressed the view that they got along only with people in their own group. This was a larger percentage than that of the heavy metalers in both locales.

Society Responding to questions about their attitudes toward society, over one-third of the California punkers and metalers felt that a nuclear war would occur in their lifetime. This more nihilistic view expressed by the California teenagers is possibly due to the greater presence of a nuclear threat in the United States compared to the more geopolitically neutral and more remote region of New Zealand.

Slightly more teenagers in New Zealand compared to California expressed the view that they did not want to get involved in society. One-fourth of the New Zealand punkers and metalers shared this sentiment. Quite possibly these New Zealanders were expressing discontent and an unwillingness to conform to and accept the more traditional strictures of their society.

Nearly half the punk rockers in both countries said they would not fight in a war to protect their country. A similarly high proportion of New Zealand metalers expressed an unwillingness to fight in a war. Among California metalers, however, only a very small group expressed an unwillingness to fight for their country. This was one of the major differences between the California punkers and metalers, reflecting their different political philosophies—with punkers more typically liberal and metalers more uniformly conservative in their views.

Nearly half of all the sampled groups expressed the belief that it was good for people to be rebellious. Interestingly, this view was also shared by the California control group, who also valued teenage independence and autonomy—if not some youthful rebelliousness. Only the New Zealand control group expressed some reservations in this area, with just one-fourth agreeing with the statement.

A more egalitarian view with respect to females being treated equal to males was shared by the punk rockers in both countries and by New Zealand youths as a whole. For instance, four-fifths of the New Zealand metalers agreed that females were equal to males compared to only slightly more than half of the California heavy metalers. The California metalers, it appears, were the most chauvinistic.

In summary, with regard to alienation and isolation, the punk rockers' estrangement from their families also extended to an alienation from self, others, and society. Punk rockers in both countries expressed views that reflected the greatest degree of estrangement (They had contemplated suicide, had few close friends, and shared a belief that there would be a nuclear war.). The California punk rockers expressed the highest degree of alienation and isolation of all groups studied.

School Relations and Delinquency

Several statements on the questionnaire detailed the youths' attitudes toward school, peer pressure, patterns of delinquency, musical tastes, and social issues, as Table 6.2 illustrates.

School Relations A much higher percentage of the New Zealand sample in all groups expressed a dislike for school compared to the California groups. Close to two-thirds of the New Zealand punkers and metalers expressed a strong dislike for school compared to two-fifths of the California punkers and metalers.

Punk rockers in both countries were also more likely to feel that their teachers treated them poorly, compared to the metalers and control groups. A greater percentage of all the New Zealand respondents, moreover, felt that their teachers treated them poorly compared to the California sample.

More California respondents in all three groups (punkers, metalers, and controls) felt that schools should not have dress codes compared to the New Zealand group. (It should be pointed out that in New Zealand, uniform dress in school was often the norm.)

Peer Pressure One-fourth of the punkers and metalers in California and metalers in New Zealand felt pressured by peers, expressing the view that they were easily influenced by others. However, only a small percentage of the punkers and metalers in both countries expressed the view that they were put down by their peers if they did not do drugs. These percentages are somewhat lower than what one might expect based on the public's common perception of these youths as being subjected to intensive peer pressure.

Table 6.2 Punk Rockers and Heavy Metalers in Cross-Cultural Perspective: Youths in Southern California and New Zealand

School Relations and Juvenile Delinquency	CP	CHM	CC	NZP	NZM	NZC
I do not like school.	42%	44%	20%[1]	69%	62%	28%[1]
Teachers treat me poorly.	35%	15%	5%[1]	46%	33%	8%[1]
Schools should not have dress codes.	96%	74%	68%[1]	53%	66%	39%[7]
I am not easily influenced by others.	24%	26%	15%	12%	23%	17%
I am put down if I do not do drugs with the group.	12%	12%	4%[9]	10%	10%	5%
Other people my own age consider me to be a troublemaker.	34%	11%	5%[1]	35%	14%	9%[5]
In the past I have been in trouble with the law/police.	49%	37%	14%[1]	53%	36%	19%[7]
I am an aggressive person.	38%	46%	38%	44%	45%	38%
My friends are involved with drugs or alcohol.	71%	58%	35%[1]	80%	57%	44%
Kids today are more streetwise than their parents.	78%	68%	58%[3]	70%	71%	74%
Punk rockers are delinquents.	18%	44%	25%[1]	12%	29%	38%[8]
Punk rockers are a new form of gang.	37%	18%	22%[1]	20%	27%	28%
I listen to messages in my songs.	74%	48%	67%[5]	50%	52%	56%
Sex plays a role in the music I listen to.	54%	49%	40%[1]	47%	50%	29%[8]
My music is violent.	44%	23%	8%[1]	29%	45%	8%[1]
Kids who break the law should not be punished like adults.	47%	42%	29%[5]	53%	66%	39%
Marijuana should be legalized.	43%	54%	29%[1]	65%	60%	26%[1]
The drinking age should be lowered.	58%	55%	28%[1]	44%	50%	29%
Parents should not set dress codes for their children.	72%	54%	37%[1]	35%	42%	41%
The death penalty is not a good way to deal with criminals.	32%	27%	35%	38%	24%	47%

Code: CP = California Punk Rockers; CHM = California Heavy Metalers; CC = California Controls; NZP = New Zealand Punk Rockers; NZM = New Zealand Heavy Metalers; NZC = New Zealand Controls

[1]sig. <.001
[2]sig. <.002
[3]sig. <.003
[4]sig. <.004
[5]sig. <.01
[6]sig. <.02
[7]sig. <.03
[8]sig. <.04
[9]sig. <.05

Patterns of Delinquency One-third of the punk rockers in both countries agreed with the statement that other people consider them to be a trouble-maker. This was three times the percentage of heavy metalers in California and over twice the percentage of heavy metalers in New Zealand. Punk rockers, therefore, were statistically much more likely to agree with the view that others think of them as troublemakers.

Half the punk rockers in both countries also indicated that they had been in trouble with the police or law in the past. In contrast, just over one-third of the metalers in both countries indicated they had prior run-ins with the law.

Although the majority of youths sampled did not consider themselves to be aggressive, an alarmingly high percentage (nearly 40 percent) in each group for each country did view themselves as aggressive.

More punkers expressed the view that their friends were involved with drugs and alcohol compared to the metalers and controls in both countries. In California 71 percent of the punkers and 80 percent of the punkers in New Zealand agreed with the statement, "The kids I hang around with are involved with drugs or alcohol." For the heavy metalers, over half of the youths sampled in each country also shared this view. And for the control groups, over one-third expressed this view. In other words, a sizable portion of the total teenage sample had friends who were involved with drugs and/or alcohol.

This awareness and involvement with drugs and alcohol may help to explain the high percentage of youths in all categories for each country who agreed with the statement, "Kids today are more streetwise than their parents were at their age." Close to 70 percent in all categories agreed with this perspective.

Musical Tastes Over half the youths sampled stated that they listened to messages in their songs. Furthermore, nearly half the youths sampled in both countries for all groups agreed that sex (referring to sexual content) played a role in the music they listened to.

However, on the issue of whether their music was violent, some distinctive patterns emerged. More California punk rockers and New Zealand heavy metalers agreed with the statement that their music was violent compared to the other groups. As a whole, punk rockers and heavy metalers in both countries (compared to the control groups) viewed their music as violent.

Social Issues No sizeable differences by locale emerged for this last set of statements. Punk rockers and heavy metalers shared more liberal views—compared to the controls—with respect to the following social issues: Delinquents should not be punished like adults (with close to half of the punkers agreeing with the statement); marijuana should be legalized (with over half of the heavy metalers and nearly half of the punkers agreeing); and the drinking age should be lowered (with half of the heavy metalers in both countries and half of the punk rockers in California agreeing).

California punkers and metalers were more likely to agree with the statement, "Parents don't have the right to tell their kids how to dress," compared to the New Zealand sample. Twice the percentage of California punkers compared to New Zealand punkers agreed with this view. Finally, the heavy metalers were the likeliest of all the groups to agree that the death penalty was a good way of dealing with violent criminals. Again, this reflects the heavy metalers' more conservative views on broader social and political issues.

In summary, based on their responses to the questionnaires, punk rockers in both countries were the most delinquent and alienated of the three groups studied. Compared to the metalers and the control group, punkers shared the following statistically significant characteristics:

- They had more troubled relationships in school.
- They believed that others saw them as troublemakers.
- They reported a higher percentage of trouble in the past with the police or law.
- They were more likely to have friends who were involved with drugs or alcohol.

The teenage years, it can be said, are ones in which youth are sensitive about their appearance, lack self-confidence, and strive for acceptance and approval. With parental insensitivity to these concerns, friction often develops at home, and youths become vulnerable to the pull of their peers whose youth styles often offer excitement, unconditional acceptance, and creative freedom. As youths become steadily more influenced by a negative peer group, their problems seem to exacerbate. This, in turn, causes further estrangement from, and rejection by, family members and peers who do not share similar identities and values.

No society, it appears, is immune to such patterns unfolding. What is unique, perhaps, is the different forms that youthful identities take as well as the similarity in patterns that develop throughout the world. As this small cross-cultural study indicated, youth styles and fads—fueled by exposure to a common popular culture including movies, music, rock groups, and television—transcend national boundaries. And as the results of the youth sur-

---

Youth at the Movies—On the Streets

In the 1990s the cinema began to seriously address the problem of homeless youth. *My Own Private Idaho* (1991), with River Phoenix and Keanu Reeves, confronted the issue of prostitution among homeless boys. *Foxfire* (1996) followed a gang of homeless girls, led by Angelina Jolie, on the streets of Portland, Oregon. Penelope Spheeris's 1998 documentary, *Decline of Western Civilization 3*, chronicled the daily struggle of the gutter-punks of Los Angeles. Maybe the most powerful is *Where the Day Takes You* (1992). Starring Dermot Mulroney, Lara Flynn Boyle, and Will Smith, the film follows a group of L.A. teens who live under a bridge. It is a realistic account of crime, drugs, sex, and the daily struggle of street kids.

vey demonstrated, youths who identify as either a punk rocker or a heavy metaler in such varied settings as Southern California and Christchurch, New Zealand, seemed, more often than not, to share a similar world view.

NOTES

1. Soraya Sarhaddi Nelson, "Young and Adrift: Children, Teens Make Up Large and Growing Portion of the Homeless," *Los Angeles Times* (17 December 1999), p. A-8.

2. Ibid.

3. Nanette Davis, *Youth Crisis: Growing Up in the High-Risk Society* (New York: Greenwood, 1999).

4. Chris Lydgate, "Gutter Punks," *The Willamette Week* (11 September 1996), pp. 20–26.

5. Kathryn Joan Fox, "Real Punks and Pretenders: The Social Organization of a Counterculture," in *Constructions of Deviance: Social Power, Context, and Interaction,* ed. Patricia A. Adler and Peter Adler (Belmont, CA: Wadsworth, 1999), pp. 373–88.

6. Yehuda Jacobson and Diana Luzzatto, "Youth Culture Language: Body Adornment Communication in Contemporary Israeli Society," paper presented at the Thirty-fourth World Congress of the International Institute of Sociology (Tel Aviv, Israel, 1999).

7. James Meyers, "Nonmainstream Body Modification: Genital Piercing, Branding, Burning, and Cutting," *The Journal of Contemporary Ethnography* 21:3 (1992), pp. 414–431.

8. Gary Soulsman, "Spiritual Tattoos Engraved On God's Canvas," *The Desert Sun* (26 June 1999), p. D-3.

9. Linda Andes, "Growing Up Punk: Meaning and Commitment Careers in a Contemporary Youth Subculture," in *Youth Culture: Identity in a Postmodern World,* ed. Jonathan S. Epstein (Malden, MA: Blackwell, 1998).

10. Davis.

11. Nelson, p. A-12.

12. "Punks in Christchurch," *The Weekend Star* (7 June 1986), p. A-4.

PART II

Suburban Outlaws

7

Suburban School Shooters

"Classmate, 13, Held in Shootings of Oklahoma Students"

At least four students at a rural Oklahoma middle school were shot Monday by a 13-year-old male classmate who was taken into custody, police said. A fifth student suffered minor injuries described as bruises.

Police, who said they recovered a 9 mm handgun, knew of no motive for the shootings in Fort Gibson, a town of about 3,500 about 50 miles southeast of Tulsa. The alleged gunman, who has not been identifed by authorities, faces a detention hearing Monday afternoon.

Superintendent Steve Wilmoth said students were gathered outside before the 8 a.m. start of classes at Fort Gibson Middle School when the subject, a seventh grader, "just walked up and opened fire on them."

Wilmoth said the boy began firing shortly after getting out of a car that dropped him off at the school. "It's my understanding he fired all the rounds" in a 9 mm handgun, said Lt. Tim Brown of the Muskogee County Sheriff's Department (1).

"Boys Hoped to Top Littleton Death Toll, Prosecutor Says"

Four teenagers (in Port Huron, Michigan) plotted to buy and steal weapons for a massacre at their middle school that would top the death toll at Columbine High School, a prosecutor said Tuesday.

"This was to be a Colorado-style shooting and bombing. . . . The goal was to kill more people than in Columbine," said St. Clair County Assistant Prosecutor

Michael Wendling, referring to last month's Littleton school shootings in which two gunman killed 13 people, then themselves.

The boys also planned to rape girls at Holland Woods Middle School, Wendling said at the arraignment for the two suspects, both 13 years old. He would not elaborate on the charges outside of court (2).

THE REALITY OF SCHOOL GUN VIOLENCE

It was ironic that April 20, 1999, the day of the Columbine school shootings, was also the day the Departments of Justice and Education released their joint report on school safety that showed a significant decline in school violence (3). Furthermore, the December 6, 1999, school shooting in Ft. Gibson, Oklahoma, happened on the day that the two departments (with MTV) released a CD-ROM called *Fight for Your Rights: Take a Stand against Violence,* aimed at helping youth to develop conflict-resolution skills (4).

Despite federal attempts to demonstrate the successes in reducing youth gun violence, 1999 was a year in which Americans were transfixed on bloodshed in suburban middle and high schools.

In the late 1990s places such as Littleton, Colorado; West Paducah, Kentucky; Pearl, Mississippi; Springfield, Oregon; and Jonesboro, Arkansas, became evidence of the downward spiral of youth violence. With less mass media coverage, schools in nonurban areas such as Conyers, Georgia; Fort Gibson, Oklahoma; Moses Lake, Washington; and Blackville, South Carolina, experienced school gun violence, adding to public fear about school safety. School-yard fights were now becoming mass murders. Instead of bringing home homework, students were bringing home bullet wounds. The spate of school shootings was proof that something was horribly wrong with America's youth.

With each dramatic event, complete with commentary from traumatized "good" teens, society struggled to understand the motivation of the gunmen, who were really gunboys. Some were not yet even teenagers. Eleven-year-old Andrew Golden and his 13-year-old friend, Mitchell Johnson, killed four girls and one female teacher, wounding eleven others in Jonesboro on March 12, 1998. Someone or something must be to blame. The list of causes was expansive: absent parents, video games, Satanism, weak gun laws, bullies, the Internet, heavy metal music, antidepressants, and the always persuasive argument, "culture."

School Gun Violence Declining

In reality, according to the FBI Uniform Crime Report, violent crime rates have been steadily declining since 1992. Over 95 percent of children are never involved in a violent crime, according to the joint report by the Departments of Justice and Education (5). Titled the (1998) Annual Report on School Safety, this report—released on the day of the Columbine shootings—gave some balance to the sensationalist coverage in the press.

According to the report, the news was generally good. Gun violence in schools was following the national crime trend and declining. There was no increased risk of gun-death for America's students. In fact, the percentage of high school seniors reporting intentional injuries with a weapon had not changed significantly for twenty years. The previous year the Department of Justice had stated that a child's chance of dying in school violence was less than one in a million and that for every one child killed in a school, 200 were killed in incidents of domestic abuse (6).

The 1998 report was even more encouraging, noting that:

- The overall school crime rate between 1993 and 1996 declined from about 164 school-related crimes for every 1000 students, aged 12–18, to about 128 such crimes in 1996. Crime victimization of students outside of school also declined.

- Most school crime is theft, not violent crime.

- Fewer than 1 percent of the 7,357 school children (age 5–19) who were murdered in the 1993 and 1994 school years were killed at school. Of the 4,366 kids who committed suicide those years, only 13 killed themselves at school.

- Violent deaths in schools decreased in 1997 and 1998.

- The most likely victims of school violence tended to be upper-grade students or male teachers in larger urban schools (7).

Although the general trend is in the opposite direction of popular perceptions, the more rare multiple victim homicides have increased. There were two in the 1992–1993 school year and six in 1997–1998. An average of thirteen young people are killed every day in gun violence in the United States. On the morning of April 20, 1999, Eric Harris and Dylan Klebold killed one teacher, twelve students, and then themselves. They topped the daily average of dead in forty-six minutes. Their actions obscure the 43 percent of schools that the report said had no crime at all in the previous school year.

The report also revealed a decline in the number of high school students who brought weapons (guns, knives, clubs, and other weapons) to school from 1993 to 1997—from 8 percent to 6 percent. But for guns, the rate was relatively constant. About 3 percent of high school seniors reported bringing a gun to school in the four weeks previous to taking the annual survey. Even with increased sanctions (6,093 students were expelled from school in 1996–1997 for gun possession), 8 percent of students of the 4,291,666 high school seniors in the United States are 343,333 kids with deadly weapons.

The findings of the Report on School Safety were mirrored in other reports (the National Parents' Resource Institute for Drug Education survey in 1994 found that 7.4 percent of high school students reported bringing a gun to school) and on the state level. A report released in December 1999 by the Oregon Health Division found that one in eight teenagers carried weapons and estimated that 19,000 students (8 percent of the high school population) had brought a gun to school (8).

The Oregon Report, based on a survey created by the Center for Disease Control and Prevention, found some useful data:

- Boys were more than five times as likely to carry a gun to school than girls.

- Students without adult guidance were three times more likely to sneak a gun into school compared to youths who had at least two adults to discuss their problems with.

- Students who engaged in risky behavior, such as smoking and binge drinking, were more likely to bring guns to school.

- Students involved in at least eight fights in the previous year were five times more likely to carry weapons and fifty-eight times more likely to bring a gun to school (9).

Although half of the homes in Oregon contain firearms, school gun-toters fit a specific profile. They tend to be males in routinely violent situations, without parental supervision, who are involved in high levels of risk-taking behavior.

A similar report on guns in Los Angeles schools in 1996 helped to explain the motivations of gun carrying. One in seven Los Angeles high school students reported having carried a gun, and 49 percent said they could easily obtain one. Their reasons were not to inflict bloodshed on campus but rather to protect themselves off campus. Only 14 percent said the weapons were intended to protect themselves on campus, but 39 percent reported the fear of gang-related violence in the neighborhood, and 30 percent claimed the gun gave them protection on the way to and from school (10).

School-yard fights are now taken off campus. One student in Los Angeles said, "Students sometimes bring weapons to school to prepare for off-campus battle. You can't run to your house and pick up a gun after school" (11).

The slight decrease in guns in school is not so comforting when one considers that 5 percent of all twelfth-graders reported that they had been injured by a student with a weapon at school. There were 255,000 cases of serious but nonfatal violent school crimes, victimizing 12- to 18-year-olds, in 1996. There are 81,300 public schools in the United States, and 10 percent reported at least one serious violent crime to the police during the 1996–1997 academic year. The fact that teenagers are still more at risk at home does not negate the fact that schools are supposed to be "safe zones" (12).

Nevertheless, the relatively low numbers carry more meaning in the face of gun violence in the United States in general. Between 1985 and 1995 teen homicide increased 153 percent (13). A child is wounded by gunfire every 23 minutes in the United States, and one is killed every 100 minutes (14). There are an estimated 192 million guns in this country (15). Sometimes we must wonder why so few guns make it into our schools.

INCREASED FEAR IN SCHOOLS

The decline in school violence does not mean that our youth feel safe and are thinking more about gum than guns. From the 1993 shooting in Grayson, Kentucky (with two dead), to the 1999 Columbine massacre (with fifteen dead and twenty-four wounded)—and into the twenty-first century—random gun violence has helped to increase levels of fear among American school kids. The threat of copy-cat crimes reminded students, teachers, and administrators that a lot of potential Harrises and Klebolds are waiting in the wings.

Soon after the Columbine shootings, for instance:

- A 15-year-old Sacramento, California, boy was arrested for making a bomb threat to his high school (16).

- In Wimbery, Texas, five 14-year-old boys were charged with plotting to blow up their junior high school.

- A 15-year-old in Keystone Heights, Florida, was found with pipe bombs and napalm in his bedroom.

- In Houma, Louisiana, a 17-year-old was arrested for felony "terrorizing" after donning a black trench coat and telling his classmates he had a gun (17).

- In the week following the murders in Colorado, hundreds of schools were closed from Hawaii to Maine because of threats by students. Two bombs were detonated, and three more shootings occurred (18).

On the six-month anniversary of the shooting, in October 1999, a Columbine senior threatened to "finish the job" started by Klebold and Harris. Hundreds of kids stayed home from school until the matter was resolved (19). The copy-cats just added to the fear that school gun violence was no longer an urban problem and that any student could be a victim of anyone at anytime.

A 1993 Louis Harris survey found that 35 percent of kids aged 6 to 12 years feared their lives would be cut short by gun violence (20). That teens are carrying guns to school as a result of fear just adds to the danger. The Report on School Safety found evidence of that increased fear. Whereas in 1989, 6 percent of 12- to 19-year-olds reported that they feared being harmed or attacked at school, by 1995 that number had increased to 9 percent. In fact, 9 percent of America's school children indicated they avoided one or more places at school out of concern for their own safety (21).

After Columbine, *Time/CNN* surveyed 409 teenagers, age 13 to 17, about their fears that something similar could happen at their school. A third of the students reported that something similar to the Littleton shootings was somewhat or very likely to happen at their school. Sixty-one percent believed Columbine gave ideas to troubled kids in their school to do something similar. Perhaps most frightening was the 21 percent of respondents who claimed to know someone their age who had talked of committing a similarly violent act at school. Most did not report this fact to adults. Most of the teens felt that the availability of guns was the most obvious cause of the violence. On a more optimistic note, teenagers in the 1999 poll tended to feel that fewer parents were neglecting their kids and things were generally going well for teens, compared to teens surveyed on the same question in 1993 (22).

The threat of violence negatively affects the social climate of schools. In 1993 the American Teacher survey found that a third of teachers reported that both teachers and students were less eager to go to school. Teachers reported being afraid of disciplining problem students, which added to the negative climate. A fourth of students felt that the threat of violence lessened their educational experience and made them want to change schools or not pay attention in class. Evidence exists that this may affect struggling students even more (23). Both teachers and students are at a loss for how to respond to this.

Despite their relative rarity, the school murders were big news. The media portrayed the perpetrators as good (white) boys with no real histories of violence, adding to the paranoia that the next shooter could be anyone. "Goths," kids in trench-coats, and that boy who did not get a date to the prom might unleash their bad day in a hail of bullets. Shooters such as Luke Woodham, Kip Kinkel, and Seth Trickey had friends, but that did not stop them. Violence could happen anywhere at anytime, at a pep rally, before classes, or during a prayer meeting. Today's class clown could be tomorrow's mass murderer.

Fueled by sensationalist tabloid news accounts, today's media-weened teens are reminded of the shootings every time they walk through a metal detector or see vaguely threatening graffiti on a bathroom wall. Harris and Klebold, photographed on their murderous prowl, were back on the cover of the December 20, 1999, issue of *Time* and in the headlines when the five home videos they made before their shooting spree were released to the press. Some families of the victims expressed anger with the Jefferson County Sheriff's Department for releasing the videos, which caused students, teachers, and family members to relive the trauma (24).

How can students focus on the increasingly competitive demands of education when they are worried about random explosions of gunfire or pipe bombs? What do students learn about their rights to privacy as every backpack is searched in hopes of preventing another Columbine? Again, despite the carnage and sad loss of life because of these events, figures indicate that schools are becoming safer places for our children and that most of that fear is misplaced.

THE BLAME GAME

Americans and their media wasted no time in trying to make sense of the seemingly out-of-left-field trend of school shootings. The covers of the May 3, 1999, issues of *Newsweek* and *U.S. News and World Report* asked, "Why?" Inside, potential scapegoats were delivered to the eager public: goth kids, films such as *Natural Born Killers, The Basketball Diaries,* and *The Matrix,* the Internet, rockers such as

Marilyn Manson and KMFDM, and video games such as Doom and Duke 'Nukem. Then the blame widenened to encompass permissive baby-boom parents, the NRA-supported gun culture, and generational alienation. All the claims were made with little academic substantiation or validity, however.

Commenting on the efficiency of teen killer Michael Carneal in West Paducah, Kentucky, Lt. Col. Dave Grossman, author of *On Killing,* saw the hand of violent video games at work. Based on his research while a military scientist in the army, Grossman made the media rounds discussing contemporary video games as "murder simulators" (25).

In the weeks following Columbine, reports rolled in of goth kids in their black clothes being beaten up by jocks because they feared the goths were members of the alleged "Trench Coat Mafia." Sociologist Randy Blazak did numerous media interviews, explaining that the Trench Coat Mafia was a local clique, not a worldwide Satanic conspiracy, and that "goth" was an overwhelmingly nonviolent, non-Fascist subculture (not to mention the fact that neither Harris nor Klebold claimed to be goths [or even looked like goths] and/or fans of Marilyn Manson [who canceled his Denver concert that month out of respect for the victims]).

Moral Panics

The widespread overreporting of the alleged Trench Coat Mafia followed the pattern of a sociological phenomenon called "moral panic." British researcher Stanley Cohen discussed the public response to youth violence in his 1972 book, *Moral Panics and Folk Devils* (26).

Cohen researched the defining aspect of the riots between rival gangs of mods and rockers on the English coast in the early 1960s. Although the riots were relatively small and harmless, their deviance was amplified by the press when they portrayed the seaside towns as orgies of youth violence. The media designated the relatively unknown mods and rockers as folk devils—a convenient source of multiple social problems. This led to an orchestrated moral panic about the threat of deviant youth. Of this, Brake wrote, "This indiscriminate prosecution, local overreaction and media stereotyping suggested a 'cabalism', that is, the solidifying of amorphous groups of teenagers into some sort of conspiratorial collectivity, which had no concrete existence" (27).

The United States has had its share of moral panics over the decades: degenerate rock 'n' roll hoodlums (1950s), subversive hippies (1960s), drugcrazed punk rockers (1970s), hyperviolent, urban gangstas (1980s), and bomb-making militia men (1990s). The attempt to peg Columbine on goths or some type of conspiratorial "mafia" is another attempt to scapegoat. Reports about deviant youth groups are rich material for rating-grabbing, news magazine programs. But they do not address the more structural issues of alienation and disenfranchisement, which are harder to explain in a two-minute TV segment. Ultimately, the creation of folk devils, such as the marginal kids at Columbine or Thurston High, only further alienates and stereotypes those who feel they have no control over their own lives.

Race and Moral Panics

There is a racial component to the school shootings as well. Not that the Columbine shooters were Nazis, for there is no substantial evidence of that. Based on their videotapes, they appeared to be as antiwhite as they were antiminority. The racial element is in the reaction. According to the Annual Report on School Safety, serious violent crimes against students peaked in 1993, which was also the peak year of students carrying weapons to school. The report also reveals that the risk of gun violence has traditionally existed in urban minority schools (28).

The moral panic over school shootings in the late 1990s arose because the shooters were white. The May 3, 1999, issue of *Time* featured the smiling faces of Klebold and Harris with the caption, "The Monsters Next Door." The coded message was that, although we expect this type of wanton violence from urban minorities, we certainly do not expect this type of behavior from nice suburban white boys. The hundreds of shootings at inner-city schools barely penetrated the news magazines in the 1980s and 1990s, let alone made it to the cover.

That the whiteness of the suburban school shooters sold magazines is not unusual. Craig Reinarman mapped out the way in which the social construction of drug scares was linked to race. The moral panics of specific drugs were linked to fears of certain "dangerous classes" infecting mainstream society. Drug prohibition was created as a way to control minority groups. In an earlier time, the prohibition of alcohol curtailed the influx of the Irish immigrants. Marijuana, cocaine, and opium prohibition criminalized the behavior of Hispanics, African-Americans, and Asians, respectively (29). Similarly, LSD was not outlawed until it fell into the hands of radical hippie baby boomers.

The history of drug scares shows us that problems gain validity as significant social ills only when they affect whites (particularly middle-, upper-middle, and upper-class whites). Marijuana was not criminalized until 1937, when the media portrayed whites as picking up the habit from Mexican-Americans (30). Similarly, school gun violence did not reach "crisis levels" until white kids were pulling the trigger (even though gun violence in schools was actually declining). A clever reporter for National Public Radio interviewed black students in Harlem, New York, the day after the Columbine shootings. All the youths were confused about how the perpetrators evaded metal detectors, heavily monitored surveillance cameras, and police to get the guns into the school.

TRYING TO UNDERSTAND
SUBURBAN SCHOOL SHOOTINGS

The tendency to generate pop answers should not prevent one from looking for deeper answers to violent trends. Are suburban school shootings just a media-generated trend, kicked off by Luke Woodham in Pearl, Mississippi, in 1997, which will disappear once the media latch onto a new moral panic? Is it an institutional failure, the product of large class sizes and overworked yuppie parents? Is it a spiritual crisis in our nation? Is this the result of endless hours of media violence?

Again, the reality is not so pessimistic. The juvenile crime rate has been dropping steadily since 1994 (even though the actual number of juveniles is increasing). The rates of teen pregnancy and drug use are on the decline, and the 1990s even saw an increase in juvenile volunteerism and church-going behavior. The outlook for youth is generally good, and their optimism in popular polls reflects that. But the few that fall through the cracks defy conventional explanation. As their peers smash through economic, racial, and gender barriers to reach new heights, these other youths' fall from grace seems that much more dramatic.

Three issues have been neglected in the explanation of school violence: (1) biosocial causes of violence, or psychopathic youth; (2) the role of masculinity in violent crime; and (3) the crisis of parenting in the United States.

Psychopathic Youth

It is interesting that the proclaimed "father of criminology," Cesare Lombroso, has become popular again among criminologists after decades of dismissal. Lombroso's simplistic experiments a hundred years ago tried to link physical anomalies to criminal predispositions. Although most contemporary researchers agree that there is overwhelming evidence that people are not "born criminal," they will acknowledge that the biological causes of violence are worth addressing.

In crimes that defy sociological explanation—where race, class, gender, education, abuse, and other social factors are not causal—biological explanations become increasingly helpful. Links have now been established between fetal brain alcohol syndrome, brain-stem damage, food allergies, learning disabilities, and nutritional deficiencies and violent behavior (31).

In retrospect, most of the school shooters were clearly disturbed. Luke Woodham claimed he was under the spell of demons while he killed his mother and two classmates and wounded seven others. Kip Kinkel's parents lived in mortal fear of him and his obsession with violence and weapons. Kinkel and Woodham both tortured animals. Klebold and Harris stunned even hardened reporters with their premassacre videos. In one such video Klebold says, "I hope we kill 250 of you," and that "it" will be, "the most nerve-racking 15 minutes of my life, after the bombs are set and we're waiting to charge through the school. Seconds will be like hours. I can't wait" (32).

Spurred by the shootings in Jonesboro, Arkansas, in 1998, child clinical psychologist Jonathan Kellerman wrote the book, *Savage Spawn*. After studying the Jonesboro and Springfield cases, Kellerman concluded that the school shooters were psychopathic. His findings make even more sense in Littleton. The repeated description of both school shooters and urban gang leaders is that they are cold. Psychopaths are not crazy. As evidenced in Harris and

Klebold's sick videos, they knew exactly what they were doing and what the ramifications were. Harris expressed acknowledgement of the effect their plan would have on his parents. "They're going to (be) put through hell once we do this. . . . There's nothing you guys could've done to prevent this" (33).

From Kellerman's research, psychopaths simply love violence and will often resort to it out of boredom. "What turns them on is the kick, the high, the slaking of impulse—pure sensation—power, dominance, subjugation of the rest of us. The *fun* of crime" (34). Psychopathic tendencies begin appearing at a young age, as early as 3. Violence and cruelty become character traits by 6½ years. Kip Kinkel had been cruel to animals. Eric Harris was obsessed with violent games.

The answer to the nature-nurture debate, according to Kellerman, is "both." To place a psychopathic youth into a society that has easy access to guns is asking for tragedy. In several of the shootings, including Jonesboro, Springfield, and Fort Gibson, the boys received the murder weapons from their fathers. Kellerman's solution is to limit access of youth to guns and protect society by removing dangerous psychopaths who are unlikely to be "cured." High-risk kids must be given highly structured, loving environments and be schooled in morality (35).

Other researchers have also looked at biological explanations. James Garbarino, author of *Lost Boys: Why Our Sons Turn Violent and How We Can Save Them,* has pointed out that research shows that brain development is connected to early parent involvement. Others have shown that abuse or abandonment can create brain chemistries that end in impulsive behavior and a lack of empathy (36). Antisocial personalities may have genetic roots but more likely stem from constant exposure to pain, violence, and exclusion.

It is important to point out that Harris, Klebold, Carneal, Kinkel, and perhaps other shooters were highly suicidal. They wanted to transfer their psychic pain to others on their way out. Gang researcher Lewis Yablonsky compared the school shooters to youths in psychiatric hospitals. "Youths with suicidal tendencies by definition have limited concern for their own lives and consequently care less about the lives of others" (37).

The Masculinity Connection

The one constant in all the suburban school shootings is that the attackers were all male. Like crime in general, homicide is an overwhelmingly male activity. Ninety percent of those arrested for murder are boys or men (38).

The "Book of the Month" on the Oprah Winfrey Show in April, 1999, the month of the shootings in Littleton, was *Real Boys: Rescuing Our Sons from the Myth of Boyhood,* by William Pollack. The timing could not have been more significant. Not until the 1990s did social scientists begin to research the connection between masculinity and crime.

Pollack's thesis is that male violence is a result of masculine repression of emotions. From birth males are more emotionally expressive than females, but by age 5 or 6, they begin to squelch that tendency. Pollack offers two reasons.

First, shame is used to toughen boys up. Second, the early emotional separation of boys from their mothers stunts their emotional development. For boys, violence becomes their expression of emotion (39).

Violence becomes the result of a boy's being pushed into adulthood too early and without sufficient emotional support. Violence is often seen as proof of manhood for boys, according to Pollack. That violent crime is the second leading killer of young men, after accidents, reflects that masculinity connection. Both reflect risk-taking behavior, where "boys will be boys."

Pollack explains Michael Carneal's shooting spree in West Paducah that left three dead and five wounded in this light. Carneal was a shy 14-year-old with no violent history, who was often teased. Pollack writes, "I believe that among other things it is shame that makes a boy like this snap. When enough shame collects inside him—when he feels disconnected, unpopular, less than 'masculine,' maybe even hated—the boy tries to master his feelings and reconnect with others through violence" (40).

Earlier in the 1990s, criminologist James Messerschmidt explored crime as a way of "doing gender" for boys. As discussed in Chapter 2, Messerschmidt linked the maleness of crime to the masculine value structure (41). School shooters Wodham, Carneal Kinkel, Harris, and Klebold all had histories as victims of bullies. In one of their videotapes, Harris lamented being a military kid, always having to move and start over at the bottom of the social ladder. "People constantly make fun of my face, my hair, my shirts," he said (42). This experience, on top of normal surrendering of autonomy that high school boys face, led to the inevitable counterswing. The boys tapped into the dominant image of masculinity present in popular Arnold Schwartzeneger, Sylvester Stallone, and Bruce Willis films—gun violence. Using Messerschmidt's theory, the dramatic killing sprees were the result of repeated experiences of emasculation that created a situation in which the boys needed to "do gender" to reclaim their manhood. Harvard psychologist James Gilligan concluded, "Nothing stimulates violence as [much as] the experience of being shamed or humiliated" (43).

Neither Pollack nor Messerschmidt sees the forces that would undermine patriarchal power as the root of the problem. It is, instead, the construction of masculinity that prevents emotional expression and promotes violent expression. In a culture in which the nonviolent boy is called a "wimp," a "fag," or a "sissy," the need for boys to become men often offers easy paths to hegemonic masculinity. Michael Carneal and a classmate had been named in the school paper "Rumor Has It" column as "having feelings for each other" (44). Only football stars and violent rebels can hope to survive the adolescent gender-magnifying glass. But with generations of John Wayne role models, "kicking ass" wins autonomy and the veneer of manliness.

Where Have All the Parents Gone?

The issue of uninvolved parents came to the forefront after Columbine. With their obsession with violent video games, threatening web sites, and their garage bomb factory, how could have the parents of Harris and Klebold not known? The statement issued by Dylan Klebold's parents claimed, "We will never understand why this tragedy happened or what we might have done to prevent it. . . . We never saw hatred in Dylan until the last moments of his life when we watched in helpless horror with the rest of the world" (45).

It is very possible that they never really saw their son. Besides the inclination of teens to be secretive, parents are working longer hours to afford their children a comfortable existence in a consumer-oriented, status-driven culture. The average work week is now sixty hours. Nine-to-five has become eight-to-six with work brought home. The increase in two-income households takes more of the child-management out of the home. Sociologist Barbara Schneider has recently found that the average teenager spends 3.5 hours alone every single day (46).

That lack of supervision is directly correlated to delinquency is well established. Juvenile crime is highest between 3 and 6 P.M., that is, after school and before parents get home from work. Effective parental supervision can reduce delinquency. Lisa Broidy found that kids who believe their parents care little about their activities and friends are more likely to engage in crime than those who feel they are being tightly watched (47). Recent research has demonstrated the importance of close parental bonds.

David May's work found three key factors in predicting the likelihood of a child's carrying a gun to school. Following from social control theory, kids who were less bonded to their parents and came from single-parent homes were more likely to carry guns. Second, unsupervised youths who spent time with gang members and older kids were also at greater risk. Finally, kids who feared criminal victimization, primarily from disorderly neighborhoods, carried guns (48). Interestingly, May's research also found that the greater the household income, the more likely the students were to bring guns to school.

Patricia Jenkinks's work also used social control theory to explain three levels of school delinquency: crime, misconduct, and nonattendance. High levels of family involvement were related to low delinquency. School involvement was a weak predictor of delinquency, but commitment to school was a strong predictor. The most important factor in this commitment was the education of the mother and the student's math ability (49). Again, students with consistent loving bonds to parents did not act out in school.

We already know the bad news about the children of single parents. They face greater risks of criminality and early violent death (50). Community crime rates and school disruption rates increase when single-parent families move into neighborhoods (51). Some of the problems in single-parent households may be due to the lack of consistent male role models. But much of it is a simple matter of supervision. Two sets of eyes are better than one. The problem is now that even in two-parent families, increasing workloads and adult activities remove parents from the lives of their teens. Their adolescents become "unbonded" and free to engage in dangerous activities such as bomb making.

IS CULTURE THE CAUSE OR THE EFFECT?

Shortly after the Springfield, Oregon, shooting in 1998, a local mayor tried to ban violent video games in his town. It was largely a symbolic act that would probably have only added to the frustration of the town's teenagers. Few things have been studied more than the impact of media violence on criminality, and nothing close to a strong link has ever been established (52). Convincing results were produced in a laboratory setting or were only short-term. Everyone *knows* it is true, yet no one can prove it.

Yet millions of kids saw the 1999 movie *The Matrix* (which allegedly had *something* to do with the Littleton shootings) and did not shoot anyone. Media violence is another form of moral panic, and each generation has an art form to blame. In the 1950s it was comic books, Elvis Presley, and rock 'n' roll. In the 1960s it was the Beatles. The 1970s gave us the threat from kung-fu movies, and in the 1980s it was slasher flicks and heavy metal. Finally, in the 1990s it was gangsta rap, Quentin Tarantino movies, and video games. As parents and preachers scrambled to find some electronic demon, they did not stop to look at themselves.

It has been argued by postmodern sociologists, such as Donna Gaines and Tricia Rose (discussed in Chapter 2), that cultural forms, such as rap and heavy metal, are more of a reflection of real experiences lived by consumers. Venise Berry writes of rap, "There is an obvious struggle going on in these kids' lives that links them to the conflict-oriented nature of cultural rap. The violent urban environment, a prominent theme in rap music, is also a prominent reality (53). Similarly, teens flock to violent movies, such as *The Matrix,* because they live in a violent society and need to process it safely.

Of course, media violence is not just a coping mechanism for young people. It has become its own source of socialization. As the influence of working parents and overburdened teachers fades, the media become the cultural parents. Children are being pacified by *The Jerry Springer Show,* teens are finding *Doom II* under the Christmas tree, and toddlers are being dragged to R-rated movies by parents who do not want to pay for a babysitter. The average child sees 8,000 media murders by the time he or she leave elementary school. Can there be a cumulative effect of all this media-weening? The escalation has scholars worried. Sissela Bok of Harvard and author of the 1998 book *Mayhem* said, "We have introduced forms and amounts of media violence beyond anything achieved in other countries" (54).

No, there is no evidence of a direct link between media violence and real violence. Japan has a higher percentage of violent video game players and violent cartoon watchers and a lower violent crime rate. Japan also has a more intact family system. The problem in the United States is the mixed messages kids receive about violence and the absent parents who do not straighten the messages out for them. The day after the Columbine shooting, U.S. Attorney General Janet Reno appeared on the nightly news deploring the act and stating that using violence to solve problems is unacceptable. The next story was about U.S. military forces dropping bombs on Serbians—using violence to solve problems. The air force even sent F-16s over the funerals of the Columbine victims in case the message was missed: Sometimes violence is OK.

The wave of school shootings was done by boys who were either extreme psychopaths or responding to serious emasculation by bullies and others. They fell through the cracks because no one heard them even though they tried desperately to be heard. The thousands of kids who bring guns to school every day carry those guns mainly to protect themselves from the kids who fall through the cracks. Despite the fact that schools are getting safer, those kids know it takes just one disgruntled teenager to put their school on the violence map.

The kids who get picked on now too have a weapon: fear. Goths, punks, geeks, drama clubbers, bandies, and the math club all have a tool against the popular cliques in the *threat* of gun violence. A fan site for Kip Kinkel went up on the Internet soon after the Springfield shootings. Other students claimed to be members of the Trench Coat Mafia, a term they had never heard of before Columbine. Some, like a 14-year-old in Alberta, Canada, got their fathers' guns and killed their tormentors. Others just put up pictures of Klebold and Harris in their lockers. All over the United States, alienated teens empathized with the shooters (55). It was the ultimate revenge of the nerds.

If "culture" is how we explain random school shootings, then we should be more specific. Easy access to hand guns is part of our culture. Popular kids who bully unpopular kids is a part of our culture. The inability to identify and treat disturbed youth who are addicted to violence is also part of our culture. A definition of masculinity that includes "might makes right" is part of our

---

Youth at the Movies—School Revenge

Teenagers in film have been rebelling against their high school peers since *The Blackboard Jungle* in 1955. But things did not get violent until the 1970s. Stephen King's *Carrie* (1976) was the ultimate revenge fantasy against the popular kids, in which most of the senior class was wiped out. Lighter fare was *Rock 'n' Roll High School* (1979), in which the punk band, the Ramones, helped the students to blow up Vince Lombardi High School. The best of the era was *Over the Edge* (1979), Matt Dillon's first film. In it, alienated suburban teens lock their parents inside a meeting hall and then destroy it. Twenty years later, while the gun violence in *The Matrix* (1999) and *The Basketball Diaries* (1995) was seen as causing the Columbine shootings, another film was closer to the root of the problem. In *The Rage: Carrie 2* (1999), which was in theaters during the Columbine shooting, Rachel Lang, a trench-coat clad "freak" with a Marilyn Manson poster on her wall is harassed by a popular clique. The jocks in Spur Posse-fashion humiliate her and in the film's climax, Rachel uses her telekinetic power to kill them all and anybody else who gets in the way.

culture as well. Finally, a consumer ethic that drives parents to work longer and supervise their children less is part of our culture. Cultural problems require cultural solutions.

NOTES

1. "Classmate, 13, Held in Shootings of Oklahoma Students," *CNN Online* (6 December 1999), www.cnn.com.

2. "Boys Hoped to Top Littleton Death Toll, Prosecutor Says," Associated Press (19 May 1999).

3. Department of Justice, Department of Education, *1998 Annual Report on School Safety,* 1999.

4. Department of Justice, Department of Education, MTV, *Fight For Your Rights: Take A Stand against Violence* (CD-ROM), 1999.

5. Barbara Dority, "The Columbine Tragedy, Countering the Hysteria," *The Humanist* 59:4 (July 1999), p. 7.

6. 1998 DOJ report.

7. Ibid.

8. Janie Har, "Survey: 1 in 8 Teen-Agers Totes Weapons," *The Oregonian* (8 December 1999), pp. D1–11.

9. Ibid.

10. Lewis Yablonsky, *Juvenile Delinquency into the 21st Century* (Belmont, CA: Wadsworth, 2000).

11. "Guns in Los Angeles Schools: A Report." Los Angeles, CA: Los Angeles Unified Schools, 1996.

12. Phillip Kaufman, Xianglei Chen, Susan P. Choy, Kathryn A. Chandler, Christopher D. Chapman, Michal A. Rand, and Cheryl Ringel, *Indicators of School Crime and Safety, 1998,* Department of Education and Bureau of Justice Statistics (Washington, D.C., 1998).

13. J. Cloud, "Of Arms and the Boy," *Time* (6 July 1998), pp. 58–62.

14. The State of America's Children Yearbook, 1998, Children's Defense Fund (Washington, D.C., 1998).

15. C. Archambault, "Young Killers," *U. S. News and World Report* (1 June 1997), pp. 18–21.

16. M. S. Enkoji and Ralph Montaño, "Student Arrested in Threat," *Sacramento Bee* (1 May 1999), p. B-1.

17. Paul Hoversten, "Copycat Behavior Emerges: Kids Mimicking Acts of Violence," *USA Today* (27 April 1999), p. 4-A.

18. T. Trent Gegax and Matt Bai, "Looking for Answers," *Newsweek* (10 May 1999), pp. 31–34.

19. Andrew Goldstein, "The Victims: Never Again," *Time* (20 December 1999), p. 53.

20. Louis Harris and Associates, Inc., "A Survey of Experiences, Perceptions and Apprehensions about Guns among Young People in America" (New York: L. H. Research, Inc., 1993).

21. *1998 Annual Report on School Safety.*

22. "Time/CNN Teen Poll," *Time* (10 May 1999), p. 30.

23. Delbert S. Elliot, Beatrix Hamburg, and Kirk R. Williams, "Violence in American Schools: An Overview," in *Violence in American Schools,* ed. Delbert S. Elliot, Beatrix Hamburg, and Kirk R. Williams (New York: Cambridge University Press, 1998), p. 8.

24. Michael Janofsky, "Rage Fills Videos Made by Columbine Shooters," *The Oregonian* (14 December 1999), p. A-2.

25. Lt. Col. Dave Grossman, *On Killing* (Boston, MA.: Little, Brown and Co., 1995).

26. Stanley Cohen, *Moral Panics and Folk Devils* (London: MacGibbon and Kee, 1972).

27. Michael Brake, *Comparative Youth Culture* (London: Routledge, 1985).

28. *1998 Annual Report on School Safety,* 1999.

29. Craig Reinarman, "The Social Construction of Drug Scares," in *Constructions of Deviance,* ed. Patricia A.

Adler and Peter Adler (Belmont, CA.: Wadsworth, 1999).

30. Ibid.

31. Larry Siegel, *Criminology* (Belmont, CA.: Wadsworth, 2000).

32. Nancy Gibbs and Timothy Roche, "The Columbine Tapes," *Time* (20 December 1999), pp. 40–51.

33. Ibid.

34. Jonathan Kellerman, *Savage Spawn: Reflections on Violent Children* (New York: Random House, 1999), p. 20.

35. Ibid., p. 52.

36. Sharon Begley, "Why the Young Kill," *Newsweek* (3 May 1999), pp. 32–35.

37. Lewis Yablonsky, *Juvenile Delinquency into the 21st Century* (Belmont, CA: Wadworth: 2000), p. 147.

38. Federal Bureau of Investigation, Uniform Crime Reports 1998, 1999, U.S. Government Printing Office: Washington, D.C.

39. William Pollack, *Real Boys: Rescuing Our Sons from the Myth of Boyhood* (New York: Random House, 1998), p. 11.

40. Ibid., p. 356.

41. James Messerschmidt, *Masculinities and Crime: Critique and Reconceptualization of Theory* (Lantham, MD: Rowman and Littlefield, 1993).

42. Pollack, p. 346.

43. Nancy Gibbs and Timothy Roche.

44. B. Dority, p. 4.

45. Lisa Belkin, "Parents Blaming Parents," *New York Times Magazine* (31 October 1999), p. 67.

46. Barbara Kantrowitz and Pat Wingert, "How Well Do You Know Your Kid?" *Newsweek* (10 May 1999), pp. 36–40.

47. Lisa Broidy, "Direct Supervision and Delinquency: Assessing the Adequacy of Structural Proxies," *Journal of Criminal Justice* 23 (1995), pp. 541–54.

48. David C. May, "Scared Kids, Unattached Kids and Peer Pressure: Why Do Students Carry Firearms to School?" *Youth and Society* 31:1 (1999), pp. 100–27.

49. Patricia H. Jenkins, "School Delinquency and the Social Bond," *Journal of Research in Crime and Delinquency* 34:3 (1997) pp. 331–47.

50. R. Kelly Ralley, " A Shortage of Marriageable Men? A Note on the Role of Cohabitation in Black–White Differences in Marriage Rates," *American Sociological Review* 61 (1996), pp. 973–83.

51. Daryl Hellman and Susan Beaton, "The Pattern of Violence in Urban Schools: The Influence of School and Community," *Journal of Research in Crime and Delinquency* 23 (1986), pp. 102–27.

52. Kellerman, p. 72.

53. Venise Berry, "Redeeming the Rap Music Experience," in *Adolescents and Their Music,* ed. Jonathan S. Epstein (New York: Garland Publishing, 1995), pp. 176–77.

54. John Cloud, "What Can the Schools Do?" *Time* (3 May 1999), p. 39.

55. Mark Fritz, "Alienated Teens Empathize with High School Gunmen," *New York Times* (28 April 1999), p. A-1.

8

Tagger Crews and Members of the Posse

"Complex Dynamics Shape Local Graffiti Phenomenon"

On a backyard wall, 17-year-old Shawn Carter and fellow taggers crackle mixing balls of Krylon spray paint cans and fill the air with hiss and vapors of red and black, turquoise blue and cream white.

"It's addictive, once you get started, it's like a real bad habit," said Danny Canas, 17, of his "tagging"—scrawling on everything he can find. "I quit because I've got to go to college."

Canas, a Cleveland High senior who plans to attend California State University, Northridge, said he has left his tagging crew CMF—Criminals Murdering Families. But he visits his friend's house where Carter's mother lets him spray "pieces"—short for masterpiece—in peace on the backyard wall.

The addiction has drawn thousands of teenagers—who call themselves and their rivals "toys," "taggers" or "piecers"—to devote their time to "getting up" to attain "fame" by tagging poles, benches, utility boxes, signs, bridges and freeway signs in the San Fernando Valley with graffiti.

The taggers "battle" to see who can damage as much property as possible in a set period and area to achieve greater fame (1).

"Life's an Exciting Game of 'Tag' for This Valley Youth"

As the war on graffiti escalates, so does the rhetoric. It thundered inside a Riverside convention hall Wednesday when about 400 frustrated and angry parents from across the county spent the whole day strategizing against presumably frustrated and angry teenagers. "I have a problem with the term 'taggers,' " said one sheriff's deputy. "Visual terrorism is a more accurate term."

The adults shared tips on stopping the terrorists. Impose tougher sentences. Take away their driver's licenses. Show them healthy ways to find adventure. Teach their parents how to raise them.

If 18-year-old Paul had been there, he would have been a damper. Paul is convinced that adults can't do a thing about tagging—conference or no conference.

Paul was 13 when he began tagging, but the real rush came in high school where he found plenty of competition. "I'd say: I can do better than that. Then I made a crew. Me and a friend of mine. We went bombing together. . . . You just go out with your can. The bigger the letters, the better the bomb. The best place would be an intersection where everybody's going to pass and no one's going to miss it." Then came his arrest. "I was like, bummed. I still didn't stop though." On he sprayed, right up until he was sent to juvenile hall. "Before I left, I was one of the best writers in this town."

"The whole point of being a writer is to be up the most. To be up more than everybody else." Up. As in: up on walls. Up on billboards. And not just up. Up with style. The best taggers practice on paper, over and over, doing justice to their obsession. "Half of them are in it to do the right thing—the way it's s'posed to be."

Style or no style, it's vandalism. Paul doesn't deny it. But he regards it as you might regard driving. It pollutes the air, but you do it anyway. An unfortunate but unavoidable reality of modern life. Besides, "I never write on anyone's house. Or on a church."

The payback of tagging is respect. "Respect from your crew and respect from everyone in the valley. That's what it's about. Respect." And good times. "You know people are looking for you, but they'll never get you. It's night. You're undercover. You're slick."

He hated juvenile hall. He hated boarding school. He hated disappointing his parents. Yet .;tn.;tn. "I still would like to be up." Especially when he sees the competition. "Every morning when I drive to school. I look up and say: Ooooo. That's a good hit! I could be there! I wanna go out and burn 'em" (2).

Welcome to the world of hip-hop culture. Once mostly the work of street gangs staking out their turf, graffiti—or tagging as it has come to be known—is now considered sport by youth from every type of neighborhood. The newest youth culture on the suburban horizon during the 1990s was that of tagger crews and posses.

According to police officials, as of 1993, 422 crews were active in Los Angeles County, with names such as NBT, or Nothing But Trouble, that claim 400 or more members. More alarming, there were about 30,000 taggers countywide (3).

Referred to by a variety of names—including "graffiti bands," "tagger crews," "posses" (or mob or tribe), "piecers" (because they draw masterpieces or works of art), "housers," or "snappers"—taggers have sprawled their three-letter monikers over the landscape of Southern California. And as their fad gains more fame, the markings of taggers have spread across the country and the world as well.

Dressed in the standard garb of cockeyed baseball caps, flannel shirts, hoop earrings, and low-slung, often oversized trousers, the taggers—armed with spray-paint cans, which they often shoplift, or Mean Streak marking pens—are ready for play. Some tagger crews, according to police officials, even carry beepers to call for backup when they are challenged by rival crews.

Some parents, knowing their kids are into tagging, let them tag the walls of their room or the inside of a backyard wall. According to one press report, one mother whose son was in the eighth grade told her he had joined a tagging crew. She indicated that setting aside the wall meant that her son and his friends would have a safe outlet to express themselves:

> My first reaction was to be really upset. I had just heard of graffiti. I'm a cool mom, is what I am. I allow them to express themselves within boundaries. Parents don't understand what tagging represents. I didn't understand it at first. It took me a long time to understand it. It's their identity. It's who they are, it's what they are all about (4).

DYNAMICS OF TAGGING

Why do youngsters tag? Similar to standard explanations for the presence of traditional, inner-city ethnic gangs is the view that tagging provides these suburban youths with a form of status. It is a declaration that says, "Here I am." Being a member of a group or crew and splashing their tags on overhead freeway signs—referred to as "mapping the heavens"—for instance, tells others "who we are" in a big way. Another view explains the presence of suburban taggers as a response to the ethnic gangs that may be spreading into their geographical areas. To more middle-class youths, tagging becomes a symbolic defiance of inner-city urban gangs—a stark means of saying, "I'm (or we're) not afraid of ethnic gangs!"

The fact that, to many people, tagging seems senseless or nonutilitarian has led some psychologists and psychiatrists to claim that vandals suffer from mental or emotional disturbances. But the large amount of vandalism unveiled in self-report research show how widespread the activity actually is (5). This research has lead sociologists to look for a connection between youth culture and graffiti. According to British sociologist Stanley Cohen, graffiti and vandalism may be a solution to problems that adolescents experience. Cohen contends that graffiti enable alienated youth to attain excitement, trouble, toughness, action, control, and risks (6). From this perspective, tagging—like graffiti and vandalism—becomes a voice for youth who feel voiceless.

But tagger crews are not merely the newest form of youth culture. On the contrary, according to police, their behavior has moved beyond being a simple fad. Older taggers now carry guns for protection and to be "cool." This is referred to as "tag-banging." Yet most taggers insist they are peaceful and do not want to "tag bang," or escalate the use of weapons to attack tag rivals. Still others, according to police, have turned to committing other crimes such as burglary and auto theft.

What is tagged varies with the tagger's age. The younger taggers, ages 10 to 15, typically mark school grounds and property. Older teenagers, besides defacing overhead freeway signs, target walls, public transportation such as buses and trains, and other public areas such as traffic signs, bridges, and street poles. In effect, anything that the public can view is fair game to these graffiti vandals. Less geographically bound to protecting a particular neighborhood turf than are the ethnic and inner-city gangs, the taggers spread their marks far and wide on their nightly runs.

Typically, taggers declare all public buildings and edifices as their "turf" to display their art, whereas ethnic gangs limit their gang graffiti to the gang's neighborhood boundaries. Taggers are driven by a need to gain "instant fame" as everyone views their "works of art." They "battle" with rival tagger crews to see who can damage as much property as possible in a given area in a set period of time—typically a week—with someone preselected as judge to declare the winner.

Lexicon of Taggers

Along with the dress and behavior has come an entire lexicon of tagger terms including, but not limited to, the following, listed in a Southern California newspaper:

- *all city*—tagging all over, not just in one area
- *homies*—fellow members of your crew
- *kicking it*—to relax with your homies
- *toy*—a novice, a amateurish tagger
- *ranker*—a person who chickens out, does not defend his tag
- *slipping*—being caught by rival taggers without homies to back you up
- *kill or kill a wall*—to completely cover with graffiti
- *seek and destroy*—to tag everything in sight
- *to be down*—to be a dedicated tagger, accepted by your crew
- *to get up*—to spread your tag in as many places as possible
- *to be rank*—to have the privilege of deciding who is in and out of your crew
- *hero*—an adult who would turn in a tagger
- *landmarks*—prime spot where a tag will not be erased
- *to be buffed*—to have a tag cleaned off by authorities
- *to be crossed out*—to have a tag erased by a rival tagger (7)
  Still more terms were found in another newspaper:
- *bomb*—to put a series of large letters on a wall usually in more than one color
- *bombing run*—when a tagging crew comes together for the express purpose of putting up as many of their tag names and the name of their crew as they can

- *def*—a really good tagger who is considered to be "cool"
- *dis*—to disrespect someone by writing over or on another tagger's work
- *fresh*—pieces of tagging styles that are considered good
- *head*—the best tagger in a crew artwise
- *jack*—to steal a tagger's supplies, usually by robbery
- *jump-in/out*—like street gangs, several members will beat a person who wants to get into the crew or who wants to leave the crew
- *mob*—putting as much graffiti on an object as possible; usually in a short period of time
- *rack*—stealing, shoplifting paint, markers, and so on
- *rolled-up*—arrested
- *slash*—to cross out another tagger's/crew's name; meant as an insult or challenge
- *spot*—a store to shoplift from, which is kept a secret from other taggers
- *take-out*—to defeat another tagger/crew in battle
- *throw-ups*—put large bubble-style letters on an object
- *wild style*—unique style of tagging that exhibits overlapping letters (8)

Police Definition of Taggers

Because of the widespread, wanton destructive nature of taggers, police have had to come up with definitions and criteria for tagger identification. They have developed four such criteria that assist authorities in arresting and charging graffiti vandals. These criteria include the following: (1) when an individual admits to being a tagger; (2) when a reliable informant identifies an individual as a tagger; (3) when an informant of previously untested reliability identifies an individual as a tagger and the identification is corroborated by independent information; and (4) when an individual has been arrested several times in the company of identified taggers for offenses consistent with usual tagger activity (9).

THE PROLIFERATION OF TAGGERS

With over 600 tagger crews identified by the police in Los Angeles County alone in the early-to-mid-1990s, the tribes have developed a variety of names or monikers. For instance, AAA stands for Against All Authority. Some of the more prolific crews include the following: TIK (Think I Kare), KMT (Kings Making Trouble), CMF (Criminals Murdering Families), EWF (Every Woman's Fantasy), KNP (Knock Out Posse), and INF (Insane Family).

Other tagger names colorfully depict the nature of the group's activity: ABC (Artist By Choice), ACK (Artistic Criminal Kings), AIA (Artists in Action),

APT (Ambushing Public Transit), BCA (Best Creative Artist), BLA (Bombing Los Angeles), CFK (Crazy Fucking Kids), CMC (Creating Mass Confusion), DFA (Defiest Boys Around), DCP (Destroying City Property), and ETC (Elite Tagger Crew), to name but a few.

Taggers are not just limited to white juvenile males. Several tagger crews reflect both ethnic and gender diversity: TWM (Tagging With Mexicans), TUL (Three United Ladies), UMK (United Mexican Kings), and RSK (Rasta Social Kings).

To the critics of taggers and to the general public fed up with the mess these youngsters have caused, TWY—Totally Wasted Youth—seems, unfortunately, to aptly describe the situation.

What Brought about the Rise of Taggers?

The tagger scene appears to be behavior that started out as an innocent form of youth culture. Known initially as "party crews" or "housers," these were youths who organized underground parties and liked to invent new dance steps. A spin-off of "house parties" and the hip-hop dress of the early 1990s, they came up with unusual-sounding names for themselves. Like every type of clique, they travel in a group, make up T-shirt designs, and on weekends and after school gather for social occasions.

The popularity of becoming part of the tagger scene also stemmed from suburban white youths' interest in gangsta rap, the popular music in the 1990s of some black urban youths. Enjoying hip-hop music and "getting down" becomes, for these white "home boys," their form of replicating inner-city, black ghetto "chic."

To one observer, tagger crews and posses are merely a new form of seeking a distinctive identity and gaining recognition:

> For kids, the hip lexicon of the day is to call your friends your posse.
> It's the influence of the street culture on kids who don't necessarily want
> anything to do with the street. You know, (it's) suburban kids who listen
> to rap and hip-hop music. They think they're Marky Mark and the
> Funky Bunch. Posses are the way kids seek recognition (10).

But others see taggers as not a new youth phenomenon at all, pointing to a group of people in the early 1970s in New York City who called themselves "TAG" for "Tough Artist Group." In fact, according to one police official, tagging crews in Southern California first appeared in the early 1980s when youngsters began writing graffiti in an exaggerated balloon-type style of writing referred to as "bombing." The most famous "graffiti artist" in the late 1980s was a youth who used the moniker "Chakka."

Another explanation given for the presence of tagger crews is the response by suburban youths—at least in Southern California, where they first emerged on a grand scale—to the increasing diffusion of traditional inner-city ethnic gangs outward into suburbia. Rather than merely mimicking the delinquencies and vandalism of these urban youths, suburban tagger crews are forming to compete with or oppose them. In effect, the taggers have reversed the direction of gang diffusion from inner city outward. That is, the tagger's movement patterns—and night runs—frequently are from suburban areas along the freeways back toward the inner city, leaving their marks or pieces (calling cards) to indicate their presence and influence along the way.

In this regard, tagging is to these blue- and white-collar suburban youths what traditional graffiti is to lower-income, traditional ethnic gangs. Tagging becomes a response to gang diffusion. As stated earlier, it is a rallying cry that says, "We will not be overlooked. We will not be trampled on."

According to this view, the actions of taggers are similar to that of racist skinheads, the topic of the next chapter, in that they have arisen in response to ethnic diffusion. Teenage racist skinheads emerged in suburbia in response to ethnic and minority families moving into formerly generally all-white neighborhoods. Whereas taggers symbolically leave their mark, racist skinheads have resorted to different forms of recourse.

In some ways tagging is more of a "passive-aggressive" act. For example, one is not striking out against a particular person or group. Instead, one is attacking—through tagging—the symbols or mere edifices of society. Like juvenile fire-setters (the focus of a previous study Wooden and Berkey conducted), a youngster who tags buildings is being less confrontational than overtly or personally attacking his or her enemy or antagonist. Defacing a street sign, moreover, is a less drastic form of "crying for help" than torching the local school.

Differences between Taggers and Traditional Gangs

By contrast, sociologists have viewed traditional graffiti and acts of vandalism around the world to be more complex. Stanley Cohen views such acts as taking one of six forms: *ideological* vandalism, *acquisitive* vandalism, *tactical* vandalism, *vindictive* vandalism, *play* vandalism, and *malicious* vandalism (11). Although these categories are somewhat arbitrary, tagging might best follow the lines of tactical and/or play vandalism. Tactical vandalism, in the sense, that, as Cohen describes, tagging can be a means to achieve some other end (e.g., reprisal, status, or identity). Play vandalism, on the other hand, may merely be "high spirits," motivated by a competitive sense.

Gang-related, inner-city vandalism, on the other hand, perhaps better fits into the categories of acquisitive, vindictive, and malicious behaviors. Acquisitive vandalism is used to acquire money or property; vindictive graffiti is used for revenge or to settle a grudge; and malicious graffiti is wanton destruction of property and serves as a primary form of confrontation with other gangs.

Several differences have been noted between tagger crews and traditional inner-city ethnic gangs. For one, the name of an individual tagger as well as one's crew can often change. However, like the traditional gang, one's name, nickname, or moniker—which becomes one's personal tag—may reflect one's physical appearance or personality quirk. One youngster interviewed is named "Lurk" because he lurks or hides behind bushes.

Not all taggers belong to a tagging crew. Some prefer to work alone. By contrast, gang members—or "OGs" for "Original Gangsters" as they are now more commonly called—nearly always "hang with their homies," maintaining steady group interaction.

Interview with Members of a Tagger Crew

As part of the research for this chapter, an extensive interview was conducted with four members of one tagger crew, the KMTs, or Kids Making Trouble (not their real name). The adolescents said their group had no detailed organizational structure. One 15-year-old, "Jerry," explained, "The only organization we have is when we are in a battle. A battle is when two or more crews get together and pick an area to tag. When we do it, the battle lasts one week. Whichever crew has their name up the most is the winner."

These tagger members also contend that, unlike gangs, they do not have any special type of initiation process. None of them were "jumped in" as is the case with traditional gangs. (Police, however, claim that tagger crews are starting to use jump-ins to initiate new members.) One 16-year-old, "Travis," maintained, "The only thing that matters is if the other members like your (art) work. You just give them a sample and they will tell you if they like your style. That's what's important to get you accepted."

Unlike traditional gangs, taggers are not territorial. Taggers rarely have any boundaries. Whereas traditional gangs build up and maintain their group, taggers drift in and out of crews, often changing their names whenever they tire of the old one. The number of taggers within a crew fluctuates because it is so easy to join or leave these groups.

The taggers interviewed indicated that the members of these crews come from all socioeconomic backgrounds and races.

As another teenage tagger, "Kevin," explained,

> Taggers want to get along with gangs. We are afraid of gangs in our community. All we want is to be able to write on walls. So long as we do not write over the gang names, we are safe. However, if a crew does write over a name of a gang, they must arm themselves. This is when taggers become violent. Some gangs now require "payoff" for taggers to move through their areas.

In response to a question about the type of weapons taggers might use to defend themselves, this juvenile replied, "Taggers will disguise chisels in pens. These are not only for protection but to permanently write on windows. One of our greatest concerns is that at night, gangs will mistake us taggers for a rival gang member and shoot us."

Kevin maintained that at first they tagged because it was fun and exciting, but fame soon replaced the initial fear they experienced.

> Everyone knows who you are. They recognize your tag. My parents at first were angry and upset, particularly when the police arrested me. But after a while they compensated for my behavior. They told the police, "Well, at least my kid's not shooting people. He's still alive."

Another teenager, "Fred," a self-proclaimed 18-year-old "former tagger," indicated that tagging, for him, was just a fad.

> Tagging is associated with clothes and music which always changes. My friends and I quit tagging because after a while, it became boring. Now we throw rave parties. This is much more profitable. (Taggers often overlap in membership to "dance crews," who attend rave parties.) We have mandatory searches for weapons on entering guests. No one is discriminated against. Anyone can attend these parties for a couple of bucks. The goal of these parties is to make money. The profits go toward throwing bigger and bigger parties."

The taggers interviewed for this study did not believe that what they do is a crime. They felt strongly that their tagging was art and an expression of themselves. "When confronted by the police," one tagger mentioned, "I felt insulted because he called my 'pieces' graffiti!"

PENALTIES FOR TAGGING

Unfortunately, taggers are driven by a desire to inflict increasing destruction in order to achieve notoriety among fellow crew members. In the past, taggers knew that, if caught, they would be charged with only a misdemeanor offense. However, this is changing. Community officials and the law, in order to develop a deterrent for these juveniles, have passed legislation to make graffiti and "vandalism with priors" carry stiffer penalties.

In the past, depending on the jurisdiction, youths arrested for tagging were charged with the crime of vandalism and sentenced to 200 hours of community service or work. The California state legislature in 1996, for instance, passed a bill to amend the state penal code on vandalism to include anyone who "maliciously sprays, scratches, writes on, or otherwise defaces, damages, or destroys any real or personal property not his or her own." The bill distinguishes between types of punishment based on the amount of defacement, damage, or destruction. In general, a youth may not only be charged or fined for the amount of damage caused, up to $50,000, but may also face imprisonment for up to one year.

Others have argued for a variety of ways to deal with the problem. Some people have indicated a desire for a "graffiti court" to prosecute vandals apart from the traditional juvenile justice system and to offer different forms of community-diversion programs to assist these delinquents. Others want a civil lawsuit filed against the parents of taggers for not being more responsible in the upbringing of their children.

Ordinances in several cities now require parents to pay criminal fines or participate in the cleanup if their children are convicted of vandalism. First Offender programs and others such as Short-Stop in Orange County mandate that parents and their delinquent offspring attend joint meetings and workshops to address the problem. Other communities have proposed fining parents up to $1,000 for tagging by their teenagers as well as denying the youth a driver's license until age 18 if convicted of vandalism. These are similar responses to those recommended by concerned citizens.

Other communities in Southern California have ordinances that require merchants to place spray-paint cans and large marking pens behind the counter or in locked shelves where they can not be easily obtained. Varnish, paint thinner, and other materials that can be used as inhalants are now kept out of reach so that juveniles do not gain access to them to get high. In San Diego, for instance, the city has begun a program called "Responsible Retailers," which assists stores with ways to reduce the theft of graffiti tools.

Also included in the 1996 California legislation were several new laws restricting the sale and possession of aerosol containers of paint. Under the new ruling, for instance, it would be unlawful for anyone under the age of 18 to purchase an aerosol container of paint that is capable of defacing property. Further, retailers who carry aerosol cans must post a sign informing potential customers that anyone who maliciously defaces property with paint will be guilty of vandalism punishable by the new fine, imprisonment, or both.

Other communities make it illegal to allow graffiti to remain on private property. In San Diego this law is strictly enforced. According to an editorial in the *San Diego Union-Tribune,* "Tracking Taggers," a law should extend to public property as well, along with one that would call for the expeditious removal of graffiti from freeway signs. To further crack down on these visual terrorists, city officials make presentations to community groups on how to prevent graffiti, how to organize paint-outs, and how to tell whether one's children are involved in tagging. The city also provides free, recycled paint for covering up unwanted markings (12).

Politicians hope that such restrictions will serve as deterrents and cut dollar losses created by these graffiti vandals. The National Graffiti Information Network reports that tagging and other graffiti are a $4.5 billion problem nationwide. The city of Los Angeles spends $4 million per year on cleanup. According to Rapid Transit District officials, removing graffiti from buses and RTD facilities costs $13 million per year or $1.1 million per month! The RTD made close to 1,000 arrests for vandalism on buses in the early 1990s, a 101-percent increase over the prior year (13).

California is not the only locale in recent years where taggers have left their mark. On the East Coast as well, city councils have drafted new measures that would require buyers of spray paint to give their names and addresses to the salesperson. According to one report, more than 8,000 spray cans are used daily to deface property nationwide. New York City outright bans the sales of spray paint to minors (14).

Other Deterrents

New legislation is not the only line of attack to combat graffiti vandals and taggers. Police now use high-tech infrared equipment to spot them. Other departments not only set up stings to arrest taggers, but they also use a computer system to identify and track them by their tags and locations. Further, once a tagger is apprehended, police can use the information they learn from questioning to log and track other graffiti vandals.

The planting of more plants and shrubbery close to freeway walls also deters graffiti artists. And the placement of coils of razor wire—such as that used to prevent inmates from escaping from prisons—has been effective in keeping taggers off the freeway signs and overpasses.

Community watch groups are also on the lookout for taggers. According to one newspaper report, citizens have joined nighttime surveillance missions, some using infrared video cameras operated by remote control or peering from rooftops with binoculars, to help police arrest more of Los Angeles's thousands of taggers. Police also are asking residents to assist them by filing crime reports and taking photographs so that they can catalogue damage (15).

Other public officials say another way to combat tagging is to develop more art and recreation programs for youngsters, similar to those developed elsewhere in the world to combat the "scourge of graffiti," as Frank Coffield describes it in his 1991 book, *Vandalism and Graffiti: The State of the Art* (16).

Other communities have developed antigraffiti curricula for grade-school students with a special emphasis on kids' responsibilities to their community. Still other communities have set up twelve-step recovery programs dubbed "Taggers Anonymous" for juveniles addicted to the rush of adrenaline they get from tagging. Youths on probation for tagging offenses are ordered by the courts to attend these group self-help meetings.

Nonetheless, the presence of tagger crews points to a general breakdown in society—a lack of respect for other people's property and the increasing indifference and insensitivity that some youths have toward others and society in general.

The destruction of the public landscape by tagger crews and traditional gangs has increased the anger of the citizenry and sparked a desire for retribution. Fueled by a sense of duty to one's community, antigraffiti activism now has a militant edge to it. "Enough is enough," people seem to be saying.

One Southern California newspaper account reported the following:

> At a recent San Pedro meeting to discuss the battle against graffiti, a member of the audience suggested cutting a tagger's hand off for a first offense. The comment drew cheers. In Encino, those at a meeting of a new anti-graffiti group spoke facetiously of hanging, shooting and castrating the vandals. The name of that group, Residents Against Graffiti Everywhere, or RAGE, emphasizes the emotions surrounding the issue (17).

These actions, of course, are not the answer. More appropriate social responses would be those previously mentioned in this chapter. But there is no doubt that the public is getting weary, warning their politicians to take action against these graffiti outlaws who, by their actions, are further breaking the spirit of neighborhood after neighborhood, suburb after suburb!

Youth at the Movies—Tagging

The early 1980s featured lots of films about hip-hop graffiti art, such as *Breakin'* (1984) and *Beat Street* (1984), but portrayals of tagging are much rarer. The act pops up in films such as *Where the Day Takes You* (1992) and *Kids* (1995). Only *Turk 182* (1985) captured the risky business of tagging. In this film Timothy Hutton plays a 20-year-old who uses the tag, "Turk 182," to needle the mayor of New York City by getting it in increasingly difficult, but public, spaces. In the process Turk 182 becomes a New York folk hero.

NOTES

1. Jaxon Van Derbeken, "Complex Dynamics Shape Local Graffiti Phenomenon," *The Daily News* (28 February 1993), p. A-1.

2. Shellee Nunley, "Life's an Exciting Game of 'Tag' for This Valley Youth," *The Desert Sun* (2 October 1993), p. A-3.

3. John M. Glionna, "Pals in the Posse: Teen Culture Has Seized the Word as a Hip Name for Groups; Not All Are Harmless," *Los Angeles Times* (26 February 1993), p. B-3.

4. Van Derbeken, p. 14.

5. Frank Coffield, *Vandalism and Graffiti: The State of the Art* (London: Calouste Gulbenkian Foundation, 1991), p. 12.

6. Stanley Cohen, "Sociological Approaches to Vandalism," in Claude Levy-Leboyer, ed., *Vandalism: Behavior and Motivations* (Amsterdam: Elsevier Science, 1984).

7. John M. Glionna, "Leaving Their Mark: Youths Risk Everything to Tag Walls, Buses and Traffic Signs with Graffiti," *Los Angeles Times* (10 March 1993), p. B-1.

8. Van Derbeken, p. 14.

9. "Taggers" pamphlet, Los Angeles and Orange Counties LASD-Transit Services Bureau, February 9, 1993.

10. Glionna, "Pals in the Posse," p. 4.

11. Stanley Cohen, "Property Destruction: Motives and Meanings," in Colin Ward, ed., *Vandalism* (London: Architectural Press, 1973), p. 49.

12. "Tracking Taggers: Police Use New Methods to Combat Graffiti," *San Diego Union-Tribune* (28 November 1993), p. G-2.

13. Hector Tobar, "County OKs New Graffiti Crackdown," *Los Angeles Times* (3 March 1993), p. B-3.

14. Robert Hanley, "Jersey City Escalates Graffiti War: Proposed Law Would Take Names of Spray-Paint Buyers," *New York Times* (11 June 1992), p. B-1.

15. Richard Lee Colvin, "Teaming Up on Taggers," *Los Angeles Times* (13 April 1993), p. B-1.

16. Coffield.

17. Colvin., p. B-4.

9

▼

Skinheads: Teenagers and Hate Crimes

"A Chilling Wave of Racism: From L.A. to Boston, the Skinheads Are on the March"

In San Jose they threatened to hang a black woman who was attempting to enter a public park. In another Bay Area community, a teenage boy was thrown through a plate-glass window when he tried to stop a group of them from posting up an anti-Semitic poster. In Chicago one of their leaders was indicted after a spree of anti-Semitic vandalism. The bizarre force behind the wave of racist incidents: skinheads, loosely organized groups of violent youths who may be emerging as the kiddie corps of the neo-Nazi movement (1).

"Man Held in School Break-in: 'Skinhead' Painted Swastikas, Police Say"

An 18-year-old man who police said is a white-supremacist "skinhead" was arrested Thursday and charged with breaking into a second-grade classroom and spray-painting swastikas on the blackboard. Detective Bob Farman said Derek James Smart, a transient, was linked to the break-in Sunday at Jamison Elementary School by instant photographs he took of himself and left in the classroom (2).

"Skinhead Convicted of Racial Killing"

A teen-age skinhead was convicted of manslaughter for killing a homeless black man during a drunken celebration of Adolf Hitler's birthday. Mark Lane, 19, of Liburn,

Georgia, said he was extremely drunk when Benny Rembert was stabbed to death under a Birmingham bridge in April, 1992, during a skinhead celebration of Hitler's birthday. Lane, convicted Thursday, faces up to 20 years in prison when sentenced next month (3).

"Arrests of Teen Members of 'Skinhead' Faction Spell End to Spree of 'Hate Crimes,' Police Say"

When nine police officers burst through the door of Mark Coven's home 10 days ago, the 18-year-old Monrovia High School dropout was asleep in his bedroom, comfortably surrounded by the trappings of the youth gang he both founded and led. Police said they found in Mark's room a gang photo album and newsletters, a 9-millimeter handgun and a .22-caliber rifle, a membership roster and a book that described gang rules, dress and tactics.

But the surroundings were not like those the officers had seen in connection with most youth gangs in the San Fernando Valley. Hung side by side on the wall of his bedroom were the flag of the Confederacy and the Federal Republic of Germany. On the nightstand next to the bed was a copy of Adolf Hitler's manifesto, "Mein Kampf." In the photo album, the pictures were of young men wearing Nazi arm bands, posing in sieg-heil salute, according to police.

Mark, known as "Peanut" by other members of the gang he named the Reich Skins, was taken in handcuffs after the raid at the two-bedroom Monrovia home he shared with his mother. In the days following, Los Angeles police arrested seven younger members of the gang. Police said the group, which had operated primarily in the western part of the Valley, was involved in racial terrorism activities— "hate" crimes—for the four to six months before the arrests. Now, they say it has been effectively stamped out.

Mark is being held in lieu of $100,000 bail at the Los Angeles County jail on charges of attempted burglary and using unlawful, violent acts to effect political change. Under an obscure 1919 Criminal Syndicalism Act, he is charged with distributing the racist literature and painting the racist graffiti.

The complaint also alleges that on Oct. 7 he and a juvenile companion tried to break into the Granada Hills home of a Latino high school student. The complaint says that Mark carried a gun and yelled "white power," "down with Mexicans" and "down with blacks." Mark, who has pleaded innocent to the charges, was described by school officials as an average student who was a loner on the Monrovia High School campus before dropping out.

Police said Mark's mother was as astonished by what her son was accused of as the parents of other Reich Skins members and some school officials were. Some parents were surprised to find that their sons had swastika tattoos. What the parents, school officials and investigators still find puzzling was how and why youths from mostly middle-class Valley families became aligned with such extremist views (4).

Teenagers involved with the skinhead youth style have been present in the United States since the early 1980s. But not all youths who embrace the lifestyle share racist views. This chapter explores both types of teenage youths: those who identify with the skinhead style in its traditional, racist form, as well as those who identify in nonracist ways, such as SHARPs (Skinheads Against Racial Prejudice) or SARs (Skinheads Against Racism).

The American skinhead youth movement appears to have been an outgrowth of English and other European patterns with some major differences, which this chapter examines. Besides discussing skinhead teenagers in general, this chapter presents an analysis of data collected from questionnaires given to several youths in Southern California who identify as either "hard-core" skinheads or as nonracist skins, along with interviews and case files of skins incarcerated for delinquent behavior.

The late 1990s saw a gradual decline in hate crimes but an increase in hate-group activity. The FBI points out that only 5 percent of hate crimes are committed by members of hate groups. More than half are committed by young people under the age of 22 (5). But hate-group recruitment of suburban teenagers fuels a wide variety of hate activity. Although many teens never actually join groups such as the Hammer Skins and World Church of the Creator, many adopt the style and philosophy of the skinhead subculture. This chapter also looks at how certain types of youth are targeted for recruitment by the skinheads.

CONTEMPORARY TEENAGE SKINHEADS

Not until the second wave of the British skinhead movement did American youths pick up the skinhead lifestyle. By the mid-1980s, American skins had organized to the point where their racial views came to public notice. In 1985, for example, several dozen skinhead youth attended a three-day gathering of white supremacist organizations at the farm of a former Ku Klux Klan leader in the Midwest (6).

Although not all youths who favor skinhead dress styles support white supremacy, racist skinheads—as their name implies—express prejudice. They most typically identify with Nazi insignia and preach violence against blacks, Hispanics, Jews, Asians, and homosexuals.

Throughout the decade of the 1980s, the skinhead movement also appeared to be growing. In 1985 the Center for Democratic Renewal of the Anti-Defamation League claimed that white power or racist skinheads (including teenagers) numbered only about 300 in the United States. By the end of the decade, however, their numbers were believed to have increased to over 3,000, peaking in 1989 and showing a decline in the early 1990s (7). Much of that decline is credited to hate crime legislation that mandates enhanced prison sentences, police assigning "bias crime officers" and "task forces," the federal use of RICO statutes (Racketeer Influenced and Corrupt Organizations Act of 1970) to prosecute criminal skinheads, and an expanding economy.

Early Roots of the English Skinhead Movement

The development of the early skinhead movement in England can be traced to the late 1950s when distinctive youth styles first emerged. Basically composed of working-class males, these British youth wore "Edwardian" coats and tight pants. British society viewed these youths, known as "Teddy Boys," as a threat to everything the traditional family stood for.

The British media described these adolescents as "folk devils," harmful to society and the social order, and the youths created "moral panics" by heightening concern over their actual numbers and significance. The cult heroes of these "Teds" of the 1950s included such imported American heroes as Marlon Brando, James Dean, and Elvis Presley (8).

By the early 1960s, however, the Teddy Boys had evolved into "modernists" or "mods." Their flashy dress imitated the styles of young blacks in the United States. The music of the British mods was "ska," songs with a popular West Indian beat. Toward the end of the decade, those mods who were more aggressive and shared a working-class dress, developed into skinheads.

Ironically, the original skinhead's inspiration were black Jamaican immigrants to England, known as "Rude Boys," whose close-shaven hairstyle and music were quickly adopted by white working-class youths. Although the early British white skinheads were not necessarily racist, their values revolved around reclaiming the traditional working class community from these new immigrants (9).

By the end of the 1960s, British skinheads were identified as a separate youth culture because of their distinctive behavior, attitudes, and dress style. The new youth style was surprising in that the skinheads' values seemed to be a reversal of the liberal trends common to the 1960s. The skinheads, from the beginning, embraced an ultraconservative, working-class view.

In 1972 police harassment and increasing political pressures led to the decline of the London skinhead movement. But in 1976, with the emergence of punk, the skins resurfaced, possibly in reaction to the punks' anarchical attitudes. The new skins revived the most extreme elements of the earlier skinhead styles in even more exaggerated ways. The boots, jeans, and suspenders were revived, and a new symbol was added—the swastika. The swastika had already been worn on the punks' T-shirts, but the skinheads took this a step further by having the swastika tattooed in several different locations on their bodies, including the face. Their aggressive racial and working-class attitudes made them easy targets for recruitment by the adult-based, neo-Nazi National Front (10).

Today skinheads in both England and the United States are characterized by a uniform appearance: Doc Martens or industrial boots, such as those commonly worn by fire fighters—which can now be purchased in most large chain department stores; heavy jeans rolled up over the boots; suspenders; green flight jackets; and, most of all, short and manageable hair resembling servicemen in boot camp. All of these are an exaggeration of a stereotyped, working-class image reflective of traditional masculinity.

In the United States, skinhead gangs—like other youth gangs—initiate their members in a ritual act of "jumping in," which involves the potential member getting "jumped" (for example, attacked with fists) by four to twelve of the strongest members of the gang for a set period of time. If the potential members do not last that long or are unable to "hold their own" by defending themselves, they will not be admitted to the group.

As in other traditional gangs, there are many symbols that relate to dress style in contemporary American teenage skinhead philosophy. If a skinhead has scuffed the steel tips on his boots, for instance, he is considered to be tough. The more scuffed the boot tips, the more likely the skinhead has been involved in physical violence.

Likewise, if one sees a skinhead wearing his suspenders down, this may mean that he is ready to fight. If a skinhead wears white laces in his combat boots, it means that he embraces white pride. Red laces stand for a more aggressive white power. Yellow laces signal hatred for police or claim that the wearer has killed a police officer. Recently, graffiti drawn by skinheads in Southern California include a circle with a cross in the middle, with lines extending outside the circle (11).

Skinhead Violence

What links most skinheads is an embracing of violent acts. Skinheads use violence to dispel anger they feel toward those they feel are different—homosexuals, and racial, ethnic, and religious minorities. As the media have noted, skins are responsible for an increase in violence around the country and the world. In the early half of the 1980s, according to one source, the brutal tally of skinhead violence was 121 murders, 302 assaults, and 301 cross burnings (12).

This violence has continued, but the trend may have peaked in Southern California (although it continues to grow in European communities such as Germany and Italy). Incidents over the years, for example, have been recorded in such varied locales as Los Angeles and Santa Clara County, California; Las Vegas, Nevada; and Tampa, Florida, as the following summary accounts from newspaper stories demonstrate.

- In Los Angeles, "Kill the faggot!" was screamed as a homosexual man was repeatedly beaten with a metal pipe by two neo-Nazi skinheads. These particular skinheads went to the area to specifically harass homosexuals.

- In Los Angeles three skinhead youths began shouting racial slurs and beat an Ethiopian immigrant with baseball bats for no apparent reason. A pair of teenage girls watched from a nearby car and shouted, "Kick him. Kill him," as encouragement to the attackers.

- In Los Angeles a black security guard was stabbed to death when he tried to eject a large group of skins from a grocery store.

- In Santa Clara County a 19-year-old skinhead was convicted of manslaughter after he fatally stabbed another white youth who had taken a black man to a party.

- In Las Vegas five white supremacist skins were accused of attacking blacks and Hispanics and of planning to exterminate Jews by placing cyanide in the air-conditioning units in a synagogue to remind them of the Holocaust where millions of Jews were gassed in Nazi concentration camps.

■ In Tampa a 16-year-old skinhead was sentenced to life imprisonment for beating and stabbing to death a 41-year-old black transient (13).

As these news clippings indicate, a majority of the violent attacks displayed by skinheads are unprovoked and racially motivated. The usual victims are typically unarmed, outnumbered, and defenseless. Skins use baseball bats, steel-toed combat boots, brass knuckles, lead pipes, and knives in their violent acts.

From the beginnings of their roots in the late 1960s, skinhead youths have been violent. In England much of this violence was initially directed toward immigrants such as Pakistanis ("Paki-bashing") because of jealousy over their affluence. When the skinheads first appeared in the United States, their anger was expressed in similar ways but took the form of hostility toward African-Americans ("black-bashing") and homosexuals ("gay-bashing"). As *Rolling Stone* magazine noted in an extensive 1988 cover story on skinheads: "It doesn't matter if you've done nothing wrong. If you're the wrong color, religion, sexual orientation, or you look at them the wrong way, they'll stomp on you (14).

Types of Skinheads

Though the appearance and dress of all skinheads tend to be similar, differences among them exist in thoughts and actions. Not all skinhead youths are racist and violent. In fact, distinctions can be drawn between them and three other types of skinheads: *nonracist, separatist, and political.*

The nonracist skins tend to exist in reaction to the racist skins, and their membership is racially mixed. Common names for them include both the previously mentioned SHARPs and SARs. Other similar nonracist youth groups include the "Two-Tones," gangs that comprise more than one race and who share similar views, and "Straight-Edge," skinheads who do not carry weapons and are against racial violence and the use of drugs and alcohol.

Unfortunately, the antiracist skins are often attacked by the Nazi skins for refusing to enter the racist fold. And these nonracist skins are often harassed and approached by the police and the general public who mistake them for racist skinhead youths. Few people in society realize that antiracist skins actually exist. More often the public assumes that all youths who dress in jeans, suspenders, combat boots and have shaved heads are racist and violent.

Also typically nonracist are the separatist skinheads. These youths (and adults) consider themselves more as survivalists, concerned only with their own personal welfare and survival in the likelihood of a nuclear holocaust or natural disaster. Separatist skins do not care much about what is going on around them and try to stay clear of overt racial violence. The separatist skins, who tend to be loners, tend also not to affiliate with gangs.

More similar to the racist skinheads are the political skins, who often follow the orders of such groups as WAR (White Aryan Resistance) and the Aryan Brotherhood. Political skins are critical of the U.S. government, claiming that it supports minorities to the detriment of the white race. These political, adult skinhead organizations often now recruit the more youthful teenage racist skins to be their "frontline" attack force in working toward a "whites-only" society.

Skinhead gangs are often found in U.S. prisons, where white convicts are frequently pressured to join the White Aryan Brotherhood, the Ku Klux Klan, and other white supremacist groups. These white gangs are often formed in response to the presence of other ethnic groups who have formed their own gangs in adult prison (for example, Black Guerrilla Family and Nuestra Familia in California's prisons).

White gangs—so-called stoner gangs—are also present in California institutions that house juveniles (a topic of the next chapter). Similar to the situation in adult prison, white youth join these gangs as a defense against—or in opposition to—the wide variety of ethnic gangs in the various camps and institutions of the California Youth Authority (for example, the black Crip and Piru or Blood gangs; an array of both Northern and Southern California Hispanic gangs; and Asian gangs.).

Apart from these specialized situations, teenage skinheads appear to be most frequently involved with the racist or nonracist skinhead groups and less likely to be involved with either the separatist or political movements.

Skinheads' Racial Views

Much of the violence that teenage racist skinheads display originates from their racial views. Whereas black gangs are often motivated by power, money, and drugs and Asian gangs are motivated by profit, skinhead gangs are motivated by racism. Racist skins, approximating the patterns of ethnic gangs, now are viewed by authorities as roaming the streets and doing whatever they feel is necessary to protect their own white race (15).

Although the total number of teenage skinheads involved in gangs is small (250 to 300 in California, according to the State Department of Justice in 1990), skinhead juvenile street gangs maintain a presence, particularly in suburban areas in Southern California, where there is continued ethnic movement outward from the inner city of Los Angeles. The presence of such skinhead gangs is malleable as well. Neo-Nazi skinhead gangs nearly doubled in size in a single year during the late 1980s (16).

Such individuals and groups are of special concern to authorities because of their propensity for violence and racist behavior. One 17-year-old youth, "Bob," who was interviewed for this study, recounted, "I used to frequent the punk clubs, drink heavily, and listen to heavy metal music. I also enjoyed surfing. I became attracted to the skinheads at about the age of 13 largely as a way to stand out from the other kids."

Sporting the standard look with a shaved haircut and the skinhead dress of military flight jackets, pants rolled above Doc Martens or combat steel-toed boots, and suspenders and boot laces whose color identified the specific skinhead gang he belonged to, this juvenile had carved a small swastika on his leg. Bob also indicated he had served time in the California Youth Authority for aggravated assault.

Racist American skinheads, like the earlier British skins, are opposed to immigrants and nonwhites and view them as a threat, believing that they steal employment opportunities. Jealous of and angry at the affluence that many immigrants acquire—while they perceive many whites to be struggling, unemployed, and homeless—racist skinheads want to establish a nation only for whites. To accomplish this they plan to ban all other races, whom they refer to as "God's mistakes" (17). Tom Metzger, the California founder of the White Aryan Resistance movement, is quoted as saying, "White people are on the way out unless they do something. The worst invasion is the biological invasion. Third World immigrants come here, have children, and take over" (18).

In the past several years the White Aryan Resistance (WAR), located in Southern California, has frequently been accused of encouraging and inciting teenage skinheads to commit violent acts against blacks and other minorities in order to promote white supremacy. Supplying the teenage skinheads with their WAR newspapers and comic books featuring the killings of blacks and Jews, the movement's main target has been to stop nonwhite immigration. In fact, mainly white racist skinhead gangs take the name WAR as part of their title—such as the Huntington Beach WAR Skins or the La Habra WARS.

Racist teenage skinheads follow the same line of thought as the Aryan Youth Movement (AYM) and the White Student Union (WSU). Unable to create their whites-only society, they express their frustration and anger by beating and harassing all minorities. As "Bob" stated, "I'm white and proud of it, and if that makes me racist, so be it."

Religion is often a tool of skinheads, who traditionally fall in two categories: Christian Identity or Odinists. Christian Identity adherents, such as those skinheads who call the Aryan Nations compound in Idaho their headquarters, believe in a recent racist interpretation of the Christian Bible. Here Adam is viewed as the father of the white race. By contrast, Jews are seen as the "race of Cain," the product of Eve's unholy union with Satan. Nonwhites are descendents of the beasts in the Garden of Eden. Christian Identity skins believe that whites are the chosen people and that a prophesied race war will "cleanse" the United States of all Jews, nonwhites, and race-traitors.

Other skinheads, such as Volksfront in Oregon, are Odinists, who cling to the Norse mythology of Scandinavia. The Viking Gods, such as Thor and Odin, are portrayed as fierce racial warriors. Odinists often get their racist propaganda into prisons as "religious matter" and appeal to young people interested in European paganism.

A third new religious position became more popular among skinheads in the late 1990s. Known as the World Church of the Creator (WCOTC), it was founded by a state chairman for George Wallace in 1973 and holds that "race is religion" and that Christianity in general is a Jewish plot. The WCOTC is now led by Matt Hale, who runs the "church" out of a spare room in his father's house in East Peoria, Illinois (19).

Through his web site Hale actively recruits skinheads. Between 1997 and 1999 young WCOTC followers were arrested for assault, attempted murder, robbery, intimidating witnesses, and arson, and on July 4, 1999, Hale ally and WCOTC adherent Benjamin Smith went on a three-day racist shooting spree, killing two and wounding nine.

Skinheads versus SHARPS

The reasons some teenagers join the antiracist skinhead movement appear less complex. According to one authority, youngsters join SHARP in reaction to the racist views of their parents or other family members. In other words, according to this source, "Some SHARPs hate their parents because their parents are racists" (20). Many SHARPs spent time as Nazi skinheads and rejected the racist position because of the lack of autonomy. SHARPs claim to be more independent (21).

The teenage skinhead movement is varied. Because of its secrecy and its suspicion of authority, it also proved difficult to study. But to gain some understanding into both the teenage racist and nonracist skinheads, we decided to interview several youths in Southern California who identified as one or the other of the two groups.

A questionnaire was developed, using seventy-four questions from the "Youth Survey" that had been distributed to punkers and metalers in Southern California and New Zealand (see Appendix A, "Youth Survey 2").

Attempts were made to distribute the questionnaires through various sources and contacts to self-identified skinheads in Southern California. Through these efforts we contacted thirty-two youths who completed the questionnaire and agreed to be interviewed in some detail. Twenty-three of these youths self-identified as hard-core, racist skinheads, and nine defined themselves as nonracist skinheads. An analysis of the thirty-two questionnaires and the three case files served as the basis for the following discussion.

Results of the Youth Survey

In examining the statistical analysis of the thirty-two questionnaires administered by Wooden, several key patterns emerged that differentiated the two groups of teenage skinheads (see Table 9.1). Because of the small number of respondents, however, these findings should be viewed with some reservation.

Table 9.1   Racist versus Nonracist Skinheads

Identify as a Skinhead

Believe it is good to be rebellious	<.001
Believe skinheads are a new form of gang	<.003
Believe the drinking age should be lowered	<.003
Spend a lot of time away from home	<.01
Peers see them as troublemakers	<.01
Teachers treat them poorly	<.01
Other students treat them poorly	<.01
Disagree they are against racism in any form	<.01
Feel kids should not be punished like adults	<.02
Was considered a bully in grammar school	<.03
Believe there are too many immigrants	<.03
Do not like their parents	<.04
Parents do not approve of their lifestyle	<.04
Feel minorities should be excluded	<.04

Identify as a Member of SHARP

Believe there will not be a nuclear war	<.0003
Believe there are not too many immigrants	<.001
Less likely to exclude minorities	<.01
Less likely to view skinheads as delinquents	<.02
Do not spend a lot of money on drugs	<.02
Affiliate with a religion	<.04
Believe blacks and Hispanics are equal to whites	<.04
Was not considered a bully in grammar school	<.04
Less likely to spend time away from home	<.04

Those Who Were Considered Bullies in Grammar School

Peers see them as troublemakers	<.001
Spend a lot of time away from home	<.01
Do not like school	<.01
Believe there will be a nuclear war	<.01
Have been in trouble with the police	<.02
Are less likely to like their mother	<.02
Parents do not approve of their lifestyle	<.03
Identify as a skinhead	<.03
Spend a lot of money on drugs	<.03
Peers treat them poorly at school	<.03
Believe music they listen to is violent	<.04
Hang out only with their own group	<.04
Believe drinking age should be lowered	<.04
Have tattoos	<.04
More likely not to be a SHARP	<.04

Music They Listen to Is Violent

Believe that life is boring	<.01
Abused by parents as a child	<.02
Participate in gay- or black-bashing	<.02
Spend a lot of money on drugs	<.03
Friends use drugs	<.03
Was a bully in grammar school	<.04
Are less likely to be happy	<.04
Do not like their mothers	<.04

Have Friends Who Use Drugs

Parents do not approve of their lifestyle	<.01
Believe music they listen to is violent	<.03
Have considered suicide	<.03
Are less likely to favor the death penalty	<.03
Was a bully in grammar school	<.04

Hard-Core Racist Skinheads Those youths who clearly identified themselves as racist skinheads, compared to those who self-identified as nonracist skinheads, differed in their responses to fourteen of the forty-six statements on the survey (or 30 percent of the items). These hardcore racist skins agreed, for instance, that it was good to be rebellious, that skinheads were a new form of gang, and that the drinking age should be lowered. They also were likely to say that they spent a lot of time away from home, feel that their peers viewed them as troublemakers, and believe that both their teachers and fellow students treat them badly.

These hard-core skinheads disagreed with the statement that they were against racism in any form. They believed that kids should not be punished like adults, agreed that there were too many immigrants, and stated that they had been considered bullies while in grammar school. The racist teenage skinheads reported not liking their parents, having parents who disapproved of their lifestyle, and believed that minorities should be excluded.

Furthermore, those youths who identified as hard-core skinheads were also most likely to share these additional characteristics: They were bored with their life, had been in trouble with the police, had family members who were themselves racists, had contemplated suicide, and admitted to spending a lot of money on drugs.

Non-racist Skinheads By contrast, those youths who completed the questionnaire and who identified themselves as nonracist skinheads, or members of SHARP, shared views that distinguished them from the racist skinheads in nine of the forty-six items (or 20 percent of the statements). The nonracist skinheads believed there would not be a nuclear war in their lifetime. They disagreed with the statement that there were too many immigrants in the United States and were less likely to want to exclude minorities.

The nonracist skinheads also indicated that they were less likely to view skinheads as delinquent (because as skins themselves they were not necessarily delinquent). Furthermore, they did not spend a lot of money on drugs, they maintained a religious affiliation, and they viewed blacks as equals with whites. They indicated they had not been considered bullies in grammar school, and they were also less likely to spend time away from home compared to the hard-core racist skins.

Moreover, the SHARPs reported that they were happy with their lives. They also shared these additional characteristics: They were affiliated with their own group; they agreed they would fight in a war to protect their country; they felt that their parents were happy with their own lives; they felt close to their families; and they had parents who approved of their lifestyle.

These youngsters, however, were not totally nondiscriminatory in their views. These nonracist teenage skinheads agreed with the statement that society should discriminate against homosexuals or gays (a view that may have been influenced by their stronger religious affiliation), and they reported that they had family members who were themselves racists.

Cross-tab statistical analyses were also conducted on three other items from the Youth Survey that are germane to this study: being a bully in grammar school; listening to music that advocates violence; and having friends who use drugs.

Being a Bully in Grammar School Those skinheads who agreed with the statement, "In grammar school I was considered to be a bully,"—compared to those who disagreed with the statement—were also more likely to have peers that now perceived them to be troublemakers. They also indicated that they spend a lot of time away from home, they did not like school, and they believed there would be a nuclear war in their lifetime.

These youths who had been perceived as bullies in grade school were also more likely to share these characteristics: They indicated they had been in trouble with the police, they did not like their mothers, they spent a lot of money on drugs, they felt that their peers treated them poorly at school, and they agreed that their parents did not support their lifestyle. These teens also expressed the belief that the music they listened to was violent, they reported hanging out only with their own group, they felt that the drinking age should be lowered, and they admitted to having tattoos.

In looking at these patterns, it appears that their antisocial behavior has been associated with these teenagers since early adolescence at least. It should not come as too much of a surprise that some juveniles who were bullies as youngsters grew up to become racist skinheads as teenagers. The fact that delinquent teenagers (in this case, the hard-core racist skinhead), in general, were also likely to have been bullies in grammar school is borne out by behavioral science research on bullies (some of which was discussed in Chapter 2).

Bullies—or "schoolyard menaces" as one psychologist terms them—are a subset of aggressive kids who seem to derive satisfaction from being psychologically or physically abusive with other youngsters. Harming others becomes a way of life for them, the means by which they gain power. Such behavior results from a combination of parental influence, aspects of the child's home environment, and an unruly temperament. Too little parental love and care and too much freedom in childhood contribute strongly, according to one researcher, to the development of these aggressive personalities (22).

Others have speculated that the defenseless child who ends up as victim reminds the bully of his or her own defenselessness against abuse while at home and of the humiliation and shame it caused. Bullies, in other words, feel threatened by their victims' vulnerability. In the classic pattern of "the victim who becomes the victimizer," these bullies lash out at others in ways similar to what they had experienced (23).

In another study of what happens to bullies in later life, the researchers found that such children carry their aggression with them into a relatively unsuccessful adulthood. They are more likely than their less aggressive classmates to abuse their spouses and tend to punish their own children more aggressively, thus raising a new generation of bullies (24).

Listening to Music That Espouses Violence Besides having been considered bullies in grammar school, the racist teenage skinheads in this study also agreed with the statement that the music they listened to espoused violence. More important, those whose musical tastes were more violent were also significantly more likely to agree with the statement, "As a child I was abused by my parents". This raises an interesting question: might exposure to violence in childhood (that is, being abused by one's parents) condition one to more readily embrace violence in one's musical preferences?

Six other characteristics were associated with those skinheads who listened to violence in their music. They reported having participated in minority bashing; spent a lot of money on drugs; had friends who used drugs; had been considered a bully in grammar school; were less likely to be happy; and did not get along with their mothers.

Having Friends Who Use Drugs Finally, one other pattern was evident from an analysis of the thirty-two questionnaires. The teenage skinheads in the sample who said their friends use drugs were more likely to have parents who did not approve of their lifestyle; to believe that their music was violent; and to have considered suicide. They were also less likely to favor the death penalty, and they, too, had been considered a bully in grammar school.

Results of the Interviews

Examples of Racist Skinheads Very typical of the hard-core, racist skinhead youths that completed the questionnaire was "Paul," a 17-year-old ward of the court who was residing in a group home when contacted and interviewed. The youngest of three kids, Paul came from a working-class family.

Based on his responses to the interview and the questionnaire, Paul disliked school and believed his teachers and peers at school mistreated him. He also did not get along with his parents. In response to the open-ended, "fill-in" questions (see survey), Paul contended that a skinhead was one who "stands up for what he believes" and that anyone who was not a skinhead was a "wimp." According to Paul, anyone who did not like his kind of music was either a "fag" or a "fairy."

Paul claimed that blacks and Hispanics were not equal to whites and felt that our society has too many immigrants. To support his beliefs, Paul reported having participated in both gay- and black-bashing. Such violent behavior appeared to begin for him at an early age. Paul came from a family that definitely agreed with his strong racist views. He also indicated that he was a loner, socializing with only those in his own racial group.

A second youth, "Tom," further exemplified the typical racist skinhead that completed the survey. At age 18, Tom felt that his parents were too authoritative. He also did not like school and did not care what his teachers or peers thought about him although he indicated they considered him a troublemaker. Tom also believed that the United States has far too many immigrants, and he admitted to participating in gay-bashing, claiming that our society should discriminate against homosexuals.

Tom believed that it was important to be rebellious, which may have something to do with his drug abuse and past problems with the police. He also indicated he had been considered a bully in grammar school. Politically, Tom was very conservative and believed that our society should employ the death penalty. He also said that he would fight in a war to protect his country.

"Joe" exemplified the racist skinhead attitude as well. He is a 17-year-old who was brought up in a racist environment. An only child from a middle-class background, Joe shared, along with his parents, the view that blacks and Hispanics were not equal to whites and that there are too many immigrants in our society. Joe also reported having participated in black-bashing in support of his beliefs. To Joe, a skinhead is someone who "believes in the white race."

Joe disliked school and felt his teachers and peers treated him poorly. At an early age he became violent. He reported that he was a bully in grammar school. Due to these factors, perhaps, Joe indicated he socializes only with those in his own racial group.

Another youth interviewed who affiliated with the violent White Aryan Resistance movement was "Rhonda," age 18. Rhonda was brought up in a racist environment and her answers reflected this. She comes from a large family, having seven siblings. Rhonda gets along with her parents, who both have working-class backgrounds. Her father is a factory worker and her mother is a housewife or "domestic engineer," as Rhonda wrote on the form.

Rhonda defined nonskinheads as "gutless pinkos." She was against blacks and gays and had participated in "bashing them with a club." Also, she felt that the country has too many immigrants and that they should not be allowed to live in white communities. She strongly disagreed with the nonracist SHARP's views—crossing that group out on the survey form with a white power symbol.

Examples of Nonracist Skinheads One female interviewed, "Julie," reflected the skinhead identity but identified herself as a member of SHARP. As noted previously, some teenagers embrace the look and demeanor but reject the racist overtones of the skinhead subculture. Other nonracist youths reject the drugs and alcohol that seem part of the outlaw stance. Julie sported a shaved head with long bangs and dressed, according to her, "alternatively." Julie reported getting along with her mother but not with her father because he had abused her as a child. Julie enjoyed school and was happy with her life although at one time she had felt like committing suicide.

Julie considered herself to be neither aggressive nor a troublemaker, and she reported never having been in trouble with the police. She believed that blacks and Hispanics were equal to whites, was against racism in any form, and did not think that society should discriminate against homosexuals.

One youth, "Rod," also reflected the nonsupremacist attitude. He viewed racist skinheads as violent and too publicized for his liking. He believed in the Two-Tone doctrine of "black and white unite" and freely associated with people outside of his own racial group. He appeared to be positive about life and comfortable with his views.

Rod enjoyed school and got along with his parents, who were both teachers. He also indicated that he got along well with his two sisters. Rod was a part of the Straight-Edge scene, commenting, "It's our little way of trying to set examples for the younger kids and even the older ones. Drugs are a bad scene and we should stay away from them."

"Greg," a 17-year-old Native American, also followed the Straight-Edge view. He, however, seemed more ambivalent than most. He spent a lot of time at home and reported that he got along with his parents, teachers, and peers. Greg believed, however, that there are too many immigrants in the country and that society should discriminate against homosexuals. On the other hand, he believed that blacks and Hispanics were equal to whites. Greg also expressed the view that everyone was responsible for their own actions and that they should be punished accordingly—including minors who break the law.

Another nonracist skinhead, "Steve," also identified with the Straight-Edge movement. This was emphasized with a "Drug-Free" tattoo on his arm. Steve, age 16, saw himself as an individualist and encouraged others to be themselves. He reported getting along well with both parents and enjoying school. He was happy with his life and has never contemplated suicide. Although not a member of SHARP, he felt that all races were equal. He, too, however, felt that society should discriminate against homosexuals.

Table 9.2   Strain Factors and Skinhead Recruitment

Threats to ethnic/racial status
Growth in minority student population
Minority student organizations or events
Shifts to multicultural curricula
Racial conflict in which the institution appears to support the minority group

Threats to gender status
Conflict over female participation in typically male activities
Feminist activist groups
Antisexual violence, events, or programs

Threats to heterosexual status
Sexual minority organizations
Gay pride events
Movements that sponsor dialogue or advocate inclusiveness

Threats to economic status
Factory lay-offs
Large-scale employer downsizing

RECRUITMENT OF TEENAGE SKINHEADS
BY RACIST GROUPS

Researching skinheads since the mid-1980s, Blazak has found that Merton's strain theory (as discussed in Chapter 2) is crucial in explaining the motivations of skinheads. The response to blocked opportunity explains not only why teens become skinheads but also which youths are singled out for recruitment by racist groups.

Blazak's research is based on fourteen years of enthographic study. His ongoing research project includes the results of 65 formal interviews with skinheads, approximately 200 informal interviews, interviews with three skinhead recruiters in Oregon, and survey data collected from a "High School Anomie and Racist Recruitment Study."

According to preliminary findings, the recruitment of skinheads employs a systematic process based on the identification of social strain. Such strain can take the form of threats to ethnic and/or racial status, threats to gender status, threats to heterosexual status, and/or threats to economic status, as Table 9.2 notes.

Racist skinhead leaders are adept at targeting potential recruits. Frequently they best operate in a social milieu in which a perceived threat to the status quo exists (e.g., the infusion of racial and ethnic minorities into a given area the presence of gay and lesbian youth, and the economic downsizing of local workers in blue- and white-collar occupations). Racist skinheads are quick to address these perceived threats and other concerns of disaffected youth, who are easy prey, especially those who have a reputation for fighting or dress in a defiant manner compared to the general student population. These youths may be pursued by skinhead recruiters who present themselves to the youths as a collective "problem solver" (25).

Such a tactic is evident in the following passage from a Nazi group called New Order, whose "Action Program for Aryan Skinheads" dictates how to recruit marginalized youth:

> Recruit Skins or covert activists from Punk Rockers and from the group of disaffected White kids who feel "left out," isolated, unpopular, or on the fringe or margin of things at school (outsiders, loners). There are some very effective people among such kids, and working with Nazi skinheads will give them a sense of accomplishment, attainment, success, and belonging. In recruiting, proceed from such "outsiders," inwards towards the mainstream, conventional, average students (26).

In summary, groups such as the New Order teach their recruits the vivid philosophy of white supremacy, including the belief that the United States is manipulated by foreign Jewish interests, known as the Zionist Occupation Government (ZOG). With this conspiracy theory the "threat" or strain is "explained" (for example, that Jews are behind multicultural curricula), and a solution is presented (which may involve the commission of hate crimes).

The Selection of Anomic Populations

Members of organizations such as Youth Corps (the youth wing of the KKK), the Aryan Youth Movement (the youth wing of the White Aryan Resistance), and Volksfront (an Oregon Nazi skinhead group) conducted strategy meetings to discuss target populations with which their recruitment activities would have the greatest success. Leafleting was the most common method, but members might also stage a violent confrontation with an "enemy" to raise their visibility and awareness. Recruiters manipulated the power of rumor and the knowledge that young people will quickly spread forbidden information.

"Trey," 22, a Portland skinhead, recounts the following incident:

> There was this fight at Milwaukee High School between a black kid and a white kid and everyone was supporting the black kid who had been picking on this white forever. Typical bullshit, right? But we knew that there were whites there who were sick and tired of being called "racists" just for sticking up for themselves. So we went down there one day right when school was letting out and beat the shit out of some gangsta looking Nigger. The next day everyone at Milwaukee was talking about, "Oh man, did you hear that the skinheads kicked some Nigger's ass?" It was the talk of the school so we went back a week later and put up a

bunch of flyers and got a bunch of calls from kids wanting to know what they could do."

This tactic was not uncommon. The skinheads like to view themselves as rescuing the cultural underdogs in heroic macho fashion. One of the more common images in skinhead art and tattoos is a Viking warrior who comes to rescue his people from the "evil Jews and subhuman mongrels." During the ethnographic research one ritual was regularly observed. Racist skinheads would often mix with other youth subcultures at all-ages alternative music clubs that would attract punk rockers (both left-wing and right-wing), hippies, minority youth, and mainstream "slummers." The skinheads would stay in the background, drinking beer and talking to girls. But as soon as a conflict arose, the skinheads bounded into the fray to attack the group that was the least "skinhead." Most commonly the victim was a SHARP who was seen as a racial traitor, but occasionally it was an ethnic or sexual minority. The goal was to show skinheads "kicking ass" in answer to the problem of threats to ascribed status.

"Jack," age 20, from Orlando, Florida, recounted his adventure:

It's a fun Saturday night for us. We go down to Visage and drink beer, slam dance and pick up some punk chicks and fight. All it takes is one Spic to start something and we just open a can of whoop ass. It's great for us because we know that half the white kids there are getting harassed by the Hispanics in their school and they are just waiting for someone to stick up for them. I've had these totally straight looking kids come up to me later, maybe a month later, and say, "Hey, that was really cool what you did. I wish you guys would come to my school and kick some ass."

The selection of schools or neighborhoods for recruitment usually involves two factors. First, are there any racist skins already in the school or younger siblings of older skins who can be used as contacts? The second factor represents more awareness of the value of anomie. Is there a perceived threat to straight white (male) students that the racist group can manipulate? As noted in Table 9.2, this threat can be ethnic or racial, sexual, or economic.

The following quotes by skinheads represent these categories:

■ The suburbs are the new battle zones. We hardly even go into the city anymore. But the burbs are supposed to be white! I mean, whites moved out here to get away from all the crime and Niggers and shit and here they come. And now we have gangs out here and drugs and these nice clean white kids gettin' jumped. We know that white parents are tired of moving and white teachers are scared to death and the young people are on the front line.

—Bryan, 25, Atlanta skinhead

- The feminists are as bad as the queers. We try to get our guys to talk to dudes who think feminism is cool. You know, they're into it because they think they'll get laid. But we say, hey you know what happens if the feminists gets their way? No one's gonna listen to you because you're a man and you're gonna be cleaning out the toilet. And even fewer white babies are gonna be born because *if* a chick has sex with you and gets pregnant she's gonna have an abortion so she can keep her paycheck. Do you think the Niggers and the Mexicans are having abortions? Hell no! So then they see feminism as the nail in the coffin. It's like, who wants to be a minority?

—Harley, 24, San Francisco skinhead

- I'll tell ya, as much as I hate all this "gay pride" shit, it's been the best thing for skinheads. Our numbers have tripled since they've been having these (gay pride) rallies in Cobb. It's like fag haters just come out of the woodwork and we just scoop 'em up. We can't print enough flyers. I think people see that our way of life is threatened and they want to do something. We've got an idea!

—Frank, 21, Atlanta skinhead

- The easiest place to recruit is around some big lay off which is pretty common around here (Chicago). You wait for things to get bad and you go talk to the kids, not the parents, and say, "You know why your dad got laid off? It's because the money hungry Jews sent his job to China. They care more about the fucking Chinese than they do about the white workers". You know, they're all fucked up because their world is upside down and here is someone explaining it to them in very simple terms.

—Sid, 18, Chicago skinhead

Blazak's research encountered such stories over and over again during the past fourteen years. Skinheads' leaflet neighborhoods where auto or textile workers have been laid off and blame Affirmative Action and "Jewish capitalism". Skinheads come to the "rescue" of white youths who have been victimized by minority gangs, and they present a viable model of masculinity to boys confronted with the "homofication" (a skinhead term) of American culture.

Perhaps the newest recruitment technique is to target schools that are experiencing a curriculum shift toward multiculturalism. As history and social science books are retooled to be more inclusive, the voice that is diminishing is the hegemonic, straight white male perspective. Without the proper context this shift can seem to appear as a conspiracy to write white contributions out of the standard educational curriculum. Several highs schools in Oregon have been targeted for skinhead recruitment using the backlash against multiculturalism as a reason to recruit.

One of the most common skinhead tactics is to attempt to establish a "White Student Union," a method pioneered in the 1980s by the Klan in the East and WAR (White Aryan Resistance) in the West as simply an issue of equality. The idea behind it is that, if there is a black prom queen, there should also be a white prom queen. Similarly, if there is an Asian student union, there should also be a European student union. If there are gay pride stickers, there should also be straight pride stickers. If there is a Hispanic Heritage Week, there should also be a European Heritage Week, and so on. The concept of the white student union appeals to adolescents' need for fairness and balance. Without an understanding of the cultural history that has slanted power in the direction of straight white males, the concept seems just and is enhanced by the switch to a multicultural curriculum that further removes the voice of the white student.

One interviewee, "Sam," 26, who had spent several years recruiting high school youth into the Aryan skinhead movement, explained the importance of manipulating the victim mentality.

> It's really easy. You find out what's happening in a school and then find out where the kids hang out. You get some stupid conversation going and then you ask them about school. They bitch and moan and you say, "Yeah, it was a lot better in my day when we didn't have gangs and people who can't even speak English and all this multicultural shit." I'd say, "Don't you think it's fucked up that you can have a Black Student Union but not a White Student Union? Why are the blacks allowed to be racist?" And you can see them agreeing. I'd say, "Did you ever own a slave? Did you ever kill an Indian? So why are they trying to make you feel guilty for being white?" Before they can answer, I'd start telling them about ZOG. About how the Jews are behind all this to fuck over the white man. I give them the whole line, multiculturalism, gay rights, Affirmative Action. These kids don't know shit so they just eat it up. Then I tell them they should hang out with us or start an "unofficial" White Student Club. They just look at me like I'm Jesus Christ and I just saved them.

In summary, as the "New Order" recruitment manifesto illustrates, "disaffected White kids who feel left out, isolated, unpopular, or on the fringe of things at school" are targeted for intensive recruitment. The ethnographic element of Blazak's research revealed that Nazi skinheads can serve as "big brothers" or "friends in need" to frustrated boys whose fathers have been laid off or who have been harassed by minority peers. Similar to the research on cult recruitment, skinheads provide a sympathetic ear, a critical explanation of the problem, and an action program that appears to—at least in their minds—resolve the problem.

SKINHEADS' RULES OF CONDUCT

In 1990 law enforcement officials in the Orange County area of Southern California reported teenage skinhead gangs to be one of four new gangs that had set up operation in the region. (The other three gangs included new Hispanic, Vietnamese, and multiracial gangs.) According to the report, skinhead gang members in Orange County were sometimes difficult to document because they frequently held jobs, finished school, and blended in with regular life.

The report also noted the groups' hangouts, such as video arcades and malls; their most common tattoos, such as lightning bolts, swastikas, and white power mottoes; and their mode of dress, which is similar to that of skinheads in other parts of the country, including shaved heads (in part, so that their hair does not get pulled in a fight), heavy steel-toed boots, suspenders (often worn hanging), and military-style jackets. More recently skinheads have kept a relatively low profile in Orange County. Many have become more mainstream, covered up their tattoos, and let their hair grow although they still retain their racist philosophy. Their gang names include Death Squads and Huntington Beach Skins (27).

Included in this report was an example, confiscated by authorities, of rules used by one white youth gang in the county.

Rules of the Nazi Low Riders

Don't smoke after a black. Don't drink after a black. Don't talk and associate with a black. If anything goes down like a fight and the person who's getting his butt beat is a Nazi Low Rider (NLR), you are supposed to jump in to protect that person.

Whatever the President says, goes. No doubt about it or you'll be put on a shine (suspended). You are supposed to be cool with the Chicanos because they are with the whites in a way of protection. If something big comes down, and either race needs help, you are supposed to "go down" with them and help fight, etc.

Everything a NLR has—like a "canteen," they are to share with all of their gang. Nothing should be refused to another member. When you give somebody a light off your cigarette, don't let them touch it or hold it, because you don't want to catch their germs.

Don't talk to "Kacks," people that are on a shine. For violating the rules, the penalties are either to go behind the wall and fight or get put on a shine. In some cases, both (28).

A pamphlet circulated by members of WAR Skins affords an intriguing glimpse into the group's ideology. The flier, written by two teenagers—one, the head of WAR Skins, and the other, the vice-president of the Aryan Youth

Movement—was covered with Nazi swastikas and the logos "Young Nazis" and "Skinheads." (All grammatical errors and mistakes are as they appear in the leaflet.)

> The attitude of a skinhead is generally ready to fight and on guard all the time. Skins do not usually go around and start trouble. Its only when people start to make the jump on skins. When that happens, the skins end up winning! Skinheads are mad and tired of the system screwing them over.
>
> Skinheads are the All-American white youth. They love mom and love their flag. The dress of the skin (is) rough, smart and clean. All in all, the skinhead uniform is working class, ready to fight because our heads are shaved for battle.
>
> Skinheads are against non-white immigration because, these people take our jobs and land and give nothing in return. Skinheads are Anti-Semitic, because we know the Jews have extorted us for there personnel means. Skinheads are anti-abortion, we all know that abortion is another form of genocide, the nonwhite races and the jews sit and laugh at our self-annihilation (29).

The pamphlet also recommended the standard skinhead uniform for both men and women. Women, however, were also allowed to wear miniskirts and fishnet stockings, wool kilt skirts, and a fringed skinhead hairstyle. Finally, the flier stated that skinheads should be "pro-American, pro-family and pro-work, but should violently oppose communism and homosexuals" (30).

In Northern California, a skinhead organization called the "American Front" espoused the typical message of hate aimed at Jews, African-Americans, homosexuals, communists, government, the media, and just about everyone or everything else. Their telephone hotline carried this message:

> We in the American Front feel it's high time to slay the hooknosed, bagel-stuffing, penny-pinching, gentile-sacrificing, holy hoax-preaching beast. The fact still remains that white revolution is the only solution. If you don't want to fight, then prepare yourself to be hung on the day of the rope with the faggots that you feel so equal to. Hail victory (31).

EXPLANATIONS FOR THE RISE OF SUCH GANGS

In explaining the rise of teenage racist skinhead gangs across the country, one observer, interviewed by a gang detail member under the auspices of the California Youth Authority, notes two factors. First, black drug gangs from the Los Angeles area, including both the Crips and the Bloods, have extended their market for selling and distributing their drugs (for example, crack cocaine). As these black gangs have moved into suburban white neighborhoods, their presence has fueled racist fears. Like the rise of tagger crews (see Chapter 8), white racist skinhead gangs have emerged, in part, as a challenge to these former inner-city ethnic gangs who have moved into white suburban neighborhoods and public schools.

Others might disagree with this view. In general, racist skinheads appear to vent their rage and aggression by attacking and killing unarmed, law-abiding citizens. Often they are not battling other gangs (that is, defending their turf or neighborhood). Inner-city gangs can hardly be blamed for these skins' cowardly, unruly, and criminal actions.

The second factor, according to this authority, has been the news media. The tendency has been for the press and television news to give these new skinhead gangs media coverage. By engaging in violence on television (for example, the skinheads' disruption of a "Geraldo Rivera Show" on the subject of teenagers and hate crimes), racist skinheads gain more recruits. "When they see Geraldo beaten," he noted, "membership goes up."

This observer further contends that skinheads are basically undisciplined bullies or social misfits who engage in drug abuse and are quick to fight other gangs. When asked what law enforcement should do, he replied that skinheads should have mandated, as their sentence, the completion of a high school education.

Although skinheads' views should be protected under the First Amendment, which guarantees freedom of speech, their racist views need to be countered with minority group sensitivity training. This, he feels, can best be accomplished within a school setting. Part of the judicial sentencing, furthermore, should involve the family in some type of sensitivity sessions because many of the racist views are learned at home (32).

Skinheads and Status Frustration

The question still remains, why was there such an explosion of skinhead activity in the late 1980s and early 1990s? And why do teens continue to become skinheads in the twenty-first century? Blazak's ethnographic research has found three main factors that propelled young men into the skinhead subculture: (1) The downward mobility of the middle class (Spurred by "trickle-down" economics and corporate mergers, many stable factory and white-collar workers were laid off or downsized and lost their grip on the American Dream.); (2) The patriarchal reaction (Not only was the United States changing economically, but it was also changing in gendered terms. The new power of women and homosexuals threatened many men who clung to traditional definitions of masculinity.); (3) The changing demographics of the suburbs (As urban jobs disappeared and some blacks managed to move up the social ladder, the suburbs were no longer white enclaves, which led to cases of suburban "white flight.") (33). Hate crime researcher Jack Levin points out, "There are more hate crimes in the suburbs than in the city and it's much more likely to happen where there is an influx of minorities" (34).

Youth at the Movies—Skinheads

In the late 1980s skinheads began popping up on TV and in the movies as the new bad boys. The worst was 1988's *Skinheads,* featuring Chuck Conners going back to war against the Nazis. *Romper Stomper* (1992), with Russell Crowe as the lead skinhead, was a much better, if hyperviolent, portrayal of the chaotic life of racist skinheads in Australia. By far the most accurate representation stateside was *American History X* (1998). Edward Norton was nominated for an Academy Award for his role of a middle-class youth whose family and peers drive him into the world of hate crimes. He rebels against the skinheads after a prison term and tries to save his little brother (Edward Furlong) from a dead-end life as a skinhead.

Again we see the issue of strain. Not in the classic Mertonian sense of blocked economic status but rather blocked social status. This "status frustration" was manipulated by right-wing groups who explained to teens why their father's factory was closed down, why feminists had so much power, why their suburban school was becoming "less white." The answer was always the same—Jews.

The following quotes from the field reflect the status frustration of skinheads:

- Man, it's obvious that the world is seriously fucked up. My mom and step-dad work their asses off and it just keeps getting worse for them. It really sucks, especially for the working man. Look at all the money the Jews have. For doing what? Some guy busts a gut in a factory all day long then gets laid off so the Jew owner can hire some dumb spic who will work for half the price. People wonder why things are so bad. Because no one can make an honest living, that's why. There's no good job for me, they were all given to losers.

  —Jack, 19, Atlanta skinhead

- We don't have a President. He's (Clinton) a wimp whose wife controls him. You can't be a man anymore. Everyone's screaming "sexual harassment" if you even look at a girl. It says in the Bible that God created man first. Now they even want to change the Bible!

  —Telly, 15, Portland skinhead

- Man, it happens so fast. Like in Stone Mountain. It's white one day, then the blacks take over. Now you got murderers at Stone Mountain High. Snellville (an Atlanta suburb) is next. They're already moving in. You got redneck kids smokin' crack. Where did they get it? Every neighborhood goes to hell when the blacks move in. They're fuckin' animals. We build the neighborhoods and then they want what we got. So they come in and fuck it up. I got nowhere left to go. So I'll stay and fight.

  —Ollie, 17, Snellville (Atlanta suburb) skinhead

The hostility expressed by these and other skinheads is a reflection of their anomie. They are experiencing "normlessness," as the classic sociologist Emile Durkheim described it. Their world is changing. It is less upwardly mobile, less male dominated, and less white. The skinheads do not have the education that would enable them to navigate this frightening cultural change, and hate groups use their fear of change to recruit them. Their dogma gives vulnerable youth an explanation for the change (the Jewish conspiracy) and a way to reclaim their racial, gender, and economic hegemony (a race war). To the teenager who has difficulty with shades of gray, the violent world of skinheads may seem like the only hope.

NOTES

1. John Leo, "A Chilling Wave of Racism: From L.A. to Boston, the Skinheads Are on the March," *Time* (25 January 1988), p. 57.

2. Jonathan Volzke, "Man Held in School Break-in," *Orange County Register* (9 June 1989), p. B-3.

3. "Skinhead Convicted of Racial Killing," *The Desert Sun* (23 October 1993), p. A-4.

4. Michael Connelly, "Arrests of Teen Members of 'Skinhead' Faction Spell End to Spree of 'Hate Crimes,' Police Say," *Los Angeles Times* (1 November 1987), p. B-1.

5. Jack Levin and Jack McDevitt, *Hate Crimes: The Rising Tide of Bigotry and Bloodshed* (New York: Plenum, 1993).

6. Bill Wallace, "Skinhead Crimes a Growing Threat," *San Francisco Chronicle* (3 December 1988), p. A-1.

7. "Young and Violent: The Growing Menace of America's Neo-Nazi Skinheads," (New York: Anti-Defamation League of B'nai B'rith/Civil Rights Division, 1989).

8. Nick Knight, *Skinhead* (London: Omnibus Press, 1982).

9. Ibid., p. 8.

10. Ibid., p. 23.

11. "Skinheads," *Propaganda* 6, pp. 9–14.

12. Leo, p. 57.

13. Barry Came, "A Growing Menace," *Macleans* (23 January 1989), pp. 43–44.

14. Jeff Coplon, "Skinhead Nation," *Rolling Stone* (1 December 1988), pp. 54–65.

15. Ibid.

16. "Shaved for Battle: Skinheads Target America's Youth" (New York: Anti-Defamation League of B'nai B'rith/Civil Rights Division, 1988).

17. Richard E. Meyer, "The Long Crusade," *Los Angeles Times Magazine* (3 December 1989), pp. 14–31.

18. Came, p. 43.

19. "The Great Creator," in *The Intelligence Report* (Montgomery, AL: SPLC, 1999) pp. 23–29.

20. Came, p. 43.

21. Randy Blazak, "The Suburbanization of Hate: An Ethnographic Study of the Skinhead Subculture". Dissertation, Emory University (1995).

22. Marjorie Roberts, "Schoolyard Menace," *Psychology Today* (February 1988), pp. 53–56.

23. N. M. Floyd, "Pick on Somebody Your Own Size!: Controlling Victimization," *The Pointer* 29 (2) pp. 9–17.

24. Leonard Eron et al., *Learning of Aggression in Children* (Boston: Little, Brown and Company, 1971).

25. Randy Blazak, "Strained in the '90s: Skinhead Recruitment of Strained Youth," paper presented at the 1998 Annual Meetings of the American Criminological Association, Washington D.C., November, 1998.

26. "Action Program for Aryan Skinheads," pamphlet published by the New Order, 1989, p. 6.

27. "Gangs in Orange County," *Orange County Register* (21 January 1990), p. M-2.

28. Ibid.

29. Bill Wallace, "Skinhead Crimes a Growing Threat," *San Francisco Chronicle* (3 December 1988), p. A-2.

30. Ibid.

31. Tamara Jones, "Violence by Skinheads Spreads across Nation," *Los Angeles Times* (19 December 1988), p. A-1.

32. Susan Manuel, "Former UH Professor Battling Roots of Racism," *Honolulu Star Bulletin* (21 March 1989), p. B-1.

33. Randy Blazak, "Hate in the Suburbs: The Rise of the Skinhead Counterculture," in *The Practical Skeptic: Readings in Sociology,* ed. Lisa J. McIntyre (Mountain View, Calif.: Mayfield, 1999).

34. "Youth at the Edge," in *The Intelligence Report* (Montgomery, Al.: SPLC, 1999) pp. 6–12.

10

Stoner Gangs
and Satanic Youths

Diary of a Teenage Stoner

We arrived in San Diego on Monday morning about 4:00 A.M. We woke up some time in the morning about 9:00 A.M. and went to some campground and took some showers, and, guess what? We got fucked with by some dick head, whiteboy cop who started talking shit about how we can't just go in a camping ground and take showers. He asked me if I wanted to go to San Diego Juvenile Hall. He was going to give us all tickets, but Dingy paid $3.00 for each of us. So about 11:30 A.M. we went to the beach and had raw potatoes, uncooked bacon, and cold burritos, with no fuck'en drink (hard times).

After our bitch'en breakfast it started to liv'en up a little bit. We scored a case of Schaffer and headed up to Yuma, Arizona. We cruised around for a little looking for some weed. Finally, we saw some whiteboys about 6:00 P.M. at some arcade. So we asked them for some weed and Dingy pitched in $15.00 and they pitched in $10.00 so we bought a quarter. Crazy ended up dividing it and fucked them over. He gave them about three joints. Fucked up those posers' whole day. So after that we went to the store and I got a case on credit at 7:30 P.M. Bud bottles. After that Crazy took us on a little adventure to the orange fields in Yuma. We ended up turning around and found a Motel 6. After that we were kicking back, drinking beer and smoking some weed. Me and Crazy got bored, so Dingy took us to 7-11 and got a case and a half of Bud cans on credit. These people are cool about credit. But some van was chasing us for about four blocks. Finally he turned around. So about 10:30 P.M. we got back to the motel and partied some more, and passed out. We woke up in the morning at 8:30 A.M. and started drinking some more and smoking some more weed. We were all pretty hungry so Dinky took Chuck ("Loner") to the store to get some lunch meat and bread on credit. We munched down and drank till about 1:00 P.M. and left the fuck'en food.

We then went to a gas station to get a map, and the nice people gave us a case-and-a-half on credit, but I guess they changed their mind and some bitch ran after us. So we jumped in the car and bailed to a free camping ground in the middle of the desert about 2:30 P.M. We were cruising around in the desert, then went into a little town to get some shit on credit. Me and Loner got two cartons. Loner was taking a long time so I went in to see what happened and ended up getting a carton too. Then we bailed back to the desert. We ended up almost getting busted around 4:30 P.M. The fuck'en pigs found a case of beer and a half a bottle of whiskey. The license plates were covered with a red "Suicidal" (a punk band) rag. Finally, they let us go about an hour later, but they gave Dingy and homeboy Loner a ticket. They're supposed to go to court out here on March 5th. But they said, "Fuck the court." So we found a spot to camp about 6:00 P.M. Later that night about 9:00 P.M. we all went hiking but ended up getting fuck'en lost, and were fuck'en thirsty. So we seen a camper truck and asked them for some water. They gave us all water. Then we asked them how to get back to our campground, and they told us and we got back about 10:30 P.M. I ended up falling asleep and Dingy, Crazy, and homeboy Chuck kicked back in the tent listening to the radio and playing cards.

We woke up about 7:00 A.M. and Dingy, Lisa, and Chuck went to the store and got some more stuff on credit. They got some lunch meat, bread, and paid for some water and soda. After we munched out, Crazy, Chuck, Lisa and me went hiking again. We fucked around, leaving our graffiti on some rocks.

We left the camping place at 1:45 P.M. Now we headed toward that little town again for some more shit on credit. We arrived at the store. Me and Crazy kicked back in the car checking out some old ladies. There's nothing else to look at. There's not one good bitch in this whole fuck'en state. There's nothing but old people here. Dingy got some cookies and punch, and Chuck scored some beer. He ended up buying a case and a box of matches on credit. We were ready to jam, listening to "Slayer," and headed toward the Colorado River. We arrived at the river about 3:00 P.M., and just kicked back, drinking some beer. Later we all jammed to the store to get more beer. Chuck had a case in his hands but ended up tripping on the way out and fucked up his arm. We went back to the river where we were camped and started drinking again.

We woke up at 8:00 A.M. Me, Crazy, and homeboy Chuck went and walked around for a while and then went and tipped the tent over that the girls, Dingy and Lisa, were sleeping in. After that we went swimming in the river and threw Dingy and Lisa in the cold ice water.

Later we went to Alpha Beta in Blythe, California, to get some more shit on credit. Dingy got some steaks and Loner got some hot dogs and candy bars. I got a knife from Thriftys drugstore and a frisbee to fuck around with. Chuck got some lighter fluid from Thriftys and salami from Albertson's. These people are cool about credit out here. There's a few nice bitches out here—blondes.

When we got back to the river me, Crazy, and Chuck jumped in. That was a couple of hours ago. But since then it's been pretty fuck'en boring. I want to get a case on credit but fuck'en Dingy don't want to take me until later, so fuck it. It's 5:45 P.M. and it's deader than heaven. I'm just kicking back writing this journal. Crazy is playing the guitar. Dingy's making some sandwiches. Lisa's kicking back, and Chuck's cleaning *some shit that he threw on the window of the car. There's no more fuck'en beer, and we haven't had weed for about two and a half fuck'en days. That's pretty fuck'en long.*

RUNNING WITH THE HOME BOYS

This account was written by a 17-year-old juvenile who was a member of a white, teenage stoner gang from Northern California. Currently incarcerated in the California Youth Authority (CYA) for grand theft, this home boy, "Stray," wrote in his journal (which was confiscated by authorities) about activities that seem aimless but sadly are representative of the daily lives of so many of these suburban outlaws who have no direction or purpose in life.

The juvenile justice system has been quite concerned about the proliferation of teenage stoner gang members since the early 1980s. Although the term *stoner* seems to have been first attributed to the long-haired youth of the counterculture and hard-rock music era of the late 1960s and early 1970s, it was not until the advent of the heavy metal music scene in the 1980s that youth groups collectively identified themselves as stoner gang members.

According to one official, "stoner" used to refer to juveniles who used marijuana and were "stoned" all of the time, were involved in the anti-Vietnam war movement, and were part of the "tune in, turn on, and drop out generation". The stoner groups of that period presented only marginal problems for law enforcement officials through their truancy, antisocial behavior, and delinquent activity (1).

Such groups, however, have undergone a metamorphosis in the past three decades and have been increasingly implicated in violent street crimes and numerous homicides. Instead of being merely retreatist gangs noted for their drug-using, kicks-oriented subculture, these stoner gangs have become criminal gangs noted for extremely violent activity. Some also appear to have a strong interest in the occult and Satanism, as this chapter explains.

Currently over 100,000 youths are housed in correctional institutions in the United States. The most serious juvenile offenders are housed in locked-down prisonlike facilities once called Youth Training Schools, each under the auspices of their states' Youth Authority. In 1998 California, whose locked-down facility is located in Chino (some twenty miles from Cal Poly, Pomona), changed its name from the California Youth Training School to the California Youth Correctional Facility, reflecting its real function of tight security and social control. Although the facility still embraces rehabilitation as its goal in dealing with youth, in reality its main function is warehousing violent youth. Vocational training, remedial education, drug and alcohol counseling, and peer group counseling and support are optimistic goals.

Lower-level custodial facilities include the county- and state-run camps, boot camps (or shock incarceration programs), residential treatment facilities, foster care, each one listed in decreasing levels of security. Delinquents housed in the Youth Correctional Facility can be detained until they are 25 years of age. Most wards housed there are young men who are serving time for criminal activity they engaged in while a minor. Juveniles, if tried as adults for a serious crime and found guilty, may be sentenced to adult prison. However, for the years that they are still minors, they are frequently placed in the juvenile facilities and then transferred to adult prison once they are of age. Some are even placed on death row for capital offenses.

According to information provided by the California Youth Authority, stoner groups vary in size from approximately ten to forty members and range in age from 13 to 20. Their members tend to congregate in specific locations such as video arcades and shopping malls during and after school. Their locations, however, are not treated by them as "turf," nor do they defend these areas in the traditional sense as other ethnic, inner-city gangs mark and protect their areas.

The youths involved in stoner group gangs adopt a specific style of dress, including T-shirts depicting their favorite heavy metal group. They frequently attach drug and other paraphernalia to their clothing such as upside-down crosses, pentagrams, hexagons, swastikas, coke spoons, and roach clips. Their hair is frequently worn shoulder-length.

Satanic hard-core stoners, furthermore, favor Converse tennis shoes because of the five-pointed star embossed on the shoe. This they equate with the pentagram, an evil or magic symbol. Other distinctions include having satanic and other forms of occult graffiti written on their clothing such as "666" (the mark of the Devil or the beast), "All Religion Sucks," "Death to the Pigs," LSD," and "Satan is Lord."

The stoners tend to be followers of specific heavy metal groups such as Motley Crue, Black Sabbath, KISS, Twisted Sister, and many others. The deeper the juveniles become involved with the stoner group and heavy metal music, the more rebellious and hostile they become, according to authorities.

WHITE YOUTH GANGS AS CULTS

Some criminologists view stoner youngsters as belonging to new youth cults, which are both hard to identify and differ greatly from the more traditional, inner-city ethnic gangs. One management consultant firm hired by the state of California in the late 1980s to look into the new phenomenon of youth gangs as cults raised several relevant questions including: Who is involved in these youth cults and how do they identify themselves? What role does heavy metal music play in youth cult identification? What criminal and other problem activities are youth cult members responsible for? How widespread is the problem of youth cults, and why is their membership increasing? What is being done to reduce cult membership? (2)

The firm's report argues that membership in these youth cults appeared to be growing at epidemic proportions but that the number was difficult to measure because group affiliation was both secretive and hard to identify. Although heavy metal music appeared to be the most common denominator linking these youths, membership was not a direct result of identifying with this music. The report further stated that cult members can identify one another readily through their common dress: metal-spiked wrist cuffs, collars and belts, sacrilegious or anti-Christ items, and T-shirts denoting their heavy metal heroes or bands.

The report also noted several patterns that distinguished these youths from the more traditional street gangs: Most of their cult activities were secretive and more difficult to identify. The group often held an ideological linkage (such as satanic music) and engaged in more ritualistic than territorial protection. The group followed few codes with nothing considered sacred. The group's goal was not to protect but to destroy. Cult membership was predominately white and of higher economic status than that of the more common ethnic street gang members. And these groups were located in suburban rather than urban areas (3).

The report concluded that the stoner gangs' antisocial and criminal activities included using illegal drugs, abusing girls, assaulting parents, and drawing graffiti. In its most extreme form, grave robbing and the desecration of human remains and churches were some of their more bizarre activities.

The Gang Information Services Unit for the state of California distinguishes between four types of stoner gang members. Similar to the distinctions drawn between other more traditional gangs, the first type is the *wannabe* gang member who is trying to join the gang and may dress and act the part to impress the actual gang members. A second, also less serious, type is the *peripheral* gang member who gets involved when time allows but who is also attending school or holding down a job and so has other responsibilities and priorities. He may "get down" with the gang if a serious altercation warrants his presence.

Of more serious concern is the third type, the *hard-core* gang member, who lives entirely for the gang, is frequently an officer, and is responsible for planning and carrying out the gang's activities. This third type of stoner "gang banger" is the focus of the first part of this chapter. He may or may not be affiliated with a skinhead gang. A similar threat is, finally, the fourth type, the *satanic hard-core* gang member, who is involved in more ritualistic activities. This last type is also the focus of this chapter.

Similar to classification systems previously discussed, the Gang Information Services Unit (GISU) also utilizes the following criteria for classifying a minor as a stoner gang member: "The minor is a self-admitted stoner. The minor has tattoos (e.g., a pentagram, "666"), and/or satanic-type graffiti, or markings of known stoner groups on his person, clothing, or in his possession. The minor is in the company of known stoners when he is taken into custody, and, when interviewed, the minor does not deny being a stoner. Finally, the minor's name or moniker frequently appears in stoner graffiti" (4).

Stoner Gang Members in the California Youth Authority

According to a spokesperson for the California Youth Authority who was assigned to specifically work with and monitor juvenile gangs, stoner youth gangs compose only 5 percent of the total 1,200 gangs in the state. Their membership, however, appears to be growing and is of increasing concern to authorities. Furthermore, according to this same authority, skinheads are just one faction of the stoner gangs, a term or category the CYA uses to include those "Caucasian-based youth gangs which affiliate with both heavy metal and punk identities and music, and which include youth involved with satanic cults as well."

According to one report, stoner gangs are structured similarly to other inner-city, ethnic gangs characterized by criminal behavior. That is, they have a common dress, display colors, claim a name, and sport tattoos. Stoner gangs in suburban America, including skinheads, are more likely to hail from the middle class, but in other respects they are typical gang members as they come from broken homes with high instances of drug abuse and where many had been abused as children. According to this same report, the state of California has the highest level of juvenile stoner gang membership as well as the most criminally violent activity (5).

White stoner youth are housed in the State of California's juvenile facilities. Permission was given to examine the files of those individuals so labeled by the California Youth Authority. For purposes of analysis, the files of just those whites that the CYA labeled as stoner gang members were examined. Unfortunately, the term "stoners" is somewhat restrictive although it was the closest category that corresponded with the groups of youth under study.

As noted, stoner gang members, in the eyes of the Youth Authority, encompassed an array of youth, including, for instance, youth who embraced heavy metal music, sported tattoos, affiliated with skinhead or white supremacy gangs, and even embraced Satanism. The common factors that linked these individuals was their Caucasian status, their outlaw stance, and their appreciation of heavy metal music.

Using institutionalized youths in a study of this sort means that not only is one not guaranteed that all cases fit the specific category one is analyzing, but there is also no guarantee of consistency from one case to the next. Thus, information gathered by various people and agencies on the different wards may not be uniform. The researcher, in other words, may be left to draw conclusions based on insufficient and noncollaborated reports. For purposes of analysis, however, the study had to rely on the identification protocol set up by the CYA.

Then, too, there is the problem of generalizing about stoner youth from juvenile institutional settings to stoner youths found in the broader society. For these reasons and obvious limitations, the results reported should be viewed as preliminary and investigative at best.

On the positive side, however, using case files from sources such as the CYA is valuable because each file on these youths was extensive. Most of the files numbered over one hundred pages, each with detailed notes of every commitment offense; every encounter with police; and detailed accounts of each meeting with institutional-based psychiatrists, psychologists, intake eval-

uators, probation officers, and so on. Every nuance of the juveniles' prior police records, court-ordered visits and family evaluations, as well as behavior
records within the various institutions housing the wards, were systematically
and chronologically logged in these comprehensive files.

As part of the study, case files were obtained on the fifty-two male youths
who were categorized by the CYA as stoner gang members (in 1990 when
the study was undertaken). Further, the CYA also provided a comparative
printout of these stoners' patterns, along with the overall patterns of the entire
Youth Authority population, so that parallels could be drawn between the
two groups.

Besides the overall patterns provided by the CYA on both the stoners and
the general ward population, some forty items were gleaned from a detailed
analysis of the stoner gang members' files. Per the institution's use, a stoner
gang member was defined for the analysis as a "long-haired, unkempt youth
who got into trouble with the law for drug or alcohol-related activities, and
who fit one or more of the four criteria established by the Gang Information
Services Unit" as outlined previously.

For most of these delinquents, the name of their gang clearly indicated
that they were stoners, and made their identification simple. Several California stoner gangs adopt the term "stoner" within their title or affiliation, such
as the Heavy Metal Hangout Stoners of Newport Beach. Other stoner gangs
take such clearly identifiable names as Los Angeles Death Squads or LADS;
Suicidals, whose members are followers of the Suicidal Tendencies rock
group; Hitler's Youth; and True Sons of Liberty, which stands for "Lost" spelled
backwards.

PROFILES OF STONERS

According to information provided by the Research Division of the California Youth Authority, stoner gang members represent only a small fraction
(3 percent) of all the white males in their juvenile justice institutions. Not all
information was available in the files of the fifty-two stoners available for
analysis. As Table 10.1, "Profile of Stoner Gang Members in the California
Youth Authority," notes, only percentages and actual numbers for specific patterns that were included in the files were tabulated. Further, a separate column
notes the number of wards' files that did not discuss a particular item.

Stoner Gang Members Compared to Other CYA Wards

A review of the printout on the fifty-two stoners showed that their most
common commitment offense was burglary, with 70 percent incarcerated
for this offense, followed by aggravated assault, auto theft, and armed robbery. Reflecting California's overall demographics, a high percentage of the
stoner gang wards resided in Southern California (81 percent). Likewise,

Table 10.1   Profile of Stoner Gang Members in the California Youth Authority (Number of Cases = 52)

	Information Gathered from Case Files		Information Unavailable
	% Yes (Number)	% No (Number)	Total Number
Demographic Background information			
16 years old or under at admittance	42% (22)	58% (30)	(0)
Resided in Southern California	81% (39)	19% (9)	(4)
Resided in urban or suburban areas	73% (35)	27% (13)	(4)
Offense against property/drugs	74% (35)	26% (12)	(5)
Middle-class socioeconomic status	40% (11)	60% (16)	(25)
Caucasian racial background	96% (48)	4% (2)	(2)
Religious affiliation	37% (3)	63% (5)	(44)
Family Relationship			
Ward got along with father	7% (2)	93% (26)	(22)
Ward got along with mother	14% (3)	86% (18)	(31)
Presence of a stepparent	43% (20)	57% (27)	(5)
Parents abused drugs	89% (25)	11% (3)	(24)
Parents moved when ward was young	72% (38)	28% (14)	(0)
Ward was a middle sibling	47% (18)	53% (20)	(14)
Ward had been adopted	4% (2)	96% (46)	(0)
Parents were divorced	53% (25)	47% (22)	(5)
Ward had problems with parental authority	22% (11)	78% (38)	(3)
Ward reportedly sexually abused	25% (3)	75% (9)	(40)
Ward reportedly physically abused	47% (15)	53% (17)	(20)
Peer Group Influences			
Ward influenced by peers	98% (44)	2% (1)	(7)
Peers used drugs	95% (18)	5% (1)	(33)
Ward abused drugs and/or alcohol	100% (52)	0% (0)	(0)
Ward was heavy or multiple-drug user	94% (46)	6% (3)	(3)
Ward was poor achiever in school	76% (28)	24% (9)	(15)
Ward affiliated with a gang	57% (25)	43% (19)	(8)
Ward involved with satanic activity	20% (9)	80% (36)	(7)
Ward into heavy metal music	67% (8)	33% (4)	(40)
Ward affiliated with white supremacist group	24% (10)	76% (31)	(11)
Psychological and Social Issues			
Ward had work history	88% (34)	12% (8)	(10)
Ward started taking drugs under age 13	69% (22)	31% (10)	(20)
Ward previously incarcerated	96% (44)	4% (2)	(6)
Ward in special education classes	65% (13)	35% (7)	(32)
Ward attempted suicide	12% (3)	88% (22)	(27)

Ward had dropped out of school	43% (13)	57% (17)	(22)
Ward had average or above average IQ	72% (18)	28% (7)	(27)
Ward had homosexual experiences	40% (6)	60% (9)	(37)
Ward had physically or sexually abused others	52% (11)	48% (10)	(31)
Ward had history of bedwetting	23% (3)	77% (10)	(39)
Ward was hyperactive as a child	19% (8)	81% (35)	(9)
Ward had some/many psychological problems	96% (47)	4% (2)	(3)
Ward had physical problems	32% (12)	68% (26)	(14)

they more typically came from urban or suburban backgrounds, rather than from rural areas.

In more than three-fifths of the cases (62 percent), the income level of the wards' homes of these wards had been evaluated as either "adequate" or "more than adequate," based on the standard intake information completed on all wards. Stoner gang members appeared to come from slightly higher socioeconomic backgrounds than the general ward population. Further, nearly three-quarters of the stoners tested at average or above average intelligence (72 percent). Nearly all of the stoners had a work history prior to incarceration (88 percent). And all but two were Caucasian.

These patterns contrasted sharply with the "typical" CYA ward, based on the information for the entire inmate population. Generally, incarcerated youth come from lower socioeconomic backgrounds and test at below-average intelligence (based on standard IQ tests, which have been criticized for failing to account for ethnic and racial diversity). Furthermore, typical wards have had a sporadic work history prior to incarceration, if they have had a history of employment at all. And they are disproportionately non-Caucasian.

Even with an average or better-than-average IQ, the stoner gang wards were still evaluated as low or nonachievers. None of the juvenile delinquents, for instance, had yet graduated from high school. Two-thirds had been previously placed in special education classes while in the public schools prior to incarceration. Over two-fifths had dropped out of school (43 percent), with most (68 percent) leaving high school in the tenth or eleventh grade. And three-fourths (76 percent) had overall poor school achievement, which, as prior research has noted, has been demonstrated to be one of the strongest predictors of subsequent juvenile delinquency (6).

Nearly all of the wards (96 percent) had "priors," meaning that they had been arrested for some previous offense and possibly had been incarcerated in another facility or correctional program prior to their current placement within the CYA. Further, these wards were comparatively young to be housed in the more secure, higher-custody-level institutions. Two-fifths (42 percent) were 16 or under at the time of initial admittance. By contrast, the "typical" CYA ward was more often an older teenager or young adult.

Most of the stoner gang members came from small families. Half of the wards, for instance, had only one other sibling. No specific birth order differentiated the group. For those youths from larger families, however, nearly half of the stoners were middle siblings. One of the fifty-two wards had a physical handicap. Two of the wards had been adopted, according to their files. By contrast, in Wooden and Berkeys' earlier study of juvenile fire-setters, a larger number had been adopted as young children (14 percent), and adopted children have been viewed as being at greater risk to engage in delinquent acts (7).

The data clearly indicated that both alcohol and drug abuse were these stoner gang members' majors problems. For example, as the stoner profile in Table 10.1 indicates, two-thirds of these youths (69 percent) began taking (often multiple) drugs before the age of 13. These youths were drug abusers before they were even teenagers!

The Problem of Substance Abuse

All fifty-two of the wards studied had a history of abusing drugs and/or alcohol. In fact, the commitment offenses that brought them to the attention of authorities—and that sentenced them to the CYA—overwhelmingly centered around their possessing illegal drugs, selling illegal drugs, or committing crimes against property such as burglary and theft to get money to purchase drugs or alcohol.

Furthermore, these youth frequently come from multigenerational, substance-abusing families. With regard to the wards' parents, where information had been gathered, at least one parent was noted to be a substance abuser in 89 percent of the cases. In fact, in one-fourth of the cases (25 percent), the wards had parents that *both* abused drugs. Where just one parent was noted as a substance abuser, it was more often the father (57 percent for the father versus 7 percent for the mother).

Drug abuse was not just a family activity. A careful reading of their files indicated that nearly all of the stoner gang members had been strongly influenced by their peers (98 percent). And nearly all of the peers that these wards socialized with were also known by authorities to be involved with drugs. These wards, it tragically appears, had been socialized both at home and among their peer group into a pattern of substance abuse. No wonder they are called "stoners"! And the fact that the wards began abusing drugs at an early age and are considered to be both heavy and multiple-drug users (94 percent) indicates the severity of their substance-abuse problem.

John The psychiatric evaluation of one ward, "John," was fairly typical of the drug dependencies of stoner gang members. John, age 16, had a long involvement with the law prior to his commitment offense of trespassing, stealing a gun, and receiving stolen property. According to his file, during the five years preceding incarceration, he had several counts of burglary and running away from placement. He associated primarily with other delinquent individuals involved in substance abuse and had limited work experience as a landscaper.

His history of alcohol and drug abuse indicated that John had abused alcohol since the age of 9. Prior to that age he had been on Ritalin for his hyperactivity, and as a teenager he had also abused marijuana. He reported that he used both alcohol and marijuana in order to feel good. He denied that he was depressed at any time but simply wanted to feel better. He also reported having tried cocaine, crank, and speed but did not like these drugs as well and found them to be too expensive for chronic use. He had never shot up.

Academically, the ward did well in grammar school, according to information in his file. Subsequently, however, he was identified as learning disabled and was enrolled in special education classes. It was also felt, at the time, that John used the disability as an excuse to avoid responsibility for his behavior. John reported that, currently, in high school, he was getting "C" grades. According to the case report, the juvenile got along "okay" with his teachers and found it easy to ask for help when he needed it. His test scores indicated he performed at the ninth-grade level in English and fifth-grade level in mathematics. He indicated that he did not think that the drug program in prison was helping him and that the group therapy sessions were "more or less a game" and that people were "kissing up" to the staff in order to get privileges.

John was the younger of two children. His parents separated and divorced while he was an infant. Contact with his biological father had been very sporadic. His mother raised both him and his older sister as a single parent. According to his file, there was a long history of chaotic family environment. Even though there were behavior problems on the ward's part, repeated attempts to involve the family in counseling had all failed. John's family situation had changed recently when his mother had remarried. Although John had not met the current husband, he had seen pictures of him and planned to work in his stepfather's restaurant once he was released from the youth authority.

John voiced many mixed feelings about his incarceration. As he told his caseworker, "If I were on the outs right now, I would probably be doing other drugs and getting into bigger kinds of trouble. This time I have to do all the school stuff here and that helps me."

Lawson A second stoner ward, "Lawson," also came from a disruptive family life where drug taking was common, as his psychiatric report indicated.

Lawson's background indicated a chaotic history of living with his mother, who had a series of liaisons with men who abused drugs and alcohol. Since the ward was 11, he had been involved in petty theft and had been placed at several homes with unsuccessful results. When he was 13, he became involved in burglary and was again placed unsuccessfully. At 15 he violated probation, was placed in juvenile hall, and, after assaulting a supervisor there, was transferred to the Youth Training School (now referred to as the Youth Correctional Facility), the most secure of the CYA institutions.

Lawson, it appeared, had a reasonably good education, received "Bs" and "As" in his coursework, and, according to his teachers, was at least at grade level. A moderately tall, handsome, youthful-appearing, 16-year-old Caucasian adolescent, Lawson had abused nearly every drug obtainable, including crank, coke, speed, weed, gasoline, paint, acid, and typewriter whitener. His favorite drugs were weed and typewriter whitener. The ward described in detail the effects of these various agents:

> Crank for example, made me hyper, a good feeling. Coke mellowed me out. Speed provided hallucinations. Weed made me paranoid. Gas made me hallucinate and lose control and occasionally black out. Paint was the same as gas, with an additional feature of having an echo chamber phenomenon. That is, I heard sounds as if there was an echo. Acid provided hallucinations.

Lawson never knew his natural father. He was the product of an extramarital affair. The ward's stepfather (his mother's legal husband) died of a heroin overdose when Lawson was a young child. His second stepfather was an active alcoholic, and that relationship terminated due to alcohol and physical abuse. Lawson was the oldest of seven children.

Lawson's juvenile rap sheet involved charges of petty theft, second-degree burglary, violation of probation, and battery. Reported in his thick file were numerous incidents addressing the delinquent's explosively violent behavior toward not only family members and friends but also institutional staff.

Even with this background, Lawson was currently being considered for parole. If granted, he would live with his aunt rather than his mother because his mother had a recent history of cocaine abuse. She was also getting married again, and Lawson did not know this future stepfather.

As these two case studies sadly indicate, these wards have typically had a history of dysfunctional home life. Other studies of delinquent youths have noted similar patterns. In one study preadolescents who reported that they did not get along with their family and did not feel cared for had less affectional relationships, identified less with their parents, and were more likely to initiate substance use (8).

The stoner gang members in this present study followed a similar and, unfortunately, too common path. Like youth in the other studies, the wards discussed here imitated their parents' drug taking and tried to impress their peers by engaging in "adult behavior."

Like the delinquent youth in the other studies, the stoner gang members incarcerated in the CYA did not get along with their parents. Where information was available, nearly all (93 percent) stated they did not get along with their fathers, and most (86 percent) were found not to get along with their mothers. Furthermore, indicative of dysfunctional families in general, the wards shared these disturbing patterns: The parents of these wards were frequently divorced (53 percent); a stepparent was often present in the household (43 percent); and the families of these delinquent youth had often moved when the ward was quite young (72 percent), creating a disruption in the child's early years.

Physical and Sexual Abuse

Many of these male wards had experienced physical abuse within the home. Where information was available, it appeared that nearly half (47 percent) had experienced some form of physical abuse. Information on whether the wards had been sexually abused as youngsters was less frequently indicated in their files. In only twelve of the fifty-two cases was the topic of sexual abuse even mentioned. For these wards, however, it appears that for some, sexual abuse had likely been a contributing factor in their antisocial behavior.

Edward One ward that experienced physical abuse as a youngster was "Edward." The following account was taken from his psychiatric case report. Edward's commitment offense at the age of 16 was armed robbery. He claimed he committed his offense as a means of survival because his relationship with his parents was poor and he wanted to be independent. He claimed his parents had "too many petty rules" for him.

While institutionalized, Edward had had several rule infractions such as not following instructions, showing disrespect, talking during silence, being out of bounds, and possessing contraband. Edward was the third of four children of an intact marriage. According to his case file, he grew up in a fairly strict household. Punishment usually meant taking away his personal property when it conflicted with the family's moral values.

According to his mother, the ward had been a happy child until two years before his arrest when he suddenly changed, becoming more defiant and noncompliant. It was at that time that he gave up his relationship with his parents' church and began to ingest alcohol, marijuana, and other drugs.

Edward, a tall, thin, 16-year-old Caucasian adolescent, tested as above average in intelligence. Reports in his case files indicated that he expressed anger at being at CYA, blaming his parents for his incarceration. He attributed most of his problems to the authoritarian nature of his family and the family's overly strict attitudes and behavior, which resulted in his receiving many humiliating punishments as a child and young adolescent.

His parents' use of physical punishment was administered inconsistently. He believed that this accounted, in part, for the circumstances of his three brothers. His eldest male sibling currently was serving time in a federal prison for having transported drugs while in the military. His second oldest brother had just been released from jail for burglary. Edward was in the youth authority. And his youngest brother was hyperactive and had been under psychiatric care for many years.

Edward's mother and father were strict, religious individuals. The father had served his entire career in the military. His parents ruled the family with strict guidelines, according to Edward. With all four of their sons having serious behavioral problems, the parents' "strict guidelines" had not seemed to work.

Edward, besides having an extensive drug history, was also involved with a neo-Nazi stoner gang in prison. Membership in the Nazi Low Riders (NLR), he claimed, provided him with a social group he could belong to. And although he admitted to having a sense of white dominance, he felt that it was "under control" and that it did not mean "putting down other races." He believed he got along well with all ethnic groups on the hall but was not sure how the staff responded to his NLR affiliation.

Edward's treatment psychiatrist interpreted the teenage ward's antisocial behavior in this way:

> Edward is an angry young man who clearly is defiant of all authority, probably stemming from relationships with his family. Dynamically, he has incorporated authoritarian figures and this identification with them leads to his current behavior. He defends himself by joining hostile groups, attenuating somewhat the intense rage he feels within himself, but at the same time getting into difficulty. Basically, however, he is not a violent individual, but uses it to act out especially in relationship to events occurring within the family.

According to Edward's parents, prior to their son's arrest for armed robbery at a food and liquor store, he had been influenced by a neighbor boy who gave him drugs. Within the year prior to his incarceration, Edward had begun to run away and refused to accept any direction or guidance from his parents. He also began to express opinions that they were too strict and that he could not abide by their religious expectations.

Located within his case file was this written report that Edward had given the authorities upon his arrest, recounting the circumstances that led up to his commitment offense:

> I was really fed up with my parents. I felt boxed in. I planned on running away. I needed the money to live on. I found an old shotgun that might not have worked. It was rusty. I thought I could get some food money if I robbed the store. I picked one (a convenience store) I thought would be used to robbers. I went in by myself and threatened the man at the counter verbally in a way so as to cover for the unloaded gun. I grabbed the first fist full of cash I saw because I was really scared and ran. I threw the gun in a dumpster and hid until the cops quit searching. I only got $30.

Edward was apprehended later at a continuation high school because witnesses recognized him running from the store. At the time of Edward's arrest, his father was employed as a law clerk in the local county jail. Edward's case, unfortunately, was representative of many of the stoner gang members incarcerated by the youth authority.

Many of the stoner gang members in the CYA were bullies. By their late teens they had already exhibited a history of physically and/or sexually abusing other youths either inside or outside the institution (52 percent). Having also been the recipients of parental abuse themselves when they were youngsters, these wards had shifted roles from being the victim to becoming the victimizer.

Such antisocial and self-destructive behaviors—which are unfortunately learned at home—are all too common. Our nation's juvenile justice institutions and adult correctional facilities are filled with those who were abused as children and who, unfortunately, grow up in turn to abuse others.

Furthermore, both the juvenile and adult facilities seem to perpetuate these patterns of abuse as well. In an earlier study on a men's medium-security, adult prison in California, Wooden and Parker documented the pattern whereby men who had been sexually exploited and victimized ("turned out") in one institution had frequently—upon transfer—become the victimizers or aggressors on younger, vulnerable men in the institution under study (9).

Ted One stoner gang ward, "Ted," fit this profile of the physically and sexually exploited youth that, in turn, became the exploiter. According to his prison psychiatrist, Ted, age 17, had been both physically abused by his parents and sexually molested by an adult male. Ted described a chaotic and confusing family history involving multiple moves, family conflicts, and school problems.

In Ted's case file, his psychiatrist noted that the ward was quite open about being raped by an older man who had picked him up after he ran away from home. Likewise, he readily described an incident of excessive physical punishment he received at the hands of his mother and stepfather, leading to his being removed from the home. The psychiatrist concluded that Ted had a strong tendency to strike back—to get even one way or another—for wrongs done to him. It appeared he had experienced several incidents of physical abuse from his parents.

Ted's commitment offense was molesting his younger 10-year-old half-sister, who claimed that Ted had fondled her vagina and breasts. He denied the charges, attributing her lying to jealousy.

Stoner gang members, as has been noted, are of increasing alarm to authorities in California and throughout the country. Only since late 1986 have personnel who detail juvenile gangs in California begun to track these youth involved with white youth gangs. As this investigative analysis of stoner wards illustrates, these youths, besides being abused, are serious substance abusers themselves. Further, they have come from dysfunctional families where substance abuse has been the pattern. Their primary peer group consists of juveniles who are also substance abusers.

In conclusion, any attempt at rehabilitating these delinquents must address their alcohol and/or drug-related problems and dependencies, as well as the dysfunctional family and social conditions that account for their rage.

SATANISTS: DEVIL'S CHILDREN?

"No Satan Worship at This School"

This year's handbook for students at suburban Homewood-Flossmoor High School makes the rules clear: No running in the halls, no tardiness and no worshipping Satan. School officials said the rule was included in this year's handbook to protect the

*students. Officials were told by neighboring districts and Chicago police at a recent sem-
inar that interest in the occult is growing.*

*Last spring, school officials found two markings on lockers and one scuffed on a
floor that resembled "an upside-down A in a circle," a symbol of Satan worship. According to the new policy, students may be suspended for "occult or occult-related activities,"
placing such actions in the same category as "defiance of faculty authority" or "violation
of school smoking rules" (10).*

"Police Respond to Satanic Behavior
on Gatos High School Campus"

*Police went to Gatos High School before the football game Friday night. They found a
goat that had been sacrificed and hung from the crossbars. Off to the side was a pentagram symbol. Other satanic-appearing related activities have also recently surfaced. Two
weeks ago a dairy cow was reported stolen and later found sacrificed with the pentagram
symbol next to it. It had been discarded in an open field near the high school campus
where students congregate on weekends. Police have also found a number of satanic
temples in the foothills north of the high school campus lately (11).*

"Authorities Probe Satanic Link
in Teen Murder-Suicide Case"

*In November, Thomas Manning's Catholic school teacher assigned students to research
other religions. The studious 14-year-old did his paper on Hinduism but police say he
became more interested in the subject that earned friends an A: Satanism.*

*Within weeks, the All-American, neighborhood paper boy became a defiant, hos-
tile teen buried in library books on the occult and listening to heavy metal rock music.
His teachers noticed the transformation and warned his mother on Thursday. By Saturday night, mother and son were dead. Police said Manning was entranced by the occult as he stabbed his mother at least 12 times and tried to kill his father and
10-year-old brother by setting fire to their Jefferson Township house. Then he slit his
throat and wrists with a Boy Scout knife, slumping dead on bloody snow in a neighbor's back yard (12).*

As was pointed out at the beginning of this chapter, the Gang Information
Services Unit for the state of California distinguishes between the hard-core
stoner gang member and the satanic stoner gang member. According to them,
the main difference between the two groups is that the Satanist is involved in
more ritualistic activities.

One-fifth of the stoner gang members in the California Youth Authority
group of fifty-two wards had been, or continued to be, active Satanists. None
of their commitment offenses, however, were tied to crimes involving satanic
rituals. Similar to the stoners previously discussed, all of these teenage Satanists
had engaged in burglaries or robberies as their commitment offense. And all
had, like the others, a history of drug and alcohol abuse.

All the stoner wards, regardless of category, had a socialized delinquent aspect of their lives. For both the satanic cult members and the hard-core stoner gang members, the juveniles had obviously found a subculture that accepted them and often encouraged and reinforced their drug-taking and delinquent identities.

Over half the wards in the sample proudly admitted to their treatment personnel that they were still gang affiliated (57 percent). Two-thirds (67 percent) admitted listening to heavy metal music. This behavior was noted in their case files because the authorities felt such music had been a negative influence on their lives. Several of the treatment personnel specifically noted in their evaluations of these wards that a destructive link appeared to exist between these youths listening to heavy metal music and identifying with a racist skinhead or satanic lifestyle.

PROFILES OF SATANISTS

As well as could be determined from the case files, one-fifth of the stoner wards strongly identified with Satanism. One such ward, "Greg," fit the typical profile in that he both participated in satanic activity and claimed to have been part of a satanic cult. Several incidents were described in his probation report that exemplified the typical progression for youngsters who become involved with Satanism (a pattern that will be discussed at greater length shortly).

In his early teens, Greg had, according to his parents, become interested in playing the game "Dungeons and Dragons." His parents destroyed the game after they interpreted it as an evil influence. The more the minor rebelled at home, the more his parents destroyed his personal belongings. According to his parents, they confiscated what they perceived to be "all evil influences" such as his Iron Maiden, AC/DC, Judas Priest, and Ozzie Osbourne records, his evil drawings, and his *Satanic Bible*.

When questioned about his involvement with Satanism, Greg told his probation officer that his ties were limited to self-gratification and identification. He indicated he did not concern himself with satanic rituals. He studied religions and felt Satanism met his needs. He further expressed some resentment because his parents forced him to go to the Nazarene church against his wishes. Satanism was his way of rebelling and getting back at them.

Greg told this officer that he had been involved with Satanism only since the beginning of his sophomore year in school. Although he knew other youths who were interested in Satanism, his involvement, he claimed, was more of an individual activity and those other people were not really knowledgeable. Greg did admit drawing graffiti and satanic symbols such as "666," an inverted pentagram with a goat's head in it, and upside-down crosses. The minor reported that he associated these symbols with rock bands.

Even so, the following document was written by 16-year-old Greg while he was incarcerated. It was confiscated during a room search and indicated his continued, strong involvement in the satanic youth cult. This rather bizarre account was included in his case file.

The P.S.S. (Piedmont Satanic Stoners) (not its real name) is an organization within the Satanic Church and has been planned and will be started by me and P. Jay. All who enter this organization will be given names symbolic such as these.

The P.S.S. is an organization made for spreading Satan's word and the use of drugs throughout the area. Weed will be grown on land owned by the P.S.S. and coke and horse (hard drugs) will be imported on our smuggling ships. We will also have organized robbery and burglary. All these funds will go to support ourselves and our church.

On our smuggling ships will also be smuggled guns to sell to street gangs in other areas. We ourselves will not be a street gang. We will be an organization within a church. When we are released from the youth authority, P. Jay and I are going to learn the ways of the sorcerer under Anton Le Vey, the High Priest. You are also welcome to join us and to become a leader of the P.S.S.

In a huge house we the priests will all live with our women and drugs. The house will be a hot partying house, with secret tunnels and rooms behind the walls to escape from the pigs in case of a large raid. But for the most part we will have nothing to fear of the law, for our chief warrior will be a lion. Our others will be dobies (dobermans) and pit bulls trained to kill trespassers. We will also have twenty armed men and a large arsenal of guns and explosives.

Our main ceremonies will be held in the basements and hidden cellars beneath the house. The lowest cellar will be a dungeon with torturing devices and a stone altar where we shall slay our enemies in blood sacrifice. In town we will have a stone church where we will hold services. At ceremonies we shall wear the necessary items: black hooded robes, red inside for worshippers, purple and silver pentagram medallions. But on the streets our uniform shall be: a black leather jacket, black 501's, our P.S.S. bandanna on the head or around the right leg, and a black T-shirt with P.S.S. on the front.

The shirt is not necessary, and neither is the jacket in hot weather, but the 501's and bandanna should be worn most of the time. Our women will wear tight black 501's, black spandex, a tight black leather mini-skirt, a black dress cut high on the hip and low at the breast, or some other black, revealing clothing.

Everyone should always wear the stoner pentagram, and all the men in our organization will always carry a weapon. Our colors are these: black for our evil; white for our skin (as the demons said, only whites shall be in our organization); and red for the fire in our hearts and the blood on our hands. Our numbers shall be 666, for the beast we salute, and 13, for the marijuana we smoke.

Rebellion against Organized Religion

Only three of the fifty-two incarcerated stoner gang members appeared to embrace any traditional religious affiliation. Such affiliation, however, might not have been a topic that was asked of them by their intake counselors.

If a pattern emerged at all based on a reading of their files, it was that several of the wards (such as Greg) embraced Satanism as a means of embarrassing their parents. By affiliating with a controversial religious sect such as Satanism, these misguided youth seemed to get back at what they considered to be the very rigid moral code and traditional religious values established at home by their parents. Believing in and following Satan were their ultimate acts of defiance.

By affiliating with satanic cults, these teenagers were undoubtedly behaving in ways they knew would deliberately upset their families. What better way to provoke one's father (who might serve as an elder in a more mainstream church) than by closely identifying with a belief and a lifestyle antithetical to everything the father embraced?

A similar pattern was observed in another study Wooden and Berkey previously conducted on juvenile fire-setters. They found that an unusually high number of children of fire fighters (10 percent) had deliberately set fires. This behavior was explained, in part, as a means by which the youngsters retaliated against their fathers in a decidedly symbolic way. Their arsonist behavior was also viewed as a cry for help and a means of getting their fathers to pay greater attention to them (13). Thus, in a comparable way, rejecting the traditional, religious values of ones' parents and embracing Satanism was a typical pattern for several of these CYA wards, including one named "Ken."

Ken According to the prison files, Ken was a thin, 15-year-old youth with long, stringy, recently dyed hair, who paid little attention to personal hygiene. To his caseworker he appeared antagonistic and hostile and seemed to care little for authority in any shape or form.

Ken expressed interests in music, playing the guitar, partying, and witchcraft. He claimed that Satanism was a belief, not a religion. He had a special fondness for spells calling for destruction. His career objective was to play the guitar and become a musician in a heavy metal band.

Ken grew up in Southern California. His natural parents divorced when he was 2 years old, and he was reared thereafter by his mother. He claimed to have never had any contact with his natural father, a Colombian. Ken's mother remarried when he was 12. In Ken's estimation,

> My stepdad didn't like me or my sister. He'd slap me around. He would yell at me. He was constantly abusive. My stepdad was crazy. He had to go get psychiatric help. He was a Vietnam guy. I've always hated him and

I always will. He forces all of that Seventh Day Adventist church school shit on us.

Ken told his counselor that his mother was then in the process of divorcing this man and that she had a new boyfriend. He said that he was happy to see his stepdad go. Ken said, "He'd come down on me for any little thing. My mom stayed with him because he was feeding us."

Ken claimed that the relationship with his stepfather progressively deteriorated to the point that Ken decided to move out of the house when he was 14. He moved into the home of a friend who was 16 and stayed with his friend's family for six months. When asked why he left at that point, he responded, "I got kicked out when I brought home a girl who stayed for the night."

Ken then moved back home. At that time his mother was living with her new boyfriend or with a man whom Ken described as her "boss." When Ken was asked about his relationship with this new man, he replied, "Bill's kind of cool, but he starts to play God and stuff. He ain't my dad so I don't have to listen to him." The therapist interpreted this reaction as Ken's bitterness about never having had a father to really look up to. Ken made it quite clear that he was not accepting that authority from just anyone.

It was also clear, according to the therapist, that Ken had a problem with his mother's authority as well. Commenting on his mother, Ken said, "I've never really gotten along with my mom. She's always been irrational, screaming and yelling all of the time, especially if she doesn't get her way."

Ken viewed his mother as rather unstable, and, by implication, he had not respected the relationships with men that she had had. It was also clear to him that her male friends had been far more interested in her than they had been in fathering Ken. To this point he seemed, according to the therapist, to have rejected all forms of authority.

Ken also had a younger sister, Michelle, who was 14. In his opinion, "She is the only one normal enough to talk to. We argue but I can get along with her." He described himself as a "metalist stoner" and as a "lowlifer."

When asked about his partying lifestyle, Ken related it to his satanic religious philosophy, which he had studied one year prior to his incarceration when he was 14. He said that he became particularly interested after reading the *Satanic Bible,* by Anton LeVey. Ken noted, "What I liked most was not having the moral restrictions. Morals hold you down. The Satanist philosophy takes the guilt off you when you do stuff."

Ken admitted that most of his friends in high school were into drugs. He also admitted being into drugs quite heavily himself. He said without hesitation, "I've been into everything except heroin and PCP. But I like crank the best."

As far as Ken was concerned, this was an acceptable way of life. He was critical of his use of marijuana, however. He said, "I want to give up weed because of my lungs. I want to be a lead vocalist." His ambition was to be a rock star. To him, rock stars symbolized the ultimate in human achievement. Ken also told his therapist that he was not afraid of dying, claiming, "Because when

I die I think that I'll be 'a pit beast' in hell. A pit beast is a creature who had served Satan on earth and was therefore used by Satan in hell. I'll be one of those torturing the preppies and the hypocrites. Satan won't destroy those who help him. Hypocrites are the ones who'll burn."

The therapist interpreted Ken's responses as feelings of bitterness and resentment toward others (such as "preppies and hypocrites") that Ken saw as conforming to societal norms. Although Ken derided these people, he also felt sadness at not being accepted by them.

Ken was arrested for stolen property. Four days prior to his arrest, police had been called to his home, where he was apprehended for brandishing a broken beer bottle at his parents. The police report on this incident noted that Ken was "totally out of control" and that his behavior would lead one to suspect that he may have been on drugs. The police, however, did not take action at this initial disturbance.

Ken's mother said that her son had recently told her that he was "really the son of Satan and the son of the devil." He also apparently had told his mother that she simply had him "for the devil's purposes." There was no question, according to the therapist, that some of these recent incidents were of great concern to Ken's mother and her boyfriend.

With regard to Ken's behavior inside the institution, his case file noted that he had not been a behavior problem. However, he had violated hall policies such as talking during silent periods and being out of bounds. Of greater concern to authorities was his recent involvement in gang activity, including both the Nazi Low Riders (NLR) and the Supreme White Power (SWP) groups. These two factors had played a major role in preventing him from progressing in the treatment program.

Skip Other wards in the youth authority who had been involved with satanic behavior were queried about their activities. One ward, "Skip," described what would typically take place at a satanic sacrifice:

> The most common animal used was a goat which would be hog-tied, and have its throat slashed with the blood drained into a pan. The blood would then be chilled in a refrigerator for approximately three hours. Once the blood had chilled, numerous tabs of LSD would be diluted into the blood and the concoction would then be consumed by numerous people in attendance at the ritual. They said you could then "really get to see and meet the devil." The goat was then discarded after the ceremony.

Rob Another 17-year-old ward, "Rob," who resided in a rural area in Northern California, claimed that besides animal sacrifices, he had also been involved with burning crosses in front yards. He claimed that this signified the devil. He also admitted to placing in neighbors' front yards heads of decapitated cows and goats that had been sacrificed during satanic rituals. He stated that this was a common practice with satanic groups.

Rob had also been involved in sadomasochism. According to the police report, he had numerous healed scars on both arms and hands. These, he said, had been caused by razors during an "S&M" session.

According to the police, satanic cults have been active throughout the nation for many years. These groups have reputedly been involved in ritualistic homicides, child abuse and/or molestation, kidnapping, and animal mutilations, as well as many other forms of deviant and criminal behavior.

According to these authorities, Satanism, which started out as a casual fad practiced by juveniles, has now ended up as a new delinquent subculture. In recent years youths in Southern California have been apprehended for mortuary vandalism and graveyard burglary. In one instance satanic graffiti were painted on the interior walls of mortuaries, and urns containing human ashes were stolen and never recovered. In another incident members of a stoner gang entered a mausoleum and removed marble slab covers from crypts and painted satanic graffiti on the walls. And in yet a third incident, urns containing human ashes were stolen and used by stoners in satanic rituals, according to police reports.

The self-admitted stoners who were apprehended said they broke into the mausoleum, broke open several crypts, and removed and opened caskets. Body parts were removed and thrown all over the interior of the location. Body parts were also intentionally mixed together (14).

Other youths have been involved with animal mutilations. Close to the Cal Poly, Pomona, campus, remains of goats, cats, chickens, and pigeons have been found in cemeteries. All had been decapitated and drained of their blood. Several cats were found nailed to trees. Even on the campus itself, half the young goat herd one recent year, according to campus police, had been sacrificed in ritualistic fashion. Their carcasses were left at the grisly scene, but the blood had been drained from their bodies. In spring 1994, several baby pigs were also killed, and their remains were placed in a ceremonial manner.

The Passage into Satanic Behavior

One sociologist, Martin Sanchez-Jankowski, extensively studied three satanic gangs in California in the late 1980s. He was initially approached by a member of one of the satanic gangs to study their new group. He was able to chronicle events of the gang although he asked that the gang members wear masks at their rituals so that he would not know their individual identities.

Each of the three gangs Sanchez-Jankowski studied numbered about thirty. All had similar activities but had no contact with each other. All were composed evenly of both males and females. All of the members had first become involved with the satanic gangs in their late teens. All of the members had come from white, middle-class backgrounds. And all were Christian, from "high Protestant" backgrounds such as the Methodist, Lutheran, or Episcopalian faiths.

All of the youths became involved in Satanism in a "natural way," according to Sanchez-Jankowski. They had known each other before they became involved, and none were strangers nor had any been recruited. The members of each of the three satanic gangs had attended the same high schools, and shared similar musical tastes, clothing styles, and so on.

They had initially formed as social cliques to have private parties where drugs were present and sex took place. Symbols of the devil were used to counteract Christian morality, almost as a rationalization for their behavior. What started out as a fad soon developed, however, into something more serious. As parties continued, the group wanted to learn more about Satanism. The private parties shifted to "rituals," and the meetings became a "Black Mass." At this point, according to Sanchez-Jankowski, the groups shifted into more institutionalized behavior. They developed an ideology; they met, read, and discussed the *Satanic Bible.* A theology emerged with Satan as the pinnacle.

Activities now involved more ritualistic drug taking—usually hallucinogenic drugs taken three to four times an evening—and the group began at that point to sacrifice animals. Frequently, one of the members would submit to sexual activity, abuse, and pain. The rituals also involved blood letting.

According to Sanchez-Jankowski, such activities created a bond among the members. Everyone knew everyone else and their parents as well. Pictures were taken of their events for "historical records"—but this served as a social control measure as well.

Sanchez-Jankowski noted that without the historical tradition of Satanism throughout the world, these cults would not have continued. But because these members had been reading published material and were tapping into the cultural tradition, they were able to form more long-lasting institutions (for example, the Church of Satan).

Sanchez-Jankowski concluded that these patterns suggest that cult formation can occur in quite natural ways. People do not have to exhibit psychopathological tendencies before embracing Satanism. All in all, according to his observations, it took approximately two years for the teenage group to shift from a fad into a full-fledged cult (15).

Types of Teenage Satanists

Not all youths involved in the satanic scene are equally committed to witchcraft and pagan rituals. For points of comparison (based on material provided by a student who, although not a Satanist, had numerous job-based interactions with them while she was in college), three distinct types of teenage Satanists can be delineated (16): the *soft-core* Satanists, the *noncriminal hard-core* Satanists, and the *criminal hard-core* Satanists.

Soft-Core Satanists The soft-core Satanists are usually younger than the other two types, ranging in age from 12 to 16. Although typically male, groups also sometimes include a few females. Generally they are from the same social backgrounds as members of the other two groups. The soft-core Satanists frequently are underachievers although above average in intelligence. They are generally sociable but easily angered and suffer from low self-esteem.

Soft-core Satanists get involved in Satanism as a means to upset, provoke, and embarrass their parents. Their anger, which is rooted in frustration, often is directed toward their family. These young people—who are often the product of "religious" homes—begin to feel they are living in a world full of hypocrites. This feeling usually begins as the teen matures and begins to think independently. As this happens, two things occur almost simultaneously. First, the anger and frustration build. Second, the child begins asking questions about Christianity that are not supposed to be asked. This is because many religious teachings are accepted on faith, and such questions usually have no answers.

As the questions mount and the intensity of the anger builds, this young person with enough intelligence to get into trouble (and not enough to get out of it) begins looking for trouble. About the time these people begin to experiment with drugs, they also try to find the antithesis of Christianity. They find it in Satanism.

Soft-core Satanists usually "practice" magic or Satanism with a small group of friends who also want to do what will anger their parents. For the most part, they only know what they have read in LeVey's book or in H. P. Lovecraft's *Necronomicon*. As such, they do not have access to what sets the stage for the hard core.

These youths in many ways are crying for help. Unfortunately, help is not what they get. Their actions—accompanied by heavy metal, marijuana, and alienation—are usually dealt with far too harshly by their parents and other authority figures, such as teachers. Such reactions and labels further alienate these juveniles, who retaliate by moving more deeply into the lifestyle, in a pattern known by sociologists as *labeling theory*, whereby a youth progresses from primary into secondary deviance.

Satanism, heavy metal, and drugs are merely symptoms of underlying family issues. However, they are usually thought of as the causes. More often than not this is not so. Alienation sets in long before the teen resorts to satanic behavior.

The parents of these children deny the trouble their teens are facing and do not address the issue until it reaches the boiling point. Faced with a youngster who is dabbling in Satanism, the parents' responses seem to determine whether that youngster will progress into one or the other of the next two types.

If the parents kick their child out of the house at the first sign of satanic-related behavior, for instance, that action may force the child into even greater involvement. It is critical that the family work through the other issues and concerns that the family as a unit is experiencing. In other words, a youngster's involvement in satanic behavior is not the only concern facing these often dysfunctional families. Most families, however, seem to deal with the symptoms and not the problem. This merely accentuates the pattern, pushing some children even further into the satanic realm. The kids have typically gotten behind in school, which compounds the issue as well.

At this point family therapy is essential, with honest, open communication and with each family member listening to what the others have to say. There is a need to establish programs such as Parents of Punkers to assist these families whose children are involved in soft-core Satanism.

Noncriminal Hard-Core Satanists As with the first type, these people begin soft core. However, they usually make an "adjustment," embracing more of a satanic identity while continuing to successfully function within society. They are typically older adolescents to young adults, ranging in age from 15 to 24.

These youths, composed equally of males and females, are average in scholastic work. Their satanic involvement may be an attention-seeking device, as they are typically flamboyant. They do not commit criminal acts, however. These are the Satanists who follow Le Vey to the letter. They seem to believe in Satanism for its valuing of the profane, but they generally do not believe in Satan as a deity per se. For them, Satanism is a religion (or cult) based upon worldly pleasures.

Criminal Hard-Core Satanists The third group, examples of which are the several CYA wards discussed earlier, come from all types of backgrounds, socioeconomic classes, and statuses. They are both underachievers (youngsters who are quite bright) and overachievers (those who have scholastic difficulty).

Some of these juveniles exhibit severe sociopathic characteristics. They are manipulative, suffering from low-impulse control. Typically, these are the ones that receive the media coverage. They commit human and animal sacrifices; assault; kidnapping; and sexual, physical, and mental abuse, among other atrocities.

These are the people who begin in soft core but, because of psychological and social dysfunction, become criminal. The acts this group commits go beyond a cry for help because they lose touch with what is appropriate. Sometimes these people come from abusive backgrounds themselves.

Unlike the soft core who practice alone or in small groups, this criminal hard-core type practices in "covens of 13." The covens are characteristically secretive, ritualistic, manipulative, and controlling. Initiates are typically required to prove themselves by acting as slaves to the coven and the rites, allowing themselves to be sexually and physically abused. Members are required to participate through coercion and blackmail.

The covens follow the *Satanic Bible* and the *Necronomicon* and carry the rites to an extreme. In the case of Le Vey's book, they often distort what he has written. Hard-core Satanists also use other forms of "high" magic from Norse or Egyptian myths.

Signs of Satanic Activity

In the past several decades numerous seminars have been given throughout the country by law enforcement officials, alerting authorities to the dangers of satanic cults and instructing them on how to look for signs of such groups in their jurisdictions. Pat Metoyer, of the Los Angeles Police Department, in a presentation, "Witchcraft, Devil Worship, Satanism, and Satanic Cults," distinguished between the *self-styled Satanists* and the *satanic cults.*

Self-styled Satanists were frequently young people between the ages of 12 and 24 who became involved by buying the *Satanic Bible;* by renting movies such as "Rosemary's Baby," "Damien," and "The Exorcist"; by listening to heavy metal music by groups such as Ozzy Osbourne, AC/DC, and Black Sabbath; and by consuming drugs. On the other hand, the *satanic cults* were secret groups of young people who engaged in criminal activity including animal sacrifices, grave robbery, church desecration, cannibalism, drug taking, and forced sexual activity (17).

According to Metoyer, the profile of the satanic cult member was one between the ages of 12 and 24; a Caucasian who had a high IQ; who was typically defiant, angry, a loner, and isolated; and who was a multiple-drug user—similar to those examined in the CYA. Frequently, these youngsters were overly involved with their music. They came from broken homes and were highly impressionistic, according to Metoyer. Their parents typically had problems with their children being isolated. The boys, for instance, retreated to the privacy of their own bedrooms to set up their own world.

Members of satanic cults, in contrast to the typical juvenile delinquent, come from higher socioeconomic backgrounds, in part because of the expenses involved. Dabbling in Satanism and the occult involves making purchases and obtaining implements. The activity is therefore often restricted to youngsters who have access to funds to buy drugs and satanic paraphernalia (18).

Other police officials have studied the rise of satanic cults as well. Sandi Gallant, of the San Francisco Police Department, calls teenagers' interest in Satanism "a way to get everything they want right now." Teenagers involved with Satanism also express the view that they do not have a future because of the violent nature of our society. Gallant contends that involvement of the young with Satanism began to mushroom in the early 1980s and that there may now be nearly 2,000 satanic groups in the United States with as many as two million members (19).

One spokesperson for the conservative Christian Research Center in Tustin, California, argues that Los Angeles County alone has at least 5,000 hard-core Satanists and that they have engaged in mock human sacrifices, drug abuse, kidnapping, sexual violence, and animal mutilations. Dr. Walter Miller, director of the center, is quoted as saying that at least 15,000 recorded cases of animal mutilations occurred during the 1980s (20).

Not every public official views such delinquency as satanic-cult-related, however. Many law enforcement officials believe that there remains little credence to satanic-motivated delinquency and argue that delinquent acts should be handled on a case-by-case basis. Furthermore, these officials contend, the satanic-related acts of some juveniles are sensationalized and distorted by the media. As one official explained, "Much of the interest in Satanism remains a mere fad, a trendy spin-off from the culture-wide interest in the occult. And some of it is sheer fantasy produced by drug-induced paranoia" (21).

The Influence of Heavy Metal

One common element that Satanists share is their interest in heavy metal music. One observer noted that the emergence of heavy metal music in the late 1960s corresponded with the formation by Anton Le Vey of the Church of Satan in 1968 (22). This observer also argued that heavy metal music contains satanic messages that are very important to juveniles because these youngsters often have "poor self-images." Teenagers who succumb to these influences typically are social outcasts and are frequently "the type of kids who aren't in step with their peers."

Heavy metal groups, this observer believes, are frequently linked to Satanism. For instance, AC/DC stands for Anti-Christ/Devil's Children. The heavy metal musical group KISS stands for Kids (or Knights) in Satan's Service. And the popular musical group Black Sabbath refers to the day of Satan worship (23).

Furthermore, the satanic sign made with the index and little finger extended can frequently be seen in many heavy metal rock videos and stoner gang member graffiti. Kids at concerts shout, "NATAS" (Satan spelled backward). Others contend that there are messages on records dealing with Satan and that when the records are played backward—a technique known as backward masking—the messages can be heard. This backward communicating appears to be an important aspect of satanic cults and serves as part of the mystique many stoners find attractive. The concept of backward writing is reputed to have originated with the Church of Satan (24).

Satanists and Traditional Gangs

Lawrence C. Trostle, who has extensively studied one stoner gang in the Los Angeles area, contends that stoner gangs—though known to congregate in specific areas—have no extended claim to specific land or turf. In this regard they tend not to feud or engage in gang wars with other gangs. Because of this nonterritorial pattern, stoner gangs are viewed as the "gypsies" of the gang subculture (25).

This is particularly true for stoner gangs that are also satanic cults. Frequently, the more traditional ethnic and neighborhood gangs stay clear of the Satanists, viewing them as "loco" or crazy. Also, more traditional, ethnic gang members do not see stoners as "real men" but as "wimps" and "sissies." Consequently, these stoner gangs do not pose a threat to them.

Typically, the stoners and Satanists frequent one particular location one week and move on to another the next. In this sense stoner gangs are location-oriented and not territorial. Such locations in Southern California include shopping malls, arcades, video stores, record shops, fast-food restaurants, cemeteries, freeway underpasses, and abandoned rock quarries.

Thus, when they encroach upon a traditional gang's turf, stoners or Satanists are not perceived as invaders or trespassers. In this sense, satanic cults have generally been left alone by the other types of gangs that may also be located in the area.

Youth at the Movies—Kids behind Bars

Most representations of youth incarceration are exploitative, such as 1986's *Reform School Girls*. Although the "prison film" has become a legitimate genre, few have dealt with youth. One made-for-TV movie, *Prison for Children* (1986), came close. The definitive "youth behind bars" movie is *Bad Boys* (1983). In it Sean Penn plays a juvenile offender who has to learn quickly about the inmate hierarchy and prison rape. The film portrays the way that scared children can be transformed into serious criminals inside an institution.

Some probation officers working gang detail have noted that some juveniles become stoner gang members so that they will not be required to join the more traditional ethnic street gangs of their neighborhoods. And other juveniles, upon parole, join stoner gangs to avoid breaking their parole restriction against affiliating with their own ethnic gangs (26).

Other observers, however, have argued that stoners, including Satanists, do fit the profile of a bona fide gang. For one, stoners claim certain areas as their own. Territorial boundaries, however, are used in a slightly different context by these stoners. Whereas street gang members claim certain geographical locations or portions of the community as their territory, the stoner groups will claim certain musical groups or types of music as their "territory."

Second, in terms of distinctive dress, the heavy metal accessories and T-shirts cater to the stoners' egos just as the specialized dress of African-American and Hispanic gang members set them apart. Third, the usage of graffiti is another characteristic both groups share. Both types of gangs use graffiti to mark their presence, with the Satanists often marking their areas with a "666" (27).

NOTES

1. Dennis McLellan, "Spikes and Studs: Tipping the Scales against Heavy Metal, Punk," *Los Angeles Times* (21 February 1985), p. V-1.

2. Lynne P. Cannady, "Youth Gangs as Cults," (Sacramento, CA: Evaluation, Management and Training, 1989).

3. Ibid.

4. "Stoners and the Occult," pamphlet (Los Angeles County Sheriff's Department, East Los Angeles Gang Unit "Operation Safe Streets"; Los Angeles, 1986).

5. Esteban P. Castaneda, "Report on Youth Gangs," (Sacramento, CA: State Task Force on Youth Gang Violence, 1988).

6. Martin Gold, "School Experiences, Self-Esteem, and Delinquent Behavior: A Theory for Alternative Schools," *Crime and Delinquency* 24 (1978), pp. 29–45.

7. Wayne S. Wooden and Martha Lou Berkey, *Children and Arson: America's Middle Class Nightmare* (New York: Plenum Press, 1984).

8. Jonathan Shedler and Jack Block, "Adolescent Drug Use and Psychological Health," *American Psychologist* 45 (May 1990), pp. 612–30.

9. Wayne S. Wooden and Jay Parker, *Men behind Bars: Sexual Exploitation in Prison* (New York: Plenum Press, 1982).

10. "No Satan Worship at This School," *Los Angeles Times* (9 September 1987), Part V, p. 10.

11. Frederick M. Muir, "Police Respond to Satanic Behavior on Gatos High School Campus," *Los Angeles Times* (16 August 1992), p. A-1.

12. "Authorities Probe Satanic Link in Teen Murder-Suicide Case," *Los Angeles Times* (11 March 1989), p. A-1.

13. Wayne S. Wooden and Martha Lou Berkey.

14. Lawrence C. Trostle, "Stoners Emerge as Demonic Delinquents," *California Peace Officer* 5 (October 1985), pp. 20–21.

15. Martin Sanchez-Jankowski, "Youth Culture and Satanic Cult Formation," paper presented at the Western Society of Criminology meetings, February 1988; Las Vegas, NV.

16. The typology of Satanists and some of the discussion that follows, which is presented in edited form, was provided by Lisa Collins.

17. Pat Metoyer, "Witchcraft, Devil Worship, Satanism, and Satanic Cults," paper presented at the We-Tip National Conference, April 1988; Ontario, CA.

18. Esteban P. Castaneda, "Report on Youth Gangs" (Sacramento, CA: State Task Force on Youth Gang Violence, 1988).

19. Lawrence C. Trostle, "The Stoners: Drugs, Demons and Delinquency," Ph.D. diss. (Claremont Graduate School, Claremont, CA, 1986), p. 139.

20. Ibid., p. 140.

21. Ibid., p. 144.

22. Metoyer.

23. Richard Valdemar, "Stoners, Satanism, and the Occult," paper presented at a conference sponsored by the California Youth Authority, 7 May 1986; San Luis Obispo, CA.

24. Ibid.

25. Trostle.

26. Castaneda.

27. Valdemar.

PART III

Societal Responses
and Trends

11

Reactions to Youthful Offenders

"The Rise in Kids Who Kill"

Dwayne Wright was 17 when he spotted Saba Tekle on a highway in northern Virginia, decided he wanted to have sex with her and pumped a bullet into her back when she tried to run away. Wright, now 19, awaits execution on Virginia's Death Row.

Five New Jersey teen-agers, two of them 14, allegedly strangled a pesky classmate with an electrical cord as he recited the prayer Hail Mary in his car. Three of the boys admitted to the murder in April and will testify against the others.

Two Pasadena juries Friday found teenagers David Adkins and Vincent Hebrock guilty of murder in the shotgun slayings of three girls—including Adkins' girlfriend—during a party at one of the girls' homes. A witness says Hebrock, who was 17 at the time, boasted to Adkins, who was 16: "Yeah, dude, we smoked 'em all" (1).

"Another Day in Court for Rock Music"

Rock music is back in the courtroom—on death charges. Six weeks after the British rock group Judas Priest was absolved of causing the suicide-related deaths of two Sparks, Nevada, youths, fellow British rocker Ozzy Osbourne faces similar charges in Macon, Georgia.

In two separate product-liability cases that are being considered jointly in a deposition session this week in a Macon federal court, subliminal messages allegedly hidden in Osbourne albums are blamed for the suicide shootings of two teenagers (2).

As *Renegade Kids, Suburban Outlaws: From Youth Culture to Delinquency* has noted, America's youths are faced with a multitude of choices in terms of adolescent identities. Many of the problems these youngsters face stem from our society's push to make children grow up quickly. The portrait of today's child, in the words of one observer—"dressed from birth to look like a miniature adult, pressured to read before kindergarten and left unsupervised after school"—is causing great alarm among psychologists and sociologists who suggest this trend is symptomatic of an underlying societal disregard for their well-being (3).

David Elkind, for one, contends that the hurried child sometimes develops into the hurried teen, expected not only to achieve at school but to fill in for the absent parents at home (who are forced to work). Elkind writes, "Many parents, schools and much of the media have been hurrying children to grow up fast, but they also have been abandoning teenagers" (4).

Other observers contend that children today are getting the short end of the stick. An ever-growing number of children living in poverty, increases in infant mortality, childhood obesity and lack of fitness, delinquency and teenage pregnancy, and deteriorating public education are all thought to account for the increased problems facing this generation of youngsters.

Furthermore, today's young children are bombarded with adult experiences and violence on television and in the movies, making them less sensitive and more sexually precocious than earlier generations of young people. As one expert notes, "Given the high divorce rate, children often have a front-row seat while watching one or both parents date" (5).

Forced to grow up too fast has also meant, according to the experts, that teenagers do not have the proper adult guidance, direction, and support they need to make a healthy transition to adulthood. Many are being pushed to act like adults long before they are ready. One Southern California study found that 80 percent of high school seniors held jobs. Although much public focus has dealt with the obvious return of mothers to the work force in the past twenty-five years, little attention has been given to the effects of the teenage entrance into the work force in the same period (6).

Other observers note that in addition to being rushed into adulthood, this generation seems increasingly intolerant of others. In Southern California, for instance, residents, young and old, of multiethnic Los Angeles County, are finding it increasingly difficult to cope with one another's racial and cultural differences. The Human Rights Commission has found a marked increase in hate crimes. In its report to the County Board of Supervisors, the commission noted that hate crimes, motivated by racism, religious bigotry, and intolerance of homosexuality, have been steadily rising across the county since 1986.

In 1989, 378 hate crimes were reported for the county. The commission attributed the increased intergroup tension to demographic changes across the county as well as to a rise in the general level of violent crime across the nation. African-Americans are victims in more than half of all racial crimes, Jews in 9 of 10 religious hate crimes. Violence against homosexuals and Asians is also rising, according to the report (7).

Such behavior is not limited to Southern California. In a 1993 book on the subject, *Hate Crimes: America's New Menace,* criminologist Jack Levin argues that such behavior has spread across the United States in epidemic proportions (8). In addition, Europe, from Germany to Bosnia, has been racked with a rampage of "ethnic cleansing" and violence against ethnic minorities. Election results in Russia have brought to power leaders of a right-wing nationalistic movement. Ethnic cleansing may tragically sweep beyond the borders of Bosnia.

In the United States, meanwhile, equally alarming news has been the sad statistic of the rise in the number of kids who kill. Juveniles, it appears, are arming themselves more than ever. According to FBI crime statistics, the number of juveniles arrested for homicide between 1981 and 1990 increased 60 percent nationwide. This far outpaced the 5.2 percent increase among adults (9). Furthermore, an unprecedented 2,003 youths were arrested for murder and nonnegligent manslaughter in 1990. And although juveniles are still far less likely to kill than adults, one in every six people arrested in the United States for murder in 1990 was under 18 (10).

How has society attempted to address some of these trends? And what have been some societal responses from the *school system, the mental health agencies, the juvenile justice network,* as well as *concerned citizen groups* to the varied youth styles discussed in this book? These various societal responses are the concerns of this chapter.

THE SCHOOL SYSTEM RESPONDS

On a typical day each month, nearly one of every three high school students in some areas of the country deliberately missed one or more academic classes. According to experts, soaring truancy rates reflect breakdowns in families and schools, leading to more school dropouts and more neighborhood crime. Educators echo the concern, saying they are faced with more broken families, more poverty, more joblessness, and more homelessness these days. Schoolwork takes a back seat when a kid is fighting to survive, they say.

To combat truancy some school districts have resorted to "bribing" the students. One school, for instance, makes students with perfect attendance records for each month eligible for a drawing with cash prizes. However, only 79 of the 1,600 students qualified in the month of May during a recent year (11).

Some teachers contact parents when a student starts missing class, but just contacting the parents does not always do the trick. As one counselor noted, "Parents of these students frequently respond by blaming the school, stating, 'My kids are not going to class, so why don't you do something? It's your responsibility.'"

Truancy is not the only problem. More often schools are bombarded by acts of crime. According to the California Department of Education, during one academic year in the late 1980s, 1,005 out of 1,028 school districts in the entire state reported a total of 157,597 incidents of crime on the school grounds. These crimes varied from assault, robbery, and burglary to murder. Notably, 71,351 of these incidents were against property, resulting in a total dollar-loss of $22,878,540.00 (12).

To combat such high crime rates on school campuses, the state has developed a program, "Operation Safe Schools," which sets up early intervention, prevention, and education programs tailored to assist school districts in maintaining safe, secure, and peaceful school environments.

According to the program's preliminary evaluation, there have been considerable benefits for students in the participating school districts. Benefits included improved attendance; improved academic achievement level and higher test scores and grades; an increased number of students going on to higher education; fewer discipline problems; less violence and vandalism; decreased drug and alcohol abuse; reduced negative peer pressure; increased morale level of students and faculty; improved student self-image; enhanced decision-making abilities; and goals that were set and achieved.

"Project Safe" at "Raging High"

One of the high schools analyzed in an earlier chapter ("Kicking Back at 'Raging High'") was selected to participate in this innovative program. Identified as "Project Safe" on this particular campus, the success of the program serves as a model for other school districts looking for ways to improve their school environment.

In the eighteen months prior to funding for "Project Safe," the city in which Raging High School is located had experienced numerous incidents of drug and alcohol offenses. In fact, the police department reported over 1,000 drug arrests resulting in the seizure of drugs valued at almost $1.5 million.

During this same period, juvenile felony arrests for this suburban community rose by more than 60 percent. Most of these were for possession of drugs or were drug-related offenses such as assaults, auto thefts, burglaries, and possession of weapons. Furthermore, according to police officials working gang detail, there had also been an alarming 300-percent increase in gang activity in the city in that same period. Because the city had only one high school, almost all of the juveniles arrested were students in the target area.

These delinquent activities in the community obviously had an impact on the school system. In 1988 the school district reported 176 assaults, 56 arrests for substance abuse, and criminal damage of property totaling over $21,000. Furthermore, the high school suspended 339 students for violations of the California Education Code. With a total student enrollment of 2,757, this represented 12 percent of the student body (13)!

The reasons for school suspension were possession of drugs or alcohol, selling drugs, possession of weapons, robbery, extortion, and damage to property. The work of an undercover police officer on campus led to the arrest of nineteen students in one crackdown. All of the student arrests were drug-related. In fact, during the academic year 1987–1988, 56 students were apprehended at school for use or possession of alcohol; 52 for use or possession of marijuana; 15 for use or possession of other drugs; 36 for drug sales; and 4 for driving under the influence.

Results of a Student Survey A survey of the students at Raging High School, conducted by the counseling staff in 1988, indicated that 68 percent of the student body reported consuming alcohol periodically; 31 percent smoked marijuana; and 26 percent reported using cocaine or amphetamines.

The survey data also revealed that the majority of students agreed with the statement that drugs were readily available on campus. Further, students who participated on a panel set up to discuss the findings revealed they had used cocaine in class; reported that students regularly smoked marijuana in the bathrooms; and stated that students could buy virtually any drug on campus.

The students also indicated that they did not know of resources within the larger community to assist them in dealing with their drug or alcohol-related problems. A majority of students also indicated that they did not feel comfortable going to their teachers or to other staff members to discuss such problems.

Student drug abuse was also noted by the faculty. A similar survey given to faculty and staff noted their opinion that 53 percent of their students used alcohol and drugs from two to three times a week. An overwhelming majority of the faculty (80 percent) felt that more school resources, personnel, and time should be devoted to solving this problem.

Like the other suburban high schools discussed earlier, Raging High comprised students from fairly affluent family backgrounds. Only 5 percent of the student body, for instance, came from families that received financial aid (AFDC or Aid for Dependent Children). The ethnic population of the school district was predominantly Caucasian (73 percent), followed by Hispanic (13 percent), Asian (8 percent), African-American (5 percent), and other ethnic groups (1 percent).

Besides the problems with student drug and alcohol abuse, and even with a predominantly middle- to upper-middle-class student body, the school district had seen an alarming increase in the number of gangs. In one year alone, the number of gangs identified on campus had increased from three to twelve, according to a police official assigned to gang detail at the high school.

Half of the twelve gangs composed of students on campus were Hispanic (with names such as Ninth Street Pimps, Raging Ghost Town, Playboy Z, Calle Nueve Raging, Raging Los Olivos, and Empire Villains) (some names have been changed). Two Raging High School gangs were African-American gangs (Raging High Crips and Cyco Block Gangsters). Three of the gangs were white gangs (Team Mad Dog; Raging Local Stoners, a satanic cult gang; and Master Race Youth, a racist skinhead gang). One gang was an ethnically mixed street gang (Tough City Boys).

Implementation With major drug problems as well as the proliferation of gangs, Raging High was one of the school districts funded by California in

1989 to develop strategies to address these critical concerns. A licensed school clinical psychologist (a former student at Cal Poly, Pomona, and the contact with this school) was hired as project crisis coordinator for Project Safe. The team also included a police officer assigned to gang detail and who also served as liaison officer with the school and the police department, and one other psychologist; these three professionals developed a series of workshops aimed at concerned parents.

Under the auspices of the local PTA chapter, the three discussed topics such as warning signs (for example, student dress, behaviors, attitudes, and self-esteem); interventions (for example, discipline, parental supervision, out-patient counseling, hospital programs, and probation); and successful parenting skills.

The crisis coordinator also assisted the regular school counseling staff and instructional faculty by revising the "Student Referral Form" so that early signs of student problems would be more readily identifiable. All faculty were encouraged to take a critical look at their students and to report to the counseling center or for private referral to the crisis coordinator any student who exhibited four to five symptoms from the problem areas listed on the form.

Student Referral Form

Grades. Drop in grades, decline in quality of work, obvious failure, lack of motivation (apathy);

School Attendance. Excessive absences, excessive tardies, excessive class cuts, suspension(s);

Extracurricular Activities. Loss of eligibility, lack of involvement, student drops out of activity;

Physical Appearance. Glassy or bloodshot eyes, loss of coordination, slurred speech, bad hygiene, sleeps in class, physical complaints, physical injuries, staggering or stumbling, smells of alcohol or pot, lethargic;

Disruptive Behavior. Defies rules, needs constant discipline, irresponsible, denies responsibility, blames others, fights, cheats, smokes, obscene language or gestures, gets attention dramatically, cries in class, often in unauthorized areas, hostile attitude toward authority, hyper or nervous;

Other On-campus Observable Behavior. Sits in parking lot, drug or alcohol conversations, talks freely about drug or alcohol use, avoids contact with others, erratic behavior day-to-day, drug-related doodling, changes friends or has negative relationships, acts defensively, sudden popularity, belongs to older social group, hypertension, refuses touching, uncommunicative, drug-related clothing or jewelry, sexual looseness or intimacy in public, withdrawal or becoming a loner, time disorientation, unrealistic goals, inappropriate responses, possible depression, seeks adult advice about "hypothetical" situations, draws satanic/death/gang symbols; and

Off-campus Behavior. Family relationships, runaway, job problems, law enforcement involvement, other (14).

To implement the Project Safe program, all district staff members participated in an eight-hour in-service training program on adolescent chemical dependency in the 1989 fall semester. The staff was instructed on the policies and procedures for intervention and referral of high-risk students to the Project Safe staff. Parents were also educated on youth substance abuse and informed about the referral and intervention process. In new drug education classes set up in the school, even the students were instructed on how to identify fellow students who were chemically dependent. Students were encouraged to refer themselves, their friends, and even their parents to Project Safe for counseling and assistance.

Once a student was referred, the Project Safe crisis coordinator performed assessments and interventions. After evaluating the severity of the problem, appropriate treatment was determined and the student was often referred to an outside agency, physician, or therapist. The two-year funded project also served as a resource center and monitored available community services to make effective referrals.

In summary, the Project Safe crisis coordinator filled the gaps needed in combating student substance abuse. The crisis coordinator did not handle discipline, class scheduling, career counseling, or other day-to-day functions of the existing counseling staff. Instead, by working in conjunction with counselors and teachers, the crisis coordinator and the Project Safe program were set up to combat student drug abuse, drug-related crimes, and gang activity.

Other Programs

Other innovative programs have also been introduced on high school campuses to address social concerns. One such program, "Hands across the Campus," was developed by the Los Angeles Unified School District and the American Jewish Committee with the stated goal of "learning respect for diversity."

Hands across the Campus develops awareness of the roles and contributions of people of various cultural, racial, and ethnic backgrounds and awareness of the dangers posed by organized hate groups. One program component was to develop a social science elective class that helps students relate course content to their personal experience and the pluralistic society of which they are a part.

It also includes planned activities outside the classroom. Among the many successful programs are symposia designed to improve racial harmony; plays and assemblies that focus on intercultural and interethnic themes; international fairs; and essay, speech, and poster contests to foster community sensitivity and tolerance.

School programs have also been established to reduce bullying. Based on models developed in Norway, multiple-level programs have been effectively adopted in the United States. These programs focus on the following: (1) schoolwide interventions that include teacher training and increased supervision, (2) classroom-level interventions, such as classroom rules and meetings with parents of bullies, and (3) individual-level interventions, such as discussions with bullies and victims (15). One such program is the "Bullying Prevention Project," sponsored by the Institute for Families in Society at the University of South Carolina. It targets elementary and middle school youth and uses role-playing exercises to teach students how to handle bullying scenarios (16).

THE MENTAL HEALTH SYSTEM RESPONDS

Overall, inpatient hospitalization for children under age 18 increased from 82,000 to more than 112,000 in the 1980s. Some of these adolescents are seriously disturbed and suffer from severe or acute mental disorders, or they have drug or alcohol problems. But in other cases, according to some critics, they may be simply rebellious teenagers struggling with their parents over issues such as dating, what music they can listen to, and other issues once thought of as typical "growing pains" (17).

Some of these youngsters have been held behind locked doors, virtually without civil rights. In the late 1980s the American Psychiatric Association condemned unnecessary hospitalization, calling for a wider range of affordable outpatient services.

Adolescent treatment hospitals have become big business. Large corporate chains such as Charter Medical Corporation, the Hospital Corporation of American, and National Medical Enterprises have expanded their facilities throughout the country as local laws allow. According to the National Institute of Mental Health, in 1980 only 184 private psychiatric hospitals had specialized programs for minors; in 1988 there were 450 (18).

Because insurance companies usually do not reimburse for less restrictive treatment such as outpatient therapy, private hospitals have found it lucrative to provide inpatient treatment. Typically such programs, covered by the parents' insurance policy, charge up to $900 per day for adolescents who might otherwise be treated just as well (or better) through outpatient therapy. Some policies cover up to 100 percent of inpatient costs. By contrast, insurance generally reimburses a much smaller percentage of the expenses of outpatient care. Therefore, it is often more convenient and less of a financial burden for parents to commit their children than to get them effective counseling. Most communities do not offer intensive home-based services. Parents are forced to choose between once-a-week outpatient counseling at best and full hospitalization. Furthermore, evidence suggests a correlation between the length of time a minor stays confined in such a facility and the number of days health insurance provides for inpatient care. The implication is that many facilities keep the minor only as long as the insurance policy can cover the expenses (19).

Marketing has played a part in the business of treating these adolescents. As another critic notes, hospital advertising often implies easy answers and gives the worried parent the impression that the program can "fix" anything. One local program in Southern California even set up employee-incentive programs to gather new business, offering Caribbean cruises for staff members who generated the largest number of hospital admissions. The contest was referred to by its critics as "bounty hunting" (20).

Newsweek magazine, in a comprehensive article—"Committed Youth: Why Are So Many Teens Being Locked Up in Private Mental Hospitals?"—noted that the "illness" for which many teenagers are committed is usually not the kind commonly associated with institutionalization. Instead, the teenagers are admitted for behavioral problems, "conduct disorders," or "adolescent adjustment reaction." These confined youths, according to the article, are frequently engaged in some form of antisocial behavior and do not suffer from delusional psychosis.

The article also cites the American Academy of Child and Adolescent Psychiatry's advice to parents in deciding whether to hospitalize a son or daughter. The academy offers eleven suggestions for parents, including raising such issues as the treatment alternatives other than hospitalization; the responsibilities of the psychiatrist and others on the treatment team; the way in which decisions will be made about when to discharge one's child from the hospital; and once discharged, what the plans are for continuing or follow-up treatment with the youngster (21).

In 1991 Rosenbaum and Prinsky reported the results of their study of adolescent care programs in Southern California. When these hospitals were given a hypothetical situation in which the parents' main concern with their 15-year-old son's behavior was the music he listened to, the clothes he wore, and the type of posters he displayed in his bedroom, 83 percent of the facilities believed the youth needed hospitalization. The researchers concluded that for these psychiatric treatment hospitals, the assumption that musical preference and appearance are strongly related to drug use and other mental health problems may be widespread (22).

Many patients' advocate groups believe that all teenage psychiatric admissions should be subject to stricter criteria. They urge parents to get second opinions if hospitalization is recommended for their offspring.

Despite these concerns and reservations, many adolescent treatment hospital programs have had great success in working with troubled youths. Generally, the treatment approach involves behavioral modification, group therapy, one-on-one counseling, peer counseling where appropriate, and education—including sex education as well as drug and alcohol abuse programs.

Most of the adolescent treatment hospital programs also provide concerned parents with lists of warning signs that encourage them to seek help if their children exhibit any one of the signs for several weeks. One such program in Southern California lists "10 Ways Your Teenager May Be Begging for Help!" in their newspaper advertisement. Included in their list of "frequent signs of adolescent emotional distress" are the following symptoms: fallen or lowered grades, change in eating and sleeping habits, lashing out at people or objects, putting themselves down, changed sexual attitudes, secretive and suspicious behavior, running away, withdrawal, loss of interest in personal appearance and hygiene, and preoccupation with death (23).

Other community mental health programs have been developed to assist parents with keeping their children alive and out of youth or street gangs. One program in Southern California emphasizes a parent-support group approach and even prints a brochure, "Don't Hang with a Gang," to inform other parents in the community. Parents are encouraged to know their children's whereabouts, be fair and consistent in their discipline, keep an open line of communication, hold their child responsible and accountable for his or her actions, monitor the way their child dresses for school, and try to meet their child's friends and their parents.

Other suggestions include the following:

> Confront your child whenever you suspect something is not right, chaperone parties attended by your children, and make certain you know and trust the parents who host parties your children attend, and be cognizant of the use of slang terms or hand gestures by your child to communicate with his or her peers (24).

Other Programs

The Center for the Study and Prevention of Violence at the University of Colorado has established a program called Functional Family Therapy (FFT). FFT is a low-cost solution that motivates families to deal with disruptive youth. By tailoring specific strategies for families, parents have been able to foster positive changes in family communication and problem solving and to reduce behavioral problems (25). Healthy Start is a program run by both the U.S. Department of Health and Human Services and the U.S. Department of Justice. The program is designed to strengthen maternal and infant-care systems at the community level. It was created in the early 1990s to reduce child abuse and has since been expanded to include broader forms of parent education (26).

THE JUVENILE JUSTICE SYSTEM RESPONDS

Depending on their offense, delinquent under the age of 18 may be handled by the juvenile justice system as opposed to the mental health programs. If specific crimes have been committed, as we have seen with the stoner gang members for instance, the juvenile is often sentenced by the courts to the California Youth Authority and incarcerated in one of the several different levels of security, ranging from camplike to more secure, lock-down facilities. Depending upon the offense committed, some juveniles may instead be mandated to adult court.

The highest level of security in most states is youth training schools (YTS) or youth correctional facilities (YCF). Here juveniles typically go through a drug-rehabilitation program. They are also required to participate in group therapy and either continue toward a high school diploma or learn a trade in one of the many technical programs provided in the institution.

Those youths not deemed serious offenders are often mandated by the courts to participate in some type of probation program and, depending on the nature of their offense, may be required to pay restitution or complete community service as part of their sentence. Such programs may be either publicly or privately funded.

Back in Control A program begun in Orange County, California, in the 1980s by two ex-probation officers works specifically with juvenile delinquents who have been involved with either the punk rock or heavy metal scene. The "Back in Control" program follows a "Tough Love" approach to working with these youngsters and their parents to establish strict guidelines of behavior that the youths must follow. If the delinquents do not adhere to the parents' rules, they may then be sentenced to stiffer lock-down type facilities.

The central aim of Back in Control is to depunk and demetal the juveniles. The program works to reprogram these juveniles, contending that they have been brainwashed into a youth subculture in much the same way as others have been processed into other cults (such as religious cults or communes). In order to rescue these youngsters from the control of their youth styles (including the negative influence of friends, music, and all the trappings of their deviant identities—for example, rock band T-shirts, posters, and albums), the parents are encouraged to rid their homes of all such paraphernalia.

The youths are told to disassociate themselves from their former friends who are still involved in the disruptive youth styles. Strict curfews are established by the parents, and the youngsters are informed that if they break any of the rules established by their parents (with the assistance of Back in Control), they will experience dire consequences (such as being grounded, kicked out of the house, or sent to reform school or jail).

In effect, by depunking and demetaling these juveniles and by implementing a rule-based system of behavior, the organization assists parents in regaining control over their offspring's behavior—thus, the "back in control." As the organization's brochure advocates, adults must state the rules clearly and consistently and must effectively follow through to ensure their rules are obeyed. Parents must remove all of the influences associated with their youngster's objectionable lifestyle and replace them with "family values, time, and love."

Parents are encouraged by Back in Control to abide by the five guidelines of education, involvement, supervision, enforcement, and removal. Through education, parents are to become aware of bands, lyrics, and the messages they portray. With involvement in such programs as "Parent Watch," adults are encouraged to work together in a coordinated effort to look out for suspicious activity, unfamiliar individuals, and mutilated animals. Parents are advised to supervise and chaperon their offspring at concerts and to listen to their music and monitor the literature they purchase and read.

A strict enforcement of current laws against alcohol consumption by minors, drug usage, and loitering is also recommended. Finally, parents should make every effort to remove any traces of graffiti because it perpetuates gang violence, revenge, and relays messages (27).

The organizers of Back in Control, along with representatives from other law enforcement agencies, have also developed seminar programs to alert other officials and concerned citizens about the dangers of the various white youth culture scenes including the negative aspects of punk rock, heavy metal, skinheads, and Satanism. These one- or two-day seminars are given in a variety of locations throughout the nation. At these seminars—which attract overflow crowds—various experts present videotapes, display confiscated youth graffiti and paraphernalia, and play record albums to demonstrate their concern with the negative influences that are affecting today's youths.

Although these experts caution that not all youths involved with one or more of the youth styles are equally vulnerable, these police and juvenile justice officials claim that many youngsters do get caught up in the youth culture and become antisocial, if not delinquent. At these workshops and conferences, police departments and those who work gang detail in their respective communities are urged to become aware of the danger signs in their locales such as music-related graffiti, mutilated animals, and groups of teenagers sporting unique dress and hairstyles. The presenters also recommend both mental health treatment programs or Tough Love-approach programs for parents whose children are defiant, uncommunicative, and involved.

Program Effectiveness How effective are these Tough Love-type programs? According to officials and parents, they are quite successful. But some youths take issue with this view. One juvenile who was interviewed for this study felt that he had not been helped by such a program:

> For a few years me and my family went to Back in Control. That didn't work. My folks knew there was no way they could change me. Maybe they can take your clothes, your albums, and your posters and all but they can't take away your state of thinking. Unless they send you into electroshock.
>
> They can't do it. They tried with me and my brother, and they couldn't do it. "De-punking" is what they called it.
>
> They took away everything that I had. I came home one day and they took away everything I had that was punk. My walls were stripped. My whole room was rummaged through. They threw it all away. And I had some real old shit in there—fliers from 1977. Old books that explained things about bands and stuff. Real old albums that you can't find anymore. All gone.

Other youths that were interviewed also expressed concern that the police used excessive force in dealing with them. As Skidd Marx (interviewed in Chapter 3) noted, punkers and metalers are suspicious of police because of how they typically treat these youths:

> There were trillions of cops at a youth riot in Huntington Beach at an "Exploited" gig. Cops were getting fucked up. Punks were getting fucked up. A pregnant girl got her stomach kicked in by a cop on purpose. A

friend of mine was walking down a flight of stairs and a cop pushed him down the stairs and he was on crutches with a broken leg.

About two months ago we were driving along the road and all of a sudden I see this dude running and I see this cop car speeding up. The guy is running from the cop car. The cop goes "bam" and hits him. He hit the dude! 'Cause he was drunk, he hit him. The cop took his door and went "bam" on his head. Smashed him in the head. The cop got out and sat on his stomach. He then picked him up by the hair and went "bam, bam, bam"—pounding him a number of times, smashing his head on the ground. We all saw it. He was just beating the fucking shit out of him. The cop handcuffed him, picked him up by the chain, and started dragging him all over the parking lot. The cop picked him up and started throwing him against the car. Put him in the car. Didn't duck his head down and he hit his head.

Several of the youths interviewed for this study discussed other incidents in which, in their opinion, the police had acted inappropriately and used excessive force. Such incidents made these juveniles distrustful of police and reinforced their disrespect for authority.

Several police departments, however, have consciously attempted to sensitize their officers into working more constructively with these alienated youths. Often these activities have involved developing manuals or programs alerting youths about the risks of being heavily involved in one of these youth styles.

Other Programs One law enforcement agency, for instance, developed a "Primer on Cults," which they distribute to both parents and their children. The primer includes advice about which cults operate in a given area; keeping lines of communication open between parents and their children; emphasizing love and respect for one another; and how to disengage from a cult if conversion has taken place.

Another organization, Turning Point, established by probation officers working gang detail in the Huntington Beach area of Southern California, assists school districts that have problems keeping their school environments safe. By working together, police departments and schools develop programs to increase adolescents' self-esteem and help them protect themselves against violence and crime (28).

Another recent program in Southern California, organized by law enforcement officials of the CYA, reunites groups of teens from rival gangs in a camplike mountain setting. Although initially instituted to work with inner-city ethnic gangs, the program has been successful and is used with white stoner gang members as well. In these highly structured settings, teens are encouraged to shed their gang labels and develop a shared unity of purpose. The camp offers rigorous outdoor activities such as hiking, canoeing, and backpacking. The teens attend mandatory group counseling and explore alternatives to gang activities. They learn they can be accepted outside of their gang.

The three primary goals of these mountain camp programs are the following: (1) to help teens take responsibility for effective decision making; (2) to clarify facts versus myths among gangs; and (3) to expand each youth's vision of potential opportunities (29).

In 1997 the U.S. Office of Juvenile Justice and Delinquency Prevention (OJJDP) released "Combating Violence and Delinquency: The National Juvenile Justice Action Plan." In it the OJJDP created grants for state and local programs to reduce and control delinquency. Included in this was support for graduated sanctions (or intermediate sanctions), training for the administration of restorative justice that holds offenders responsible for making restitution to their victims, and improving the research on juvenile crime made available to legislators. The Action Plan has six main objectives: (1) strengthening the juvenile justice system; (2) prosecuting serious, violent, and chronic offenders; (3) suppression of guns, drugs, and gangs; (4) enhancing positive opportunities for youth; (5) breaking the cycle of child abuse; and (6) mobilizing the community to stop crime (30). One result of the plan is the 1999 MTV cosponsored CD-ROM, *Fight For Your Rights: Take a Stand against Violence*, which teaches conflict resolution and features the music of popular teen-oriented artists such as Lauryn Hill and the Backstreet Boys.

REACTIONS OF CONCERNED CITIZENS

"Video Mimicry Backfires, Hollywood Boy Burns"

A 12-year-old boy who stayed home from school set himself on fire imitating a rock music video by Motley Crue, one of his favorite bands. He set his legs on fire and suffered second degree burns because he doused his jeans with rubbing alcohol and touched a match to them. Motley Crue's video features a band member who lights his boots and then jumps into a pond.

"I thought it was going to happen just like it happened in the video. He just set his legs on fire and nothing happens to him" (31).

In recent years the question of whether youths are strongly influenced by the music and videos they listen to has received much attention. In court case after court case, parents of youths who have taken their own lives have sued recording artists for subliminal messages that the parents allege are included in the artists' controversial songs.

In one of the more famous cases, the lyrics of the heavy metal group, Judas Priest, were scrutinized. The parents of two youngsters alleged that Judas Priest had "mesmerized" their sons "into believing the answer to life is death." The parents claimed the band's music had provoked their sons' actions by the subliminal recording of the words *do it* on the record.

When the case came to trial in August 1990, CBS and the band denied the existence of subliminal messages on any Judas Priest album. Opponents, however, denounced the group's music, saying they promoted violent, suicidal, and satanic themes. One witness for the prosecution, a medical director at a hospital for troubled adolescents, testified in court that he banned the group's music from his treatment facility because he believed it induced violent behavior in his patients. Another witness for the prosecution testified that the group's music glorifies Satan, causing youth to become self-destructive: "Putting a Judas Priest album on the turntable is like putting a loaded gun in a kid's hand" (32).

The case was decided against the plaintiffs. Judas Priest was absolved of the charges brought against them. The jury, in effect, ruled that the plaintiffs failed to prove that the defendants intentionally placed subliminal messages on the album and that those supposed messages were a cause of the suicide and attempted suicide of the two teenage boys. Even with this verdict, however, the prosecutors hoped that rock bands would get the message that they need to be more socially responsible.

Such public backlash has not been restricted to concern over the lyrics and music of heavy metal bands. Rap music, including gangsta rap, has come under greater scrutiny. In 1990 the lyrics of 2 Live Crew, for instance, were judged to be obscene and in violation of community standards. Pressures were lodged and lawsuits were filed against record stores that carried the albums as well as communities that hosted the rap band (33).

Lawsuits have been filed against other rap artists as well for alleged inflammatory messages in their lyrics. In 1992 a controversy arose over the Ice-T album that featured the "Cop Killer" rap song. Public uproar and pressure caused the removal of the song and subsequent reissues of the album.

Public outcry has not been restricted to musical lyrics and videos. In October 1993 a popular television show on MTV, "Beavis and Butthead," came under attack for promoting unsavory behavior by its two teenage, heavy metal misfits. Due to the negative publicity and concern over the incidents discussed in the following news clipping, the network, at the urging of the cartoon artist, rescheduled the show to air later in the evening at a time when it was less likely to be seen by impressionable youngsters.

"Fatal Fire Blamed On 'Beavis and Butt-head' "

The mother of a 5-year-old who started a fire that killed his younger sister blames the MTV cartoon "Beavis and Butthead" for promoting burning as fun, a fire official said Friday.

Fire Chief Harold Sigler said he wants the cable network to eliminate shows that might encourage playing with fire and would like to see violence on the show reduced.

"The mother is attributing the fact that he was fascinated with fire to the 'Beavis and Butt-head' segment where they are setting things on fire," he said.

The show features two teenagers who comment on rock videos and spend time burning and destroying things.

In western Ohio, Sidney Fire Chief Stan Crosley blamed the cartoon for an August fire that three girls started after watching the program (34).

Media Watchdogs

Public officials and elected politicians note that the increase in violence in American society stems from several factors. Some cite child abuse. Others see danger in the images of violence portrayed in television and movies as well as pop youth culture in general, including musical videos, video games, and toys. Still others argue that the prevalence of handguns has made violence a staple in the diet of many young Americans (35).

In late 1993 U.S. Attorney General Janet Reno expressed concern about the degree of violence shown on television. The attorney general's comments appeared to support the efforts by others that have long called for some kind of control, or rating system, over various forms of popular culture. Of particular concern to these media watchdogs are television shows, musical videos, and video games that depict gratuitous sex and violence aimed at the youth market.

Other politicians and citizen groups alike, although agreeing with the sentiments expressed, are concerned that setting guidelines for questionable media presentations might compromise the First Amendment rights that protect and guarantee freedom of speech.

Some citizen groups, however, banded together in the late 1980s to take action. The Parents Music Resource Center, for instance, alarmed by the content of many rock songs—specifically heavy metal, which they refer to as the "bastard child of rock and roll"—suggested that record companies develop a rating system for albums, modeled after the rating system used by the motion picture industry (e.g., G, PG, PG-13, R, and R-17) (36).

The result of this and other pending actions was the enactment of the RIAA's (Recording Industry Association of America) 1991 sticker policy in which the industry labels recordings with explicit lyrics with a parental advisory. One consequence of this action was that America's largest retailer of recorded music, Wal-Mart, refused to sell records with restrictive labels. This prevented large numbers of rural and suburban youth who did not have access to small record shops from obtaining some of the most popular (and controversial) rap and rock recordings.

To circumvent this death knell to record sales, some artists recorded "censored" versions of their albums, without explicit lyrics, to sell at Wal-Mart. Other artists, such as Nirvana, just changed the titles of their songs. "Rape Me," on their 1994 release *In Utero,* was retitled, "Waif Me" to bypass restrictive retailers.

A detailed rating system for video games was created by the Recreational Software Advisory Council at the urging of concerned parents, Congress, and the President in 1996. It ranks video games based on violence and language content by using a four-point scale (37).

According to a report by the American Academy of Pediatrics, rock videos contain too much sexism, violence, substance abuse, suicide, and sexual behavior. Urging parents to exercise control over teens' video viewing and to discuss the videos with their children, the academy cites these statistics:

75 percent of videos contain high incidences of sexually suggestive material, and 56 percent contain violence (38).

In response to pending legislation and further pressures from special interest groups, the Recording Industry Association of America recently created a standardized warning sticker to help parents identify albums that allegedly contain explicit lyrics.

Research

Even with these expressed public concerns, very little scholarly research has been done on the effects of lyrics on adolescents. Those studies that have been undertaken have reported somewhat contradictory findings regarding whether listening to some forms of contemporary music affects adolescent behavior.

In one study, "Sex, Violence, and Rock 'n' Roll: Youths' Perception of Popular Music," Prinsky and Rosenbaum surveyed nearly 300 Southern California junior high and high school students. Their conclusions were that the song lyrics—even when they included themes of sex, drugs, violence, and Satanism—had little impact on the vast majority of teens. They found that most teens could not accurately describe their favorite songs. Of 662 songs that students listed as their favorites, only 7 percent were perceived by those students as having objectionable themes. The most popular single topic in song lyrics was love (39).

Students, in fact, were unable to explain 37 percent of the songs they named as their favorites. According to the researchers, most used rock 'n' roll as "background noise." The study concluded that musical beat or overall sound of a recording is of greater interest to teens and that specific lyrics seem to be of little consequence to most kids.

In a 1985 study conducted by Vokey and Read, "Subliminal Messages: Between the Devil and the Media," the psychologists concluded that they were unable to find any evidence, based on a variety of tasks administered to participants in their experiments, to support the claim that the alleged presence of messages in the media influenced listeners' behavior. The researchers also presented evidence to suggest that the presence of backward messages in popular music lies more in the imagination of the listener than in any actual message (40).

Other academic research, however, has found that music fans do pay attention to the lyrics. In one survey, Wass, Miller, and Stevenson found that 87 percent of the metal fans reported knowing all or most of the words in the songs they listened to. The researchers also found a significantly higher degree of attitudes among the heavy metalers supportive of reckless and life-risking behavior (41).

In yet another study, Weinstein observes that although heavy metal music carries on the tradition of cross-cultural concern with social problems first depicted in youth music in the mid-1960s, heavy metal differs from such views of optimism about changing the future. Instead, heavy metal is concerned about problems but offers few solutions. Further, the music depicts a very bleak future, leaving the listener with a sense of despair (42).

In a 1993 study, "The Effect of the Heavy Metal Subculture on Violence: An Analysis of Aggravated Assault," Steven Stack contends that although the cultural symbols of heavy metal often typify violence, this symbolism does not translate to a higher aggregate level of externalized violence or violence by the listener toward others.

Although Stack notes that the album covers of heavy metal groups often symbolize a theme of violence using such symbols as skulls, monsters, violent-looking biker types, and gothic horror scenes—exacerbated by the visual dimensions of their videos and stage show—he concurs with the views of other researchers that heavy metal's theme of "chaos" can be linked with greater internalized violence, such as depression and suicide (43).

This sense of pessimism and despair was present in the punk rockers and heavy metal youths studied as well. However, one could make the following distinction. As this book has depicted, there are different forms of behavior that disillusioned youths manifest. The *renegade kids* are examples of youths, including punkers and metalers, who have, for the most part, turned their frustration inward. The *suburban outlaws,* on the other hand, particularly the racist skinheads and stoner gang members, are examples of youths who have taken similar feelings of depression and alienation and acted upon their frustration in more externalized ways.

Recall that in our discussion of the results of the cross-cultural study of punk rockers and heavy metalers in Southern California and New Zealand, over half the youths sampled stated that they listened to messages in the songs. Furthermore, both California punk rockers (44 percent) and New Zealand heavy metalers (45 percent) agreed with the statement that their music was violent compared to the other groups studied. As a whole, punk rockers and heavy metalers in both countries, compared to the control groups, viewed the music they listened to as violent.

Societal reactions to youthful offenders have been varied. In summary, parents are encouraged to be more fully involved in all facets of their children's lives. Parents should play an active role in the quality of education their children are receiving. They should work to maintain open lines of communication—to assist with their offspring's selection of friends, musical interests, and leisure activities. If they have youngsters who are involved with one of the youth styles discussed in this book, parents should seek counsel and assistance from school counselors, clergy, and community mental health and social service agencies, as well as the local police department. Programs are available to help these youths. Parents should be cautioned to examine the methods used or claims made before selecting a specific service.

Most recently, reductions in juvenile crime may have been helped by community responses to high-profile crimes committed by juveniles. After the Columbine shootings, for instance, organizations such as the Nation Alliance for Safe Schools (NASS) began to receive more attention. NASS runs training seminars and workshops to help campus security and school administrators create "Pro-Active School Safety Plans." NASS also performs school security assessments and runs a workshop for teachers called "School Survival 101,"

<table>
<tr><td></td></tr>
</table>

Youth at the Movies—In the Asylum

The treatment of youth in mental institutions is dealt with only briefly in films such as *Birdy* (1985) as compared to its extensive coverage in adult films such as *One Flew over the Cuckoo's Nest* (1975). A recent representation of youth treatment was *Girl, Interrupted* (1999). Starring Winona Ryder and Angelina Jolie and based on a true story, this tale takes place in 1969 before the institutionalization of youth for "problem behavior" became big business.

teaches how to deal with school bullies and dangerous situations, such as students with guns (44).

Responses to hate crimes have also come from the community level. Local coalitions of religious, civic, and law enforcement leaders have helped the flow of information about cultural conflicts and potential threats. Other groups focus more specifically on youth. One such group is Oregon Spotlight, which does outreach with junior and senior high school students. One of the founders, Stephen Stroud, was a racist skinhead in his teen years and explains the value of the community approach to fighting hate crimes: "The best thing to do is to educate the community about their own biases and how to overcome them. When I was a skin, we'd look for a place where we could exploit their own prejudices. We could operate there and just exploit them."

NOTES

1. Dean E. Murphy, "The Rise in Kids Who Kill," *Los Angeles Times* (16 August 1992), p. A-1.
2. Chuck Philips, "Another Day in Court for Rock Music," *Los Angeles Times* (4 October 1990), p. E-1.
3. Joan Libman, "Growing Up Too Fast: Experts Warn That Children Are Being Pushed to Act Like Adults Long before They Are Ready," *Los Angeles Times* (9 August 1988), p. V-1.
4. Ibid.
5. Ibid.
6. Ibid.
7. Marita Hernandez, "Hate Crimes Rise Sharply, Panel Reports," *Los Angeles Times* (7 September 1990), p. B-2.
8. Jack Levin, *Hate Crimes: America's Growing Menace* (New York: Plenum Press, 1993).
9. Murphy, p. 26.
10. Ibid.
11. Jim Sanders and Patrick Hoge, "Truancy Soaring: Why Go to Class When Mall Beckons?" *Sacramento Bee* (11 June 1989), p. A-1.
12. Ibid.
13. Michelle Proner, "Project Safe" (Sacramento, CA: Office of Criminal Justice Planning, 1989).
14. Ibid.
15. Larry Siegel and Joseph Senna, *Criminology* (Belmont, CA: Wadsworth, 2000), pp. 376–77.
16. Department of Justice, Department of Education, *1998 Annual Report on School Safety,* 1999, p. 40.
17. Richard Polanco, "Bad Medicine for 'Troubled Teens': Forced Private

Hospitalization Is Abuse of Process," *Los Angeles Times* (7 May 1989), p. V-5.

18. Ibid.

19. Ibid.

20. Nina Darnton, "Committed Youth: Why Are So Many Teens Being Locked Up in Private Mental Hospitals?" *Newsweek* (31 July 1989), pp. 66–72.

21. Ibid.

22. Jill Leslie Rosenbaum and Lorraine Prinsky, "The Presumption of Influence: Recent Responses to Popular Music Subcultures" *Crime and Delinquency* 37 (4) (October 1991), pp. 528–35.

23. "10 Ways Your Teenager May Be Begging for Help!" *Long Beach Press Telegram* (2 October 1988), p. A-8.

24. Coy D. Estes, "Don't Hang with a Gang," (Upland, CA: Upland Police Department).

25. Department of Justice, Department of Education, *1998 Annual Report on School Safety,* 1999, p. 40.

26. Gene Stephens, "Saving the Nation's Most Precious Resources: Our Children," *USA Today Magazine,* May 1998, pp. 54–57.

27. Darlyne R. Pettinicchio, "The Punk Rock and Heavy Metal Handbook" (Orange, CA: The Back in Control Center), p. 29.

28. "Gang Prevention and Intervention Project" (Garden Grove, CA: Turning Point).

29. Ibid.

30. "The National Juvenile Justice Action Plan: A Comprehensive Response to a Critical Challenge," Office of Juvenile Justice and Delinquency Prevention, (Washington, D.C.: OJJDP, 1997).

31. Ann Bradley and Richard Hart, "Video Mimicry Backfires; Hollywood Boy Burned," *Miami Herald* (18 February 1988), p. A-1.

32. Chuck Philips, "The Music Didn't Make Them Do It," *Los Angeles Times* (25 August 1990), p. F-I.

33. Chuck Philips, "Trial to Focus on Issue of Subliminal Messages in Rock," *Los Angeles Times* (16 July 1990), p. F-1.

34. "Fatal Fire Blamed on 'Beavis and Butt-head,' " *Desert Sun* (9 October 1993), p. A-6.

35. Murphy, p. 26.

36. David Winkel, "Rock & Raunch," *Long Beach Press-Telegram* (22 December 1985), p. H-1.

37. Chris Taylor, "Cyberguide: A Primer for Parents on What's Out There in the Digital World," *Time* (10 May 1999), pp. 44–48.

38. "Music Videos May Be Hazardous to Your Health." *Los Angeles Times* (14 November 1988), p. VI-2.

39. Lorraine E. Prinsky and Jill L. Rosenbaum, " 'LEER-ICS' OR LYRICS: Teenage Impressions of Rock 'n' Roll," *Youth and Society* 18 (4) (June 1987), pp. 384–97.

40. John R. Vokey and J. Don Read, "Subliminal Messages: Between the Devil and the Media," *American Psychologist* 40 (14) (November 1985), pp. 1231–39.

41. Hannelore Wass, M. David Miller, and Robert G. Stevenson, "Factors Affecting Adolescents' Behavior and Attitudes toward Destructive Rock Lyrics," *Death Studies* 13, pp. 287–303.

42. Deena Weinstein, *Heavy Metal: A Cultural Sociology* (New York: Macmillan, 1991).

43. Steven Stack, "The Effect of the Heavy Metal Subculture on Violence: An Analysis of Aggravated Assault," paper presented at the American Society of Criminology annual meetings, October 1993; Phoenix, AZ.

44. "Our Services," National Alliance for Safe Schools, www.safeschools.org/ (1999).

12

Generation Why?:
Crisis at the Millennium

"Y2K Generation Forced to Grow Up Fast"

The Cold War was over before they were 10. They think the stock market goes nowhere but up. They know all about sex, but also about AIDS. Their schools have computers in the classroom, but metal detectors by the front door. They wear studs in their tongues and pagers on their belts.

They are the class of 2000, more than 3 million young Americans now starting their senior year in high school, and like every generation of teens, they dare their parents to understand them (1).

"Raves Are a Rite of Passage"

Raves appear to be Gen Y's version of '60's love-ins. Several thousand young people gather for an all-night concert of music that has not yet found its way into a mainstream venue. Raves feature loud music spun together in an original way by a disc jockey.

As far as I can determine, a rave is a simple way for young people to tell their parents one thing and then do another. They must find a time and a place to prove themselves, to get themselves across some mystical barrier that prevents them from feeling fully adult. Sometimes it's dancing all night. Sometimes it's drinking oneself sick. Sometimes it's trying drugs (2).

THE POLITICS OF GENERATIONS

When does one generation end and another begin? Was the first member of "Generation X" born in 1962 or 1965? Do the baby boomers born in 1946 share the same generational experience as those born in 1961? Sociologists often use the term "cohort" to refer to a group of people who were born at roughly the same time, but that ignores the structural and historical contexts that might or might not bond them.

The sociological concept of "generations" has been pioneered by Karl Mannheim. A generation is more than a group of people who are born the same year or decade. They must have some common connection. Mannheim writes that generations "work up the material of their common experience in different and specific ways" (3). Michael Brake argues that the so-called generation gap is a product of the weak integration of age groups into society that is intensified in times of rapid social change (4). Generations have common reference points: D-Day, the assassination of John F. Kennedy, the Challenger explosion, or the Rodney King riots. A generation "knows where it was when. . . ."

In the late 1980s the postwar baby-boom generation finally began to surrender some of its cultural power to the baby-bust generation. Dubbed "Generation X" after Douglas Copeland's 1991 novel of the same name, the 44.6 million "twenty-somethings" were characterized as skeptical, apathetic "slackers" by the popular press (5).

Ten years later the next cohort of young people was struggling for its identity, separate from the Gen Xers. The media, in their rush to label a new phenomenon, has referred to the current batch of teenagers as the "Y Generation," the "Millennial Generation," "Generation Next," "Generation D," and the "Os" (as in o-o-1 and o-o-2). Although it is still early in the game to characterize the cohort of kids born after the Iranian hostage crisis, this group is still experiencing the historical and structural conditions that Mannheim said create a generation.

THE DEMOGRAPHICS OF YOUTH CULTURE

The naming of generations and the delineation of their borders is primarily the self-appointed duty of the media. For example, a person born in 1964 could be a member of the Baby Boomers or Generation X, depending on whether they read the Gen X article in *Time* (which said the baby boom ended in 1964) or *Newsweek* (which set 1961 as the cut-off date). The primary tools of sociologists and demographers for discussing the experience of generations are birth rates, which inform us of the comparative size of cohorts and the subsequent orientation of culture to certain age groups.

After World War II, the relative peace and prosperity sparked what is now referred to as the "baby boom." Between 1946 and 1964, 76 million children were born, representing about a third of the U.S. population (6). The explosion of babies who first became teenagers together and then adults together helped to create the adolescent crazes of the 1950s, the counterculture of the 1960s, the disco fad of the 1970s, and the yuppie trend of the 1980s. In the 1990s the United States elected its first Baby Boomer President, Bill Clinton (born in 1946), and boomers began to enter their fifties.

After 1964 the birth rate dropped, creating a "birth dearth" and a convenient end to the baby-boom generation. As war-era parents aged out of reproduction and their children delayed parenthood until their thirties (and beyond), the birth rate continued to decline until 1974, when the trend began to reverse. There was a significant increase in the birthrate after 1980, when baby boomers finally began settling down and starting their own families. Some argue that the AIDS scares of the 1980s helped to encourage more traditional sexual relationships, such as marriage, which also increased along with the birth rate. The 1965 to 1980 birth dearth—the "echo wave" of the baby boom—created the borders of what is now referred to as Generation X. With the low birth rate year of 1974, it is coincidental that the diagram of the generation actually looks like an "X" (See the discussion of population pyramids to follow.).

Gen Xers, who began turning 16 in 1980, came of age in the world of Ronald Reagan and the peak of the Cold War. The 45 million members of Generation X watch more TV and carry more credit-card debt than previous generations (7). They are more educated and have a greater expendable income than their parents (8). They became the voices of grunge, hip-hop, and the cyber revolution. But now the post-Gen Xers are moving into their adolescence. The birth rate increased dramatically in 1981 as boomers started families and peaked in 1991. Those born in 1981 turned 19 in 2000, and behind them is growing a "baby boom-let."

The relatively small size of Generation X will be eclipsed by the next generation. There are currently 31 million kids between the ages of 12 and 19, making up 10 percent of the U.S. population. That age group is expected to increase to 35 million by 2010 (9). There are 72 million young people between the ages of 5 and 22, which makes it close to the same size as the baby-boom generation (10). The size of this group is also fueled by the increasing youthfulness of immigrant populations, helping to make this the most ethnically diverse generation ever.

The post-X kids are filled with questions about the world that is changing around them. They know more about computers than their parents do but less about community. They experience multicultural curricula in school but never knew racial segregation. They hear that the violent crime rate is dropping but repeatedly see shootings in schools similar to their own. On the edge of a new century, it makes more sense to refer to them as "Generation Why?" than Generation Y.

Birth rates are also useful because they give one a glimpse into the future. Population pyramids give one a visual representation of a society's age structure. The triangle shape is based on a large number of births, and then the population begins to decrease through infant mortality, teen accidents,

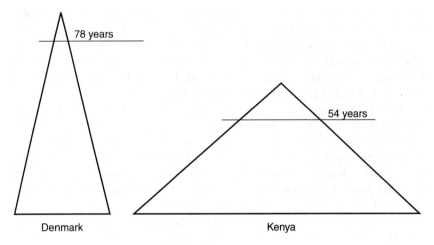

Figure 12.1

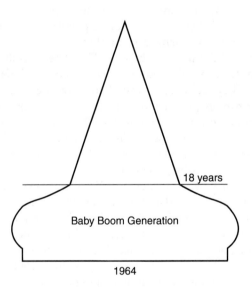

Figure 12.2

and adult disease. Finally the few very elderly people in a society create the top point of the pyramid. Figure 1 shows the population pyramids of normal societies. Developed countries, such as Denmark, where the life expectancy is 78, have lower birth rates (13 per 100,000 in 1998) and tall, narrow pyramids. Developing countries, such as Kenya, where the life expectancy is 54, have high birth rates (38 per 100,000 in 1998), creating short, squat pyramids (11).

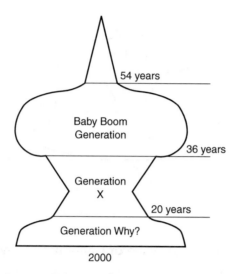

Figure 12.3

The baby boom changed the shape of the U.S. population pyramid by giving the nation a disproportionate number of children. Figure 2 shows the population in 1964 at the end of the birth explosion. One can see that in 1964 a sudden increase in 18-year-olds foreshadowed the youth movements that fueled the social changes that occurred later that decade.

The population pyramid at the turn of the century looks more like an airplane than a triangle (see Figure 3). The swell of boomers was between 36 and 54 in 2000. The smaller numbers of Gen-Xers made up the 20-to-35-year-old age group. And the sizable Generation Why? produces its first 19-year-olds. As Figure 3 reflects, there is potential for a conflict over resources between the aging baby boomers and the consumer-oriented Why? kids, with Gen-Xers squeezed out of the dialogue.

Barring any unforeseen catastrophes, such as nuclear war or a massive plague, one can project what the United States will look like thirty years from now. The baby boomers continue up the ladder into a world of improved health care for the elderly (and longer life expectancies). The middle-age bulge, evident in Figure 3, will transform into the "graying of America" (see Figure 4). By 2030 there will be approximately 50 million aged Americans, about one fifth of the U.S. population (12). A society that was youth-oriented in the 1960s will be elderly-oriented in the 2020s. By 2030 the oldest Gen Why? members will be 49.

A boom of the boom of the original baby boom ("Generation Z"?) may occur to redirect the public focus onto youth in the 2020s, but it is inevitable that the youth of the twenty-first century will have to compete for attention with their boomer grandparents.

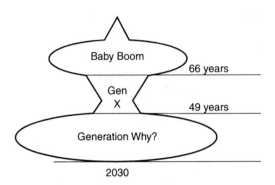

Figure 12.4

The First Wave of Generation Why?

Although it may be too soon to completely understand what makes Generation Why? unique, the first teenagers of the twenty-first century have already begun to establish a profile. The most notable characteristic is their consumerism. According to Teenage Research Limited, teens spent $141 billion in 1998. That breaks down to $89 a week spent by each teen on nonessential items. Gen Why? members earned $121 billion of that total by working (the remaining $20 billion came from their parents) (13). They are a generation that has benefited from the economic boom of the 1990s and translated that into shopping sprees, whether that involves buying clothes at mall stores such as Old Navy or hunting down Pokémon trading cards.

This is also a more racially diverse generation. The graduating high school class of 2000 had 33 percent of its students in minority groups. Only 28 percent of Americans, in general, are minorities (14). The potential for racial unity exists as more youth define themselves as multiracial, but a potential for conflict also exists as schools and communities become "less white," inciting fears among racists. The 2000 census is expected to reveal that California is the first state to have a minority white population.

As we will discuss shortly, millennial youth are more likely to spend time alone and away from their parents. But even with their isolation, a growing generational awareness of their numbers exists. The pop music charts are filled with teen artists, such as Brandy, Britney Spears, Silverchair, and Leanne Rimes, singing to their peers. Even opera music has become dominated by 13-year-old soprano Charlotte Church. Susan Mitchell, author of the *Official Guide to Generations,* said, "Look at the malls. A few years ago, there were fewer teenagers and they kept to themselves. It was kind of sad. But kids aren't hiding off in the corners so much now. They're loud and they're boisterous. They're taking over" (15).

Teens are using technology to communicate. Although chat rooms and cell phones are common, pagers have enabled youths to create a whole new lexicon. Once the domain of doctors and drug dealers, absent parents began to give their teens pagers as a way to have contact with their children, make sure they were safe, and have some form of control (16). In the hands of Generation Why? a new language of codes and "pager-speak" emerged.

Different types of codes quickly evolved—most without their parents' knowledge. Some codes are short and rely on popular culture or police codes: For instance, "411" is "I have a question," "666" is "I am angry/evil," and "143" is "I love you" (one letter, four letters, three letters). Some codes are meant to look like letters, sometimes upside down. "6000*843" is "Goodbye," "07734" is "Hello," and "7734*2*06" is "Go to Hell." Some codes relate to specific subcultures; for instance, "555" is "KKK" and "420" is "Let's smoke pot." Codes can even reflect ethnic identities: for instance, "50538" upside down is "besos" (Spanish for "kisses") and "8282" read quickly sounds like Korean for "hurry, hurry" (17).

The teen beeper culture has been coopted by companies such as MTV and Mountain Dew, who gave pagers to teens to contact with weekly advertisements (18). The pager codes are another example of teen lingo meant to bond peers (and consumer products!) and frustrate adults.

Youth Institutions in Crisis

Youth is a time of transition from childhood to adulthood. Navigating this world of "in-between" can be difficult and hazardous. As was discussed in Chapter 2, criminologists such as Walter Miller have found that many youths respond to this lack of clearly identified social expectations by retreating into youth culture (19). Nanette Davis's book, *Youth Crisis: Growing Up in the High-Risk Society,* points out that all the institutions involved in helping youths safely make the transition to adulthood are in a state of crisis, including the family, schools, religion, the juvenile justice system and the occupational structure (20).

Davis, whose research included studying homeless youth as well as delinquents, maintains that changing social institutions make it harder for kids to connect to adult expectations and actually cultivate risk-taking behavior. She outlines seven of the manifestations of cultural "crisis":

1. Modern life is uncertain. Thinking about the future is difficult with corporate downsizing and random gun violence.

2. Politicians opt for short-term solutions, ignoring long-term consequences. In the effort to get elected, many politicians put off the difficult but wise decisions in exchange for popular positions. For example, they support mandatory minimum sentences for first-time offenders instead of reducing the social causes of crime.

3. Consumerism is rampant, and status is now bought with brand names, such as Nike and Abercrombie & Fitch. (As mentioned, teens spend $89 a week on nonessential items.)

4. Race, class, age, and ethnic divisions discourage youth from believing in social institutions. If the schools or the government cannot erase poverty or racism, what hope is there for the future?

5. There is a lack of adequate child care. The increasing numbers of working mothers have limited resources for their children. New welfare reforms that force women into the work force often disadvantage their children. Parents often substitute the television for child-care providers.

6. Risk reduction attempts do not target the most vulnerable. Positions of influence are open only to those with elite educations and occupational connections.

7. There is a "cult of individualism." Self-centered and self-involved people hurt group and collective identities (21).

Davis's concerns are reflected in the results of a survey of high school youth, published in 1998. The Center for Disease Control (CDC) study found teenagers involved in a wide variety of risk-taking behaviors.

- Rarely wore seatbelts: 20 percent
- Had ridden with a driver who had consumed alcohol: 37 percent
- Had drunk alcohol: 51 percent
- Had carried a weapon: 18 percent
- Had used marijuana: 26 percent
- Had attempted suicide in the last twelve months: 8 percent
- Had had sexual intercourse: 50 percent
- Of those who were having sex, were not using condoms: 43 percent
- Had smoked cigarettes in the last month: 36 percent (22)

A similar study, the 1995 National Survey of Adolescent Boys, found that respondents were more likely to admit to engaging in risky behavior when responding over a computer than on the traditional pen-and-paper survey. Of the sample of boys, aged 15 to 19, significant percentages admitted to an involvement in dangerous behavior, including having been paid for sex (4 percent), taken drugs using a needle (5 percent), having threatened to hurt someone in the past year (26 percent), and having carried a gun in the past 30 days (12 percent). Of those who were sexually active, 25 percent said they (or their partner) were drunk or high the last time they had heterosexual intercourse, and 3 percent said they had had sex with someone who shot (used intravenously) drugs (23).

This situation is compounded by what some might refer to as low levels of social justice in the United States. The first juvenile court, founded in Chicago in 1899, was established on the idea of *parens patriae* (Latin for "parent state"), the idea that the court would serve the best interest of the "whole child" (24). Just over a hundred years later the court's philosophy of rehabilitation has been replaced with punitive motivation. Many of the over 100,000 youths incarcerated (such as the ones described in Chapter 10) are there because of "get tough" measures passed by voters, including "one, two, and three strikes, you're out" laws and mandatory minimum laws.

Oregon, which passed a mandatory minimum "one strike and you're out" sentencing law in 1995 now incarcerates youths age 15 and older for first offenses. For example, a 15-year-old who gets into a fight and is charged with second-degree assault receives a mandatory minimum sentence of five years and ten months in prison. There is no consideration of individual cases by judges. Not surprisingly, Oregon has had an increase in the number of incarcerated youths committing suicide since 1995 (25).

The movement, supported by President Bill Clinton, to try juveniles as young as eleven as adults is a reflection of the crisis of the juvenile court system. "Get tough" on youth crime policies have overloaded America's 3,000 juvenile courts. A study conducted by sociologist Charles Frazier, at the University of Florida, found that juveniles who are tried as adults have higher recidivism rates and tend to be more violent after release than those tried as juveniles (26). The trend to reclassify delinquents as adults has led many to believe that the 100-year-old juvenile court system will soon be abolished.

Nanette Davis discusses this as part of the social shift that has failed youth. Her "youth crisis" model places the problems of youth—including homelessness, suicide, and crime—as the result of three social trends: first, the "limited and arbitrary" justice that youth face; second, the high number of institutions in crisis at both the local and global level; and third, a high-risk orientation (27).

Risky behavior has become normative and Generation Why? is on the front line of this crisis. The seemingly self-destructive behavior was illustrated in the 1999 PBS *Frontline* program, "The Lost Youth of Rockdale County," which detailed a large outbreak of syphilis among seemingly well-adjusted upper-middle-class youth in suburban Atlanta. Much like the parents of the Columbine shooters, the parents of the Rockdale teens claimed to be unaware their children were involved in such risky behavior.

THE GROWING INFLUENCE OF THE MEDIA

The crisis is perhaps seen most in youths' increasing dependence on the media as a source of information. It is more than ironic that the first members of Generation Why? were born in the first year of MTV—1981. As parents spend more time away from home, at work or in other homes, the media becomes a more powerful agent of socialization than ever before. Teenagers watch an average of 11 hours of TV a week (28). After the Columbine shootings, President Clinton urged movie theaters to restrict access of teens to R-rated movies, but youth still rent thousands of violent and sexually graphic films from video stores each week. Although there is no evidence that viewing violent films makes young people criminal, as discussed in Chapter 7, the power of the media to influence increases as parents, teachers, and other members of conforming institutions withdraw from youth.

The clearest example of the media-savvy of millennial kids is their connection to the Internet. In 1998 17 million kids were online, and that number is expected to reach 42 million by 2003 (29). Mannheim's concept of generation gaps is perfectly reflected in the world of cyberspace. The rapid pace of technological change has left many parents in the dust. Kids are downloading MP3s of Blink 182 and Hot Water Music and then burning their own CDs while their parents are still listening to Neil Young on vinyl records. Gen Why? has the world on the click-stream while their parents still wait for brief reports on the evening news. Youth have access not only to limitless educational material but also to information from the most extreme hate groups and the most graphic pornography. The days of sneaking into the parents' bedroom to get a peak at their hidden copy of *Mein Kampf* or *Playboy* are long gone.

A recent *Time/CNN* poll of 409 teenagers, age 13 to 17, reflected youths attitudes towards the 'net. While about half the kids logged on regularly, 82 percent of the sample surfed the Web occasionally. Many of the subjects had visited "taboo" web sites, including porn sites (44 percent), hate sites (25 percent), and sites that explained how to build bombs (14 percent) or buy guns (12 percent) (30).

The generation gap was clear when the teens were asked about their parents. Forty-five percent said their parents know a little about the content of the Web, and 17 percent said their parents know absolutely nothing. The majority of the kids (56 percent) said their parents have rules about where they can surf, but only 31 percent said they actually always follow the rules. The good news for parents is that more kids trust their parents a great deal (83 percent) for information than the information they get from the Internet (13 percent) (31).

When kids are not "surfing the Web" or working on homework, they are often using the home computer to play video games. Nine out of ten households with children own or have rented video games. The sales of video games in 1998 topped $5.5 billion and a third of the best-selling games, such as Quake and Redneck Rampage, had violent content. The same *Time/CNN* poll revealed that 70 percent of kids surveyed played video games between one and four hours a week and that 31 percent of the boys reported they were addicted to video games (only 10 percent of the girls said they were) (32). The top three selling magazines for boys age 12 to 15 are *Gamepro, Nintendo Power,* and *Electronic Gaming Monthly* (33).

The character of Generation Why? will be shaped by its media saturation. With its multitude of options at the multiplex, the video store, and on cable and Game Boy cartridges, those born in the eighties will come to expect immediate gratification of their impulses. What will they do when those desires can no longer be satisfied? They are bombarded with mediated images of violence, but will that help them to prevent the real thing? Kim, a 17-year-old Columbine High School student, was reported to have said:

I went and saw *The Matrix* a few days before (the Columbine shootings). It was pretty realistic. But we're so used to seeing violence, it doesn't click. We're so used to seeing guns go off, people shooting each other. With me, it didn't hit until my best friend was shot (34).

Twenty-First-Century Anomie

Media consumption and the teen activity of shopping fill a void left by the transformation of traditional social institutions. As religion, family, and extracurricular school programs garner less support, teens find their community in chat-rooms and malls. Their behavior is a response to the anomie that Emile Durkheim wrote about over a hundred years ago. That "state of normlessness" produced by rapid change is as true for the members of Generation Why? as it was for those in Durkheim's 1897 suicide study.

The crucible of this anomie is the family. Parents, too busy or too self-involved to bond with their children, are letting their kids drift. Five million kids under the age of 13 are "latchkey children," left unattended after school each day (35). Half of teenagers in the United States have divorced parents, and 63 percent live in homes in which both parents work outside the home (36). A Temple University study conducted by Lawrence Steinberg found high rates of parent noninvolvement with their teens. Of the 20,000 teens studied, about 30 percent of their parents were unable to describe how the youth spent their time or who their friends were. This might help to explain the fact that, according to the Center for Disease Control, cases of teen depression have increased 300 percent in the past thirty years (37).

It is important to point out the *diagnosing* of teen depression may be increasing, not necessarily the actual occurrence of depression. Adolescence has become "medicalized" by for-profit mental facilities. A 1999 *60 Minutes* report found gross negligence and fraud at Charter Hospitals, after undercover cameras found them hospitalizing teens without formal diagnosis and rigging medical forms to bill insurance companies (38). Regardless of clinical diagnosis, the withdrawal of parents creates an enormous emotional vacuum that allows for the worst of peer and media influence to be intensified.

The Kaiser Family Foundation reports that only 58 percent of kids surveyed reported that their fathers care very much about them (and 85 percent of their mothers) (39). Angela, a 17-year-old in Chattanooga, was quoted as saying, "I've never had a father figure. It's common, so it wasn't a problem. I think with me being female, if I had just one parent, it was more important for me to be with my mother" (40).

Without parental supervision, the age-old game of teens hiding their bad behavior from their parents becomes a sport. A recent report, entitled "Millennium Hangover: Keeping Score on Alcohol," released by Drug Strategies, demonstrated how little parents know about their kids. Of the 574 parents surveyed, only 3 percent believed their high school kids have had up to five drinks in the past month. According to the CDC self-report data, actually 33 percent of youth have done that. The dramatic increase in binge drinking by teens in recent years may completely escape most parents' radar (41).

These kids with no connection to home are better examples of Bob Dylan's "rolling stone" than are members of the baby-boom generation. They are the alienated youth who identified with Kip Kinkel and the Columbine shooters. Gang researcher C. Ronald Huff compares contemporary youth to minority youth of the past. "Most people who have been marginalized will make a reasonable adjustment to compensate. A smaller percentage will become violent, either to others or themselves" (42).

FINAL THOUGHTS

Since the early 1940s and particularly since the end of World War II and the emergence of the "baby boomers," each generation of teenagers in American society has developed its own distinctive youth styles. Strongly influenced by the popular culture—particularly musical tastes, fashion, and lingo—as well as by broader societal social changes, modern teenagers have looked to their contemporaries and to the media for clues to what is hip, fashionable, and trendy.

To gain some semblance of distinctiveness and individuality, teenagers often embrace the outrageous, testing the limits of "acceptable" behavior or dress, challenging free expression, and upsetting adults and their less rebellious peers in the process.

To give some theoretical perspective to this pattern, it can be argued that youth culture follows what might be referred to as a *linear progression*. That is, the often *fluid* nature of teenage social character dictates that it continually evolves and changes in shape and form, building an identity on, and even surpassing the extremes of, the preceding generation. It is a social character quick to challenge whatever has become the recently defined status quo. Youth culture is constantly in motion, moving onward in a mad rush to some new creation, manifestation, or reinvention.

A contrasting theoretical perspective, introduced only to provide a conceptual framework by which to discuss specific forms of youth culture, is a *curvilinear progression,* which considers broader societal trends in modern society. By looking at the patterns of social change and politics, one can explain the emergence and disappearance of distinctive youth cultures within the context of the social structure. Rather than viewing contemporary teenage youth culture as constantly evolving in linear progression—embracing new forms of outrageous and even rebellious fads—a curvilinear progression sees youths as both shaping, and being shaped by, the broader cultural trends. Furthermore, these trends shift between liberal and conservative directions due to the political whims of a given historical time period.

The progression of social change that both moves forward and then curves back, to be followed by another shift forward and back once again, forms a curvilinear line. Forward movement occurs during historical periods that embrace liberal, progressive social change; backward or reverse movement occurs during historical periods aimed at restoring conservative social order and tradition.

By looking more closely at this curvilinear perspective (for purposes of this study, which examined the suburban youth cultures that emerged in the late 1980s up to those of the new millennium and beyond), one could argue that the conservative trends of the 1980s helped explain the rise of youth groups such as heavy metalers and racist skinheads who shared a more traditional, conservative ideology that embraced the status quo. These youth groups arose, in part, in opposition to the more liberal ideologies, shared by punk rockers, which preceded them during the 1970s, and by the remnants of the more liberal, Democratic policies of the 1960s, which had promoted greater racial and ethnic integration.

The youth culture of the Clinton era of the 1990s focused on issues of individual commitment. The lack of broad unifying social issues pulled young people into the world of personal ideas. Whereas some went to work in Clinton's America Corps program, more disappeared into the world of personal computers or danced with themselves at all-night raves. The economic growth of the 1990s also increased expectations of social change, leading to anomie. Unlike children in the preceding five decades, the kids of the nineties faced no great threat to bond them. External threats, such as war and nuclear annihilation, faded as did the traditionally authoritarian adult structure. Internal threats such as economic instability, although present perhaps in the recession of the early 1990s, were erased with the economic boom and growth during the remainder of the decade. The reactionary icon of Ronald Reagan was replaced by the sax-playing, baby-boomer Bill Clinton, a more centralist leader. The tough-but-fair parents who came of age in the Depression were replaced by the pot-smoking parents of the Woodstock era.

Without anything concrete to rebel against, many youths turned against each other. This is reflected in the issue of student violence. Violence by students in the Vietnam War years was targeted at symbols of *adult* power. Violence by students at the turn of the century was targeted at other students, some symbols of *peer* power.

Whereas marketing analysts try to predict the consumer tastes of the youth of the twenty-first century, academics rely on the information from past patterns and trends. Based on the curvilinear theory, Generation Why? is due for a catalyst that will shape its identity. Past generations have responded to calamities such as the stock market crash of 1929 and the 1963 assassination of John F. Kennedy. This generation's calamity could be natural (global warming), technological (a massive computer virus), or economic (the collapse of the world economy). Whatever may happen, it will push youth from their current future orientation to dealing with the present.

The United States in the new millennium will change as the sheer numbers of Generation Why? begin to eclipse the shrinking baby-boom cohort. The millennial kids are more plugged in to the global economy and reflect global ethnicity. Hints of things to come appear in both the popularity of

Latin artists, such as Ricky Martin, and the youth involvement in the 1999 protests of the World Trade Organization meetings in Seattle, Washington, in which hundreds of young people were arrested. Unfortunately, the large numbers of young people may also translate into increasing juvenile crime rates.

The urban unrest of the 1960s is likely to become the suburban unrest of the 2000s. The replacement of unionized industrial jobs and the downsizing of white-collar jobs with low-wage "temp" and service work are creating suburban ghettos that just happen to have more African-American, Hispanic and Asian residents. The mainstream media is already touting the death of suburbia in articles such as *Los Angeles Times* magazine's "Requiem for the Suburbs?" (43) and *Rolling Stone's* "I Hate the Suburbs" (44). Even youth media depicts the shift. The 1999 movie *SLC Punk* looks at the border crossing (mix) of mods and punks, as well as a pointed criticism of baby boomer suburban families.

New social movements may help to restore American institutions. At the moment the failure of the family and the state to help youth transition into adulthood is a sure recipe for calamity. As single-parent families become the norm and routinely absent fathers leave boys to construct their masculinity on their own, Generation Why? may propel a postfeminist movement in which young men and women work toward partnership systems. Noneconomic institutions, such as the family, schools, religion, and the community, may benefit from this.

The lack of status of American teens, described in Walter Miller's theory, has driven teen rebellion since the end of World War II. If that remains a part of our culture, one can expect wild and deviant youth subcultural behavior to continue into the foreseeable future. But if an energized Generation Why? has the social power to go along with its numbers, it may redefine the role of youth in our society. They might end up not as the Why? Generation but the Why-Not? Generation, in the sense of rising to address and rectify societal challenges.

Both linear and curvilinear theories have legitimate claim as to which one is more accurate in explaining the effects of social change. Both perspectives, when applied to explaining youth cultures and delinquencies, have their appeal. And it is likely that both perspectives play a part in the way a given youth culture emerges in society at a particular time. Why it—as opposed to another form—is embraced by troubled teens, and what accounts for its often rapid decline once the fad or its novelty has worn off.

In conclusion, this book examines the youth styles and identities that emerged in American society during the conservative decade of the 1980s and the anomic 1990s. It focused on a variety of youth cultures that manifested themselves for the first time in middle-class suburbia during those time periods.

Whatever the future holds, it is quite likely that the varied youth styles examined in this book—*mall rats, punk rockers, heavy metalers, school shooters, tagger crews, racist skinheads, stoner gang members,* and *Satanists*—will continue to be present in society in one form or another in the new millennium.

Youth at the Movies—Generation Why?

In the late 1990s the teen genre returned as the demographics swelled. Films such as *Scream* (1996), *I Know What You Did Last Summer* (1997), *Wild Things* (1998), *Varsity Blues* (1999), *The Faculty* (1998), *Cruel Intentions* (1999), *10 Things I Hate about You* (1999), and *American Pie* (1999) all hit big with the under-21 market by tapping into the postmodern experience of a fragmented youth culture. One of the best was *Go* (1999), starring Katie Holmes and Sarah Polley. This fast-paced drama follows one story from three teen perspectives.

This book has focused in some detail on the lives of youths involved with society's more questionable and controversial youth styles. We hope to have imparted some insight into the conditions that cause so many of our young to embrace these identities. It is critical that the destructive aspects of some of these renegade kids and suburban outlaws be rectified. If not, many more teenagers will continue to see with sharp and terrible eyes.

NOTES

1. David Foster, "Y2K Generation Forced to Grow Up Fast," *Desert Sun,* (12 September 1999), p. A-3.

2. James Conn, "Raves Are a Rite of Passage," *Los Angeles Times,* (20 February 1998), p. B-1.

3. Karl Mannheim, *Essays on the Sociology of Knowledge* (London: Routledge, 1952), p. 304.

4. Michael Brake, *Comparative Youth Culture* (New York: Routledge, 1985).

5. Margaret Hornblower, "Great Xpectations," *Time,* (9 June, 1997), pp. 58–68.

6. Ian Robertson, *Sociology* (New York: Worth, 1987), pp. 340–41.

7. Martin Miller, "Smashing the Gen-X Stereotype," *Los Angeles Times* (3 September 1999), p. A-1.

8. "Ford Focuses Attention on Generation X, Y Satisfaction," *Desert Sun* (13 November 1999), p. E-1.

9. Barbara Kantrowitz and Pat Wingert, "How Well Do You Know Your Kid?" *Newsweek* (10 May 1999), pp. 36–40.

10. "Ford Focuses Attention on Generation X, Y Satisfaction."

11. John W. Wright, ed., *The New York Times Almanac* (New York: Penguin, 1999), pp. 472–73.

12. Robertson.

13. "Class of 2000 Less Likely to Use Illegal Drugs, Get Pregnant, Drop Out," *Desert Sun* (12 September 1999), p. A-3.

14. David Foster.

15. Nathan Cobb, "Prepare for the Next Wave Teen-agers," *Los Angeles Times* (9 September 1999), p. B-1.

16. Vicki Knapp, "Beeper Culture," student paper.

17. Joe Mozingo, "Teens Create Language of Pager-Speak," *Los Angeles Times* (26 November 1997), pp. A-1, A-27.

18. Vicki Knapp.

19. William Kvaraceus and Walter Miller, "Norm–violating Behavior in Middle-class Culture," in *Middle-Class Juvenile Delinquency,* ed. Edmund W. Vaz (New York: Harper and Row, 1959).

20. Nanette Davis, *Youth Crisis: Growing Up in the High-Risk Society* (New York: Greenwood, 1999), pp. 14–15.

21. Ibid.

22. Laura Kann, "Youth Risk Behavior Surveillance—United States, 1997," in *Juvenile Delinquency: Theory, Practice, and Law,* ed. Larry Siegel and Joseph Senna (Belmont, CA: Wadsworth, 2000).

23. Julie Marquis, "Study Finds Alarming Rate of Risky Behavior by Boys," *Los Angeles Times* (9 September 1998), pp. A-1, A-47.

24. David C. Anderson, "When Should Kids Go to Jail?" *The American Prospect,* May/June 1998, pp. 72–8.

25. Pamphlet provided by the Parents against Cruel and Unusual Punishment, 1999.

26. Fox Butterfield, "With Juvenile Court in Chaos, Critics Propose Their Demise," *New York Times* (21 July 1997), pp. A-1, B-6.

27. Davis, p. 41.

28. Barbara Kantrowitz and Pat Wingert.

29. Daniel Okrent, "Raising Kids Online: What Can Parents Do?" *Time* (10 May 1999), pp. 38–43.

30. Ibid.

31. Ibid.

32. Joshua Quittner, "Are Video Games Really So Bad?" *Time* (10 May 1999), pp. 50–58.

33. Barbara Kantrowitz and Pat Wingert, "The Truth about Teens," *Newsweek* (18 October 1999), pp. 62–72.

34. David Foster.

35. Larry Siegel and Joseph Senna, *Criminology* (Belmont, CA: Wadsworth, 2000), p. 130.

36. Barbara Kantrowitz and Pat Wingert.

37. Elizabeth Mehren, "Troubled Teens' Parents Desperate for Solutions," *Los Angeles Times* (18 July 1999), p. A-3.

38. "Charter Hospitals," *60 Minutes 2,* CBS (21 April 1999).

39. Barbara Kantrowitz and Pat Wingert.

40. David Foster.

41. Judy Holland, "Parents Unaware of Youth's Drinking," *The Oregonian* (17 December 1999), p. A-10.

42. Mark Fritz, "Alienated Teens Empathize with High School Gunmen," *New York Times* (28 April 1999), p. A1, A-20.

43. Robert A. Jones, "Requiem for the Suburbs?" *Los Angeles Times* magazine (19 December 1999), pp. 24–34.

44. P. J. O'Rourke, "I Hate the Suburbs," *Rolling Stone* (vol. no. 822) (30 November 1999), pp. 35–40.

▼

Methodology

The California-New Zealand Youth Study

Teenagers in both locales were contacted in a similar fashion and asked to complete the questionnaire. Youths in both countries were approached in shopping malls, including establishments such as video arcade areas, fast-food restaurants, record shops, and other youth-oriented service areas; in and near high school campuses; in concert areas; and in other public locations where teenagers congregated.

Of the 419 surveys from Southern California, 117 youths identified themselves as punk rockers, 57 youths identified themselves as heavy metalers, and 245 teenagers identified themselves as not belonging to either the punker or metaler group. This latter group served as the controls or comparative group for purposes of the study.

For the New Zealand sample, 17 youths self-identified as punk rockers, 33 identified as heavy metalers, and 154 teenagers identified as not belonging to either of the groups, again serving as the control group.

Several hypotheses were formulated to test whether differences existed in the attitudes of the punk rockers and heavy metalers. These hypotheses included the following:

1. Punk rockers, compared to heavy metalers, would have greater difficulties in society and admit to having more interpersonal problems, regardless of locale (California or New Zealand).

2. Punk rockers, in general, would share similar identities regardless of locale.

3. Similarly, heavy metalers, in general, would share similar identities regardless of locale.

4. Where differences in youth identities did exist between locales, such differences might be explained in terms of the more rural, traditional, and conservative nature of New Zealand society.

To test these four hypotheses, an analysis of the responses to questions from the Youth Survey was completed. The findings are discussed in the following sections under the headings of *background information* and *family relations*.

Table 1 Background Information

	CP	CHM	CC	NZ	NZM	NZC
I am a male.	67%	88%	48%[1]	82%	81%	59%[4]
I am a Caucasian.	86%	81%	66%[1]	81%	94%	75%[3]
I have no religious affiliation.	44%	30%	19%[1]	73%	66%	54%[3]
I am a Catholic.	23%	35%	38%[1]	20%	10%	10%
I am from a blue-collar background.	42%	35%	29%	71%	52%	33%[2]

[1]sig. <.001

[2]sig. <.004

[3]sig. <.01

[4]sig. <.04

Code: CP = California Punk Rockers; CHM = California Heavy Metalers; CC = California Controls; NZP = New Zealand Punk Rockers; NZM = New Zealand Heavy Metalers; NZC = New Zealand Controls

Background Information

Gender Males composed the vast majority of youths who identified as punk rockers and heavy metalers in both the Southern California and New Zealand samples (see Table 1). In fact, over 80 percent of each of the three groups of California heavy metalers, New Zealand punk rockers, and New Zealand heavy metalers were males. And males composed two-thirds of the punk rockers in Southern California as well.

Racial Identity Caucasians were disproportionately represented in the California and New Zealand punk rocker and heavy metaler groups. In fact, over four-fifths of the teenagers in these groups in both countries were Caucasian (94 percent of the heavy metalers in the New Zealand sample).

Religious Affiliation The New Zealand sample indicated less interest in organized religion compared to the California youths. Three-fourths of the New Zealand punk rockers and two-thirds of the New Zealand heavy metalers reported no religious affiliation. This was nearly twice the percentages of the California punkers and metalers.

Even with regard to the California group, however, the punkers and metalers reported no religious affiliation in much greater numbers than did the control group. When religion was reported, a sizable percentage in the California group identified themselves as Catholics.

Socioeconomic Status The New Zealand punk rockers and heavy metalers were much more likely to come from working-class or blue-collar backgrounds compared to the California sample. Nearly three-fourths of the New Zealand punkers and half the New Zealand heavy metalers reported parents' occupations that would affiliate them with the working class.

By contrast, more of the punkers and metalers of the California sample listed parents' occupations that placed the family in the white-collar middle class. Perhaps the California sample's more affluent family backgrounds reflect the differential economic levels of the two countries.

Career Choices When questioned about their career choices, over half of the New Zealand punkers and metalers planned to hold jobs that would maintain a blue-collar status. In California, by contrast, only one-third of the punkers and very few of the metalers declared blue-collar jobs as their future career choices. The California sample was decidedly more middle-class oriented with regard to career choices.

Not surprisingly, therefore, the New Zealand punkers and metalers indicated they were not planning to attend college. In fact, over three-fourths of the youths sampled in Christchurch who identified as being a punker or metaler indicated they were not college bound. By contrast, nearly two-thirds of the New Zealand controls were planning to attend college.

For California, a much lower percentage of punkers and metalers indicated they were not going to college. The patterns for those youths not planning to attend college were consistent with the blue-collar occupations they had also selected as future career choices. Much more of the California sample in general indicated they were planning to attend college.

Family Relations

Table 2 ("Family Relations") makes it quite apparent that the punk rockers in each of the two countries felt more estranged from their families when compared to the heavy metalers and the control groups. The punkers in California and New Zealand indicated they spent a lot of time away from home and that they had nothing in common with other family members.

The punkers in both countries also were more likely to admit that they did not like their parents. In fact, one-fifth of the punk rockers in both countries stated they felt this way about their elders.

Punkers were also more frequently likely to state that they did not get along with their mothers; one-fourth of the punkers in both countries expressed these feelings. This was a much higher percentage than the heavy metalers or control groups in both locales.

Both the punk rockers and the heavy metalers were likely to report they did not get along with their fathers (compared to the control groups). Over one-third of the California punkers, California metalers, and New Zealand punkers reported that they were estranged from their fathers.

Accordingly, for the California sample, a greater percentage (compared to the control groups) of both punkers and metalers reported that their parents did not approve of their lifestyle and disapproved of their choice of friends. Half of the California punk rockers stated that their parents did not approve of their lifestyle. Patterns for New Zealand were less clear cut. Fewer parents of punks and metalers in New Zealand disapproved of their offspring's lifestyle and friends compared to the California group.

Table 2 Family Relations

	CP	CHM	CC	NZP	NZM	NZC
I spend a lot of time away from home.	79%	70%	62%	88%	55%	56%[2]
I have nothing in common with my family.	62%	40%	33%[1]	77%	30%	44%
I do not like my parents.	21%	11%	5%[1]	19%	10%	9%
I do not get along with my my mother.	23%	14%	7%[1]	24%	16%	13%
I do not get along with my father.	33%	37%	14%[1]	38%	21%	17%
My parents do not approve of my lifestyle.	50%	28%	13%[1]	18%	17%	19%
My parents disapprove of my friends.	34%	33%	10%[1]	27%	17%	11%

[1]sig. <.001

[2]sig. <.01

Code: CP = California Punk Rockers; CHM = California Heavy Metalers; CC = California Controls; NZP = New Zealand Punk Rockers; NZM = New Zealand Heavy Metalers; NZC = New Zealand Controls

One explanation for these cultural differences might be that California youths in this study were much more likely to still reside at home under their parents' scrutiny and therefore act out more defiantly against this dependence and parental authority. By contrast, in New Zealand many of the teenage punkers and heavy metalers had moved away from their parents' homes, which were located in the more rural farmland areas, and had migrated to the urban area of Christchurch, where they could live more independently. More New Zealand youth had also dropped out of school. Thus, they were under less adult supervision and control.

In summary, with regard to family relations, the punk rockers in both locales were the most estranged. Although the heavy metalers in both California and New Zealand reported some degree of problematic family relations, the punk rockers expressed the most discontent with their family situation.

THE BLAZAK SKINHEAD STUDY

The methodology for studying racist and nonracist skinheads was a form of participant observation. Others, such as Rapheal S. Ezekial in his pioneering work, *The Racist Mind* (1995), gained access to hate groups with their permission. He was an older Jew. Blazak was a young WASP who could gain the trust of skinheads by playing the role of a potential recruit. Someone with a shaved head and tattoos could not ask many questions without raising suspicions. By talking the talk of the white man who feared change, Blazal found it relatively easy to gain acceptance into the group. At a certain point he would ask to interview individual members for a local paper or a school project so that others could hear their story. The result was 73 formal interviews with young skinheads and over 200 informal "guided conversations."

Skinheads were interviewed in Chicago, San Francisco, Orlando, Florida, Memphis, Tennessee, Augusta, Georgia, and suburban Atlanta. Additionally, European skinheads were interviewed in London, Berlin, Prague, and Bratislava.

The formal interviews were recorded on a hand-held cassette recorder. The informal interviews were transcribed into a log book. The data from field notes (i.e., the interviews and events) were coded around value themes. Meanings were assigned to the quotes and events. From these meanings a grounded theory was inductively developed.

▼

Youth Survey 1

1. With *whom* do you spend *most* of your leisure (free) time?
   _____ by myself
   _____ with a friend
   _____ with several friends
   _____ with a date
   _____ with members of my family
   _____ other _____

2. Where do you most often go when you are with your friends?
   _____ my home
   _____ friend's home
   _____ school area
   _____ movies
   _____ video arcades
   _____ beaches, parks, or mountains
   _____ mall (village or plaza)
   _____ fast food locations
   _____ other _____

3. How old were you on your last birthday? _____

4. What gender (sex) are you? _____ male _____ female

5. What is your race?
   _____ Caucasian (white)
   _____ Black
   _____ Hispanic
   _____ Asian
   _____ other _____

6. What do you spend most of your money on? (Check three)
   _____ food (restaurant, fast food, snacks)
   _____ clothes
   _____ car (payments, insurance, repair)
   _____ video games
   _____ movies
   _____ dances/concerts/gigs
   _____ athletic events
   _____ dates
   _____ other _____

7. Religious affiliation
   _____ Protestant
   _____ Catholic
   _____ Jewish
   _____ other
   _____ none

8. Father's job (describe)
   _____

9. Mother's job (describe)
   _____

10. How many brothers and sisters do you have? _____
    Ages: _____, _____, _____, _____, _____

11. What is your favorite musical group? (name it)
    _____

12. What type of group is this?
    _____

13. What do you like about this group? (describe)
    _____

14. Do you listen to messages in their songs? (If so, describe)
    _____

15. Do you feel that your music is violent? (If so, describe)
    _____

16. What kind of clothes do you wear? (describe)
    _____

17. Describe your hairstyle and dress:
    _____

18. How do you like school?
    _____

19. How do your teachers treat you at school?
    _____

20. How do the kids treat you at school?
    _____

21. Are you a punk rocker? _____ yes _____ no
22. Which music do you like best?
    _____ country western
    _____ punk
    _____ pop or rock
    _____ heavy metal
    _____ soul
23. Which one of the following do you identify with?
    _____ punk
    _____ heavy metal
    _____ none of the above
24. Do you get along with your mother?
    _____ yes   _____ no
    Why not? _____
25. Do you get along with your father?
    _____ yes   _____ no
    Why not? _____
26. Do you plan on finishing high school?
    _____ yes

_____ no
_____ I have already graduated
27. Do you plan on going to college?
_____ yes
_____ no
_____ don't know
28. Do you currently have a job?
_____ yes
What kind of job? _____
_____ no
29. What kind of job would you like to have in the future? (describe)
_____

30. Who do you support politically?
_____ Liberals
_____ Conservatives
_____ undecided
_____ neither

For the following statements, please answer:
DY = Definitely Yes; Y = Yes; DK = Don't Know; N = No; DN = Definitely No

	DY	Y	DK	NO	DN
31. For me to like a musical group, it is important that they be political.	1	2	3	4	5
32. Punk and punk music will become "establishment, just as Elvis Presley and all other forms of rebellious music have.	1	2	3	4	5
33. Punk rockers are delinquents.	1	2	3	4	5
34. Preppies are just as likely as punk rockers to be considered deviant from an adult's point-of-view.	1	2	3	4	5
35. I am basically happy with my life.	1	2	3	4	5
36. I identify myself as part of the punk lifestyle.	1	2	3	4	5
37. Basically life is rather boring.	1	2	3	4	5
38. Most kids involved in the punk movement tend to come from poorer backgrounds.	1	2	3	4	5
39. One has to have a lot of money to afford to be a punk.	1	2	3	4	5
40. Sometimes I feel like committing suicide.	1	2	3	4	5
41. I am an above-average student in terms of grades I receive in school.	1	2	3	4	5
42. My parents approve of my life style.	1	2	3	4	5
43. I am not an aggressive person.	1	2	3	4	5
44. I like my parents.	1	2	3	4	5
45. Politically speaking, I tend to be a conservative.	1	2	3	4	5

46. I will do more with my life than my parents have done with theirs.	1	2	3	4	5
47. My parents disapprove of my friends.	1	2	3	4	5
48. Other people my own age consider me to be a troublemaker.	1	2	3	4	5
49. Punks are no different from the hippies of the 1960s.	1	2	3	4	5
50. I consider myself to be religious.	1	2	3	4	5
51. My parents are happy with their life.	1	2	3	4	5
52. Kids who dress punk-style are popular with the majority of students at school.	1	2	3	4	5
53. Schools should have dress codes.	1	2	3	4	5
54. Kids who break the law should be punished like adults.	1	2	3	4	5
55. The kids I hang around with are involved with drugs or alcohol.	1	2	3	4	5
56. I enjoy playing sports.	1	2	3	4	5
57. I have many close friends.	1	2	3	4	5
58. I am put down if I do not do drugs with the group.	1	2	3	4	5
59. Right now my relationship with my parents is good.	1	2	3	4	5
60. In the past I have been in trouble with the law/police.	1	2	3	4	5
61. New wave is my kind of music.	1	2	3	4	5
62. Most kids who are punk rockers will eventually outgrow it.	1	2	3	4	5
63. I don't like heavy metal music and heavy metal types.	1	2	3	4	5
64. I have a lot in common with my other family members.	1	2	3	4	5
65. I spend a lot of time away from home.	1	2	3	4	5
66. Punk rockers represent individuality.	1	2	3	4	5
67. Parents don't have the right to tell their kids how to dress.	1	2	3	4	5
68. Kids today are more streetwise than their parents were at their age.	1	2	3	4	5
69. Voting in a presidential election makes a difference.	1	2	3	4	5
70. Schools don't really educate kids; they just prepare them for places in society.	1	2	3	4	5
71. There is going to be a nuclear war in my lifetime.	1	2	3	4	5
72. Teenagers today pay too mach attention to their clothing and how they look.	1	2	3	4	5
73. Individuals can make a difference in today's world.	1	2	3	4	5

74. The punk lifestyle is mostly for the young.	1	2	3	4	5
75. Parents and grownups don't appreciate today's music.	1	2	3	4	5
76. I dress to impress other people.	1	2	3	4	5
77. It is important to me that I fit in with some group.	1	2	3	4	5
78. Music is a big part of my life.	1	2	3	4	5
79. The drinking age should be lowered.	1	2	3	4	5
80. I am a loner.	1	2	3	4	5
81. Preppies will become tomorrow's leaders.	1	2	3	4	5
82. The only people I get along with are the ones in my group.	1	2	3	4	5
83. I don't want to get involved in what's going on in today's world.	1	2	3	4	5
84. Sex plays a role in the music I listen to.	1	2	3	4	5
85. I am easily influenced by others.	1	2	3	4	5
86. I would fight in a war to protect my country.	1	2	3	4	5
87. Marijuana should be legalized.	1	2	3	4	5
88. The death penalty is a good way of dealing with violent criminals.	1	2	3	4	5
89. Punk rockers are a new form of gang.	1	2	3	4	5
90. It is good for people to be rebellious.	1	2	3	4	5
91. Punkers are intelligent.	1	2	3	4	5
92. Females are equal to males.	1	2	3	4	5
93. I prefer pop music to soul music.	1	2	3	4	5
94. Preppies are just spoiled rich kids.	1	2	3	4	5
95. Pop music represents conformity.	1	2	3	4	5

96. A punk rocker is someone who _____

_____

97. People who like new wave music are _____

_____

98. The heavy metal scene is _____

_____

99. Three words that describe a punk rocker are
_____, _____, and _____

100. The major difference between a non-punk rocker and a punk rocker is _____

Thank you very much for completing this questionnaire. We greatly appreciate your cooperation.

Youth Survey 2

1. How old were you on your last birthday? _____
2. What gender (sex) are you? _____male _____ female
3. What is your race? _____
4. Religious affiliation
   _____ Protestant
   _____ Catholic
   _____ Jewish
   _____ other
   _____ none
5. Are you a skinhead? _____ yes _____ no
6. Which one of the following do you identify with?
   _____ punk
   _____ skinhead
   _____ heavy metal
   _____ none of the above
7. Father's job (describe)

   _____
8. Mother's job (describe)

   _____
9. How many brothers and sisters do you have? _____
   Ages: _____, _____, _____, _____, _____
10. What is your favorite musical group? (name them)

    _____
11. What type of group is this?

    _____
12. What do you like about this group? (describe)

    _____
13. Do you listen to messages in their songs? (If so, describe)

    _____
14. Do you feel that your music is violent? (If so, describe)

    _____
15. What kind of clothes do you wear? (describe)

    _____
16. Describe your hairstyle and dress:

    _____
17. How do you like school?

    _____
18. How do your teachers treat you at school?

    _____
19. How do the kids treat you at school?

    _____
20. Do you get along with your mother? _____ yes_____ no
    Why not? _____

21. Do you get along with your father? _____ yes_____ no
    Why not? _____
22. A skinhead is someone who

    _____
23. People who like Top 40 music are

    _____
24. The heavy metal scene is

    _____
25. Three words that describe a skinhead are
    _____, _____, and _____
26. Someone who is not a skinhead is

    _____
27. Describe your tattoos, if any:

    _____

For the following statements, please answer:
DY = Definitely Yes; Y = Yes; DK = Don't Know; N = No; DN = Definitely No

	DY	Y	DK	N	DN
28. Skinheads are delinquents.	1	2	3	4	5
29. I am basically happy with my life.	1	2	3	4	5
30. I identify myself as part of the skinhead lifestyle.	1	2	3	4	5
31. In the past I've participated in gay-or black-bashing	1	2	3	4	5
32. Basically life is rather boring.	1	2	3	4	5
33. I spend a lot of money on drugs.	1	2	3	4	5
34. I am part of a satanic cult.	1	2	3	4	5
35. Most kids involved in the skinhead scene tend to come from poorer backgrounds.	1	2	3	4	5
36. As a child I was abused by my parents.	1	2	3	4	5
37. Sometimes I feel like committing suicide.	1	2	3	4	5
38. My parents approve of my lifestyle.	1	2	3	4	5
39. I am a member of SHARP (Skinheads Against Racial Prejudice).	1	2	3	4	5
40. I am *not* an aggressive person.	1	2	3	4	5
41. I like my parents.	1	2	3	4	5
42. All skinheads are sexist.	1	2	3	4	5
43. Blacks and Hispanics are equal to whites.	1	2	3	4	5
44. Politically speaking, I tend to be a conservative.	1	2	3	4	5
45. I am against racism in any form.	1	2	3	4	5
46. My parents disapprove of my friends.	1	2	3	4	5
47. Other people my own age consider me to be a troublemaker.	1	2	3	4	5
48. We have too many immigrants and racial minorities in our society today.	1	2	3	4	5

49. I consider myself to be religious.	1	2	3	4	5
50. My parents are happy with their life.	1	2	3	4	5
51. Society should discriminate against homosexuals/gays.	1	2	3	4	5
52. When I'm *not* with my friends I act differently.	1	2	3	4	5
53. Kids who dress skinhead-style are popular with the majority of students at school	1	2	3	4	5
54. Kids who break the law should be punished like adults.	1	2	3	4	5
55. Kids I hang around with use drugs or alcohol.	1	2	3	4	5
56. I have many close friends.	1	2	3	4	5
57. I am put down if I do *not* do drugs with the group.	1	2	3	4	5
58. Minorities should *not* be allowed to live in white neighborhoods.	1	2	3	4	5
59. In grammar school I was considered to be a bully.	1	2	3	4	5
60. All of my family members agree with my racial views.	1	2	3	4	5
61. Right now my relationship with my parents is good.	1	2	3	4	5
62. In the past I have been in trouble with the police.	1	2	3	4	5
63. Heavy metal is my kind of music.	1	2	3	4	5
64. I have a lot in common with my other family members.	1	2	3	4	5
65. I spend a lot of time away from home.	1	2	3	4	5
66. There is going to be a nuclear war in my lifetime.	1	2	3	4	5
67. It is important to me that I fit in with some group.	1	2	3	4	5
68. The drinking age should be lowered.	1	2	3	4	5
69. I am a loner.	1	2	3	4	5
70. The only people I socialize with are the ones in my own racial group.	1	2	3	4	5
71. I would fight in a war to protect my country.	1	2	3	4	5
72. Skinheads are a new form of gang.	1	2	3	4	5
73. It is good for people to be rebellious.	1	2	3	4	5
74. The death penalty is a good way of dealing with violent criminals.	1	2	3	4	5

Thank you for completing this questionnaire.

Index